THE SHADOWS C

THE
SHADOWS
OF
ELISA LYNCH

How a nineteenth-century Irish courtesan
became the most powerful woman
in Paraguay

Siân Rees

review

First published in 2003
by REVIEW

An imprint of Headline Book Publishing

10 9 8 7 6 5 4 3 2 1

Cataloguing in Publication Data is available from the British Library

ISBN 0 7553 1114 0

Typeset in Plantin Light by Avon DataSet Ltd,
Bidford-on-Avon, Warwickshire

Printed and bound in Great Britain by
Clays Ltd, St Ives plc

HEADLINE BOOK PUBLISHING
A division of Hodder Headline
338 Euston Road
London NW1 3BH

www.reviewbooks.co.uk
www.hodderheadline.com

Contents

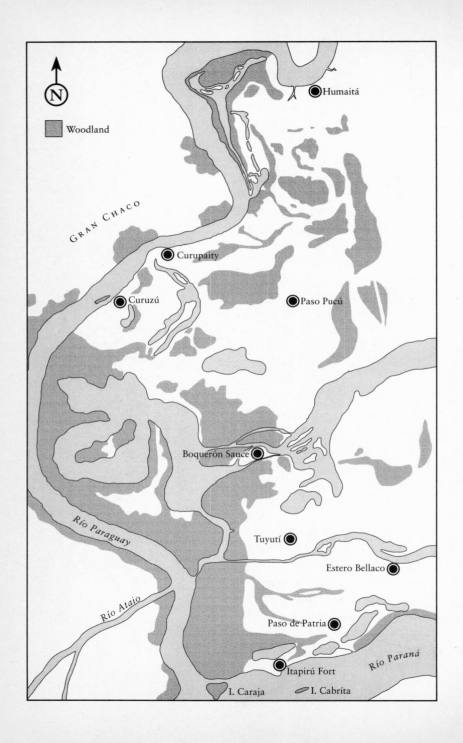

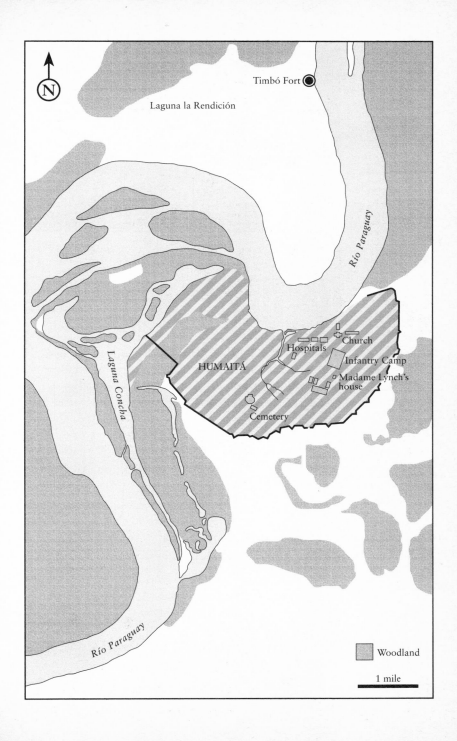

Timbó Fort

Laguna la Rendición

Río Paraguay

Laguna Concha

HUMAITÁ

Hospitals

Church

Infantry Camp

Madame Lynch's house

Cemetery

Río Paraguay

Woodland

1 mile

Acknowledgements

Jo Roberts-Miller, Heather Holden-Brown and Celia Kent at Headline; Isobel Dixon at Blake Friedmann; Jorge and Maria Rubiani, Suboficial Pablo Roberto Zarza, Carlos Barrientos, Carlos Scheffer in Asunción and Ciudad del'Este; the Biblioteca Nacional and Archivo Nacional of Asunción; Suboficial Rafael Figueredo in Luque; Oficial Ramón Benítez at the Marinería of Angostura; Bernardino Cabañas Rivas in Humaitá; Sacha Anibal Cardona in Juan Pedro Caballero; Rosa at the Gran Hotel del Paraguay; Elisa Aquino at the Embassy of Paraguay in London; the Biblioteca Nacional of Buenos Aires; the Centre des Archives Diplomatiques of Nantes; Canning House Library, the British Library and the Public Record Office of London; the Biblioteca Nacional of Madrid.

Foreword

Asunción, capital of the Republic of Paraguay
24 July 1961

A cold day in the South American midwinter. The relentless red and green of Paraguay is muted and the crowd in the Plaza de los Héroes is silent. It is the 134th anniversary of the birth of the Marshal President Francisco Solano López, *el Mariscal*, patriot, warrior and national hero. At the docks is General Alfredo Stroessner: President, Commander in Chief of the Armed Forces, brother in thought to general presidents in Chile and Argentina; heir to the Mariscal's vision of Paraguay. He wears a heavy coat and a peaked cap pulled down over a cruel and pouchy face. Behind him is an escort of cadets selected from the Colegio Militar. They have just marched from the Panteón de los Héroes, where bones lie in the half-light, tracked down to lonely places, spooned from forgotten graves, brought to Asunción with red dust on skull and femur.

An hour ago, Stroessner took a laurel wreath and descended to the crypt, where urns stand on plinths. At eight, a minute's silence began. Then a single cornet played its sad salute, an aide approached with taper and lamp and Stroessner lit an

1

eternal flame. A chaplain blessed the dead and the crowd outside watched two young men step forward, bayonets fixed, to either side of the arched door. *El Mariscal* had been honoured. Now his First Lady was to be brought home. Stroessner turned west towards the docks and the colonels, majors, captains, lieutenants, sergeants, corporals, private soldiers, priests, cadets of the Colegio Militar, surviving descendants of the great patriot and the crowd fell in behind him.

It is just after nine. Aboard the flagship of the Paraguayan Navy, a bronze urn brought from Paris and wrapped in the Paraguayan tricolour is handed down to the Commodore's launch. Stroessner and his companions watch from the dockside. Separated from them by the peeling arches of the customs house colonnade, the crowd whispers in the Plaza Isabel la Catolica and the cadets stand stiffly at one end of an empty gun-carriage. At the other are the veterans, *los mutilados*, of the Chaco War. They lack eyes, limbs, hearing, speech. Ships salute as the urn is brought across the bay at stately speed and passed from the hands of the Commodore to those of General Stroessner.

The national anthem is played on trumpets as he comes through the draughty arches with the urn in gloved hands. He places it on the gun-carriage and turns to lead the procession east through the streets of old Asunción. They walk to a slow beat and the sound of gun-carriage wheels along Calle Colón and Calle Palma, past the Panteón with its guard of honour one hour old, up Calle Estigarribia, along Calle Mexico, Calle 25 de Mayo, Calle Tacuarí, past the barracks and the cathedral to the Ministry of Defence on Avenida Francisco Solano López with the bones of an Irishwoman in their midst.

Ten o'clock: the crowd huddles in the wide *avenida* and gazes at the generals, who stand rigid on the Ministry portico with the urn between them. The police rest their hands on the butts in their holsters. The band stops playing and there is silence but for the wind, coldly blowing from the flatlands across the bay. One frail and elderly man steps forward. He is Dr Juan Emiliano O'Leary, eighty-eight-year-old Paraguayan historian, loyal follower of General Stroessner and fanatical *lopista**.

> La señora Elisa Alicia Lynch [he declared] is the greatest heroine of America.
> Surpassed by none in her courage, her selflessness and her loyalty, through pain and through sacrifice, in her contempt for danger and death and in her supreme pride in the face of tragedy. Sublime mother of children forged in the flames of her pain, she resisted five years through war, as an Extension of the Hero, and never wavered in her loyalty. She was there in the days of victory and in the days of bitterness and desolation. Her name was slandered but she rose above death and disaster and was transformed by her supreme virtue to share the fate of the Paraguayan nation . . .
> She never forgot; she lived, died and, in her dark Parisian grave, awaited her return to the country in which justice would greet her . . . to live again, today, in the admiration and gratitude of her country . . .
> Heroic companion, example of motherhood, widow of a great love, magnified by a life consecrated to supreme and infinite love . . . fill our hearts with your infinite tenderness as we raise ourselves to offer you, in this supreme hour of our history, our respect, our love and our admiration . . .'[1]

---

* An admirer of *el Mariscal* López.

Stroessner enters the Museo Militar to place the bronze urn on a plinth. An album lies alongside, its cover engraved 'To Elisa Alicia Lynch: homage from her people'.

In Père Lachaise cemetery, Paris, the bones of five bodies sag into the hole from which the sixth has been recently disinterred. In Asunción, 87,000 people signed the album.

Chapter One

Elisa Lynch's early life was obscure. She made too many false claims for any truth to emerge from among them.

'I was born in the year 1835,' she wrote, 'of honourable and wealthy parents from an Irish family. On my father's side, there were two bishops and more than seventy magistrates and on my mother's, a vice admiral of the English fleet who had the honour of fighting with four of his brothers under Nelson in the battles of the Nile and Trafalgar. All my uncles were officers in the English navy or army. My cousins still are and other relatives occupy important positions in Ireland.'[1]

These claims were made in Buenos Aires, for South American readers who would have little opportunity to check them.

Her mother, Corinne Schnock, may have had some relation to a member of the clergy. Her father, Frederick Lynch, may have been killed aboard a British gunboat when Elisa was small but the first reliable evidence of Elisa comes when she emerges as the young bride of a Frenchman in 1850. She met her husband when her mother took her from the dying peasants of Ireland to Paris, a squalid city, not yet torn apart for light and parade. These were *les années folles*, the years of madness, when the last of the Bourbons was pushed off his throne, a republic was proclaimed and every adult male was entitled to vote. People fought in the streets and insurgents lined the quays in leg-irons, waiting for the deportation boats to Algeria.

The Algerian colony was new; its conquest was precarious and incomplete. Rich visitors toured for sport and adventure, to kill lions and dress in native clothes. They followed the army and observed the engagements which subdued the last of the stubborn tribes. They saw villages burnt, crops destroyed, Arabs killed by Zouaves and the Foreign Legion, public beheadings and severed heads displayed. 'How strange!' wrote one. 'We thought we had conquered Algeria but it is Algeria which has conquered us – already our women wear shawls of a thousand colours, shot through with gold like those of the harem slaves; our young people have adopted the goat-skin *burnous*, the tarbush has replaced the classic cashmire cap, everyone smokes the *narguilé*, hashish has taken over from champagne . . .'[2] Dancing djinn and Bedouins hung in the salons. The Théâtre-Italien put on plays about harem life and fashionable drawing rooms were decorated in African prints. Algerian officers were fêted.

Lieutenant Xavier de Quatrefages, *aide major aux hospitaux militaires en Algerie*, was on leave. He saw Elisa Lynch in the city's parks or restaurants, or in some dim second-rate drawing room, and asked for her. She was a beautiful child and could have been matched to a *parti* superior to this dull medic of bourgeois line, but he was accepted. She left no explanation of the choice made by her, or on her behalf by her mother. It was said she was too young to be married legally in France and this was why the wedding was celebrated at her uncle's house in Folkestone, on her birthday, 3 June 1850. According to those reports, she was fifteen that day. According to the date on her tombstone, she was nineteen.

The couple left for Algeria.

Prince Louis-Napoleon Bonaparte was touring France. Nephew of the great Napoleon, he had recently returned from exile in England and the United States.

'I believe,' he wrote, 'that from time to time, men are created who I would call *providential*, in whose hands are placed the destinies of their countries. I believe myself to be one of these men.' This is what he told the crowds who packed theatres and halls to hear his lectures that year. There had been too many riots and too much expression of thought. Bonaparte was a man who could keep order and command the turbulent masses. In 1851, he announced he would stand for the presidency of the republic and his men contacted the Governor of Algeria. 'Assure the prince [Napoleon]', Governor General St Arnaud replied, 'that as of today he may count on me. Let him promote me Brigadier General at his earliest convenience and I will answer for the rest.' Early on 21 December, St Arnaud's men entered bedrooms in Paris to arrest the opposition. Troops surrounded the National Assembly and President Bonaparte moved to the Tuileries. General St Arnaud was promoted. Twelve thousand protesters were sent to Algeria in irons.

He was president for a year. In December 1852, he proclaimed himself Emperor Napoleon III of the Second Empire of France and political miscreants, chancers, opportunists, moneylenders, matchmakers, bar girls, dancers, entertainers, theatre managers, bored aristocrats and any who had soiled their name under older regimes flooded in. Imperial Paris was once again a mecca for New World exiles looking for fun and Europeans on the make. The Spanish Countess de Montejo gave her aging daughter Eugenie low-cut dresses and set her on display like a bowl of ripe fruit. 'What is the way to your heart?' the infatuated Emperor asked. 'Through the chapel, sir,' she said, and an impossibly splendid marriage ensued. Republican puritanism was buried with the uncomfortable *égalité* of universal male suffrage.

While Paris bloomed in pleasure, Elisa de Quatrefages and her husband lived in one of the grim army towns which pinned Algeria to the French map. News arrived late here, or not at all, of Paris, and the balls and receptions given there, of Eugenie's dresses and the splendours of the Tuileries. Like aspirant British memsahibs who sailed for the exotic East but were boxed into cantonment bungalows, army wives lived in heat and monotony, periodically scared when a tribe rebelled and attacked, periodically in danger from the diseases of camp life. In 1852, *jihad* was declared on the invaders by the tribes of the Algerian south. The fighting was bloody; grotesque operations were performed in the hospitals and cholera, dysentery and malaria swept the French garrisons.

We know nothing of Elisa's Algerian life, if she loved her husband, or hoped for a child or missed her mother and wanted to go home. We know only that she left within three years, when she was eighteen, or twenty-two. Many years later, she wrote that her departure was 'caused by my ill health', and she left 'to rejoin my mother and sister in England'[3]. The explanation was made to defend herself against accusations of sexual licence but it did not work, for a different story had already circulated. She may have visited her mother and sister, the gossips said; her health may have suffered in Algeria – but her departure was not for convalescence but love, or some variant, or compound of this with boredom, or desire, or disenchantment.

A picture survives of Elisa Lynch in these years. Her looks were arresting: red-gold hair the colour of the Empress Eugenie's, dressed in long, loosely bound ropes and studded with artful roses; blue eyes downcast beneath arched brows; a full mouth; jaw, collar and wrist bones padded with milky flesh; a slim waist and pronounced bust; a black velvet choker and one finger beneath her chin in coy contemplation. She was 'tall, delicate, flexible', her figure 'voluptuously moulded', the white of her dress 'diminished by the white of her complexion'. Her eyes, 'of a blue stolen from the heavens' were of 'ineffable sweetness' and her mouth 'voluptuous' and 'slightly moist'[4]. No woman with such a face and such a body was obliged to live in provincial monotony with a husband who came home with the smell of chloroform in his embrace.

Nasty tales were later told of the brief period of Elisa's life after she left her husband. It would be endlessly stated that she had run away to become a courtesan – some even said to become a prostitute. It was said she had ruined 'the English Lord L—'; had left him for a Spanish aristocrat and had driven a London banker to suicide.[5] It was said her sexual liaisons had been hundreds. It was said men had shot themselves and each other on her account; that she had run through fortunes. It was said she peddled her sexual services among the embassies of the Champs-Elysées in the coy guise of a language mistress and ran gaming tables. Elisa Lynch denied these tales. Of the many stories told of and against her, the one agreed to have some truth was that she left Quatrefages for a Russian whom she met in Algeria, one of the tourists who shot and observed. She eloped with him to Paris, where a Russian colony lived, supported by the vast, cold estates their owners did not visit, and became a part of the demi-monde, that twilight world of stable and adulterous couples.

Chapter Two

'*empire*', said Napoleon III, '*c'est la paix*' – 'The Empire means peace'. He did not want to go to war; he did not want *gloire*. The quarrel which forced his hand was this.

The Holy Land was Turkish, ruled from Constantinople*. In Jerusalem, Roman Catholic and Greek Orthodox priests disputed the occupation of the Holy Places. They disputed the Church of Bethlehem, the Sanctuary of the Nativity, the Stone of the Anointing, the Tomb of the Virgin at Gethsemane and the Seven Arches of the Virgin in the Church of the Holy Sepulchre. The sultan's soldiers could not stop the priests from fighting with silver candlesticks and pelting each other with crucifixes. The Catholics wanted a key to the main door of the Church of Bethlehem and both side doors to the Manger; they said a silver star must be placed above the Sanctuary of the Church of the Nativity and they must have exclusive right to maintain the cupola on the Church of the Holy Sepulchre. They wanted a cupboard and a lamp in the Tomb of the Virgin. The Belgian envoy to Constantinople demanded that the tombs of two

---

* Istanbul.

eleventh-century Belgian crusaders be restored. The dispute was absurd, but insoluble.

The Catholics appealed to the government of France. The Greek Orthodox appealed to the Tsar of Russia and the war which emerged was utterly disproportionate to the squabble of priests, for the Turkish Empire was dying and her heirs were striking at a corpse not yet dead. 'My confidence is in God and in my right,' wrote the Tsar; 'Russia, as I can guarantee, will prove herself in 1854 as she did in 1812.' To this challenge, Napoleon took up his reluctant position, Britain was brought in and the rich Russians of Paris watched with great sadness. They did not want to return to their frozen estates. In March, St Arnaud of Algeria was made Commander in Chief of French forces. In July, the Tsar destroyed the Turkish fleet at Sinope and a British–French fleet moved into the Black Sea. The Russian consul in Paris wept, and advised his compatriots that 'it was the intention of the Emperor that they should have to quit France'[1]. So, as 1853 ended and 1854 began, the rich Russians of Paris began sadly to withdraw their patronage from the city's restaurants, tailors, jewellers and beautiful women and many in the demi-monde were left stranded by the receding tide.

There was war elsewhere in the world, and it brought a young, immensely rich general to Paris. He represented the most ancient Spanish–American foundation, the Republic of Paraguay, and bore the name of a great Paraguayan saint who saved its capital, Asunción, in 1589.

Many thousands of barbarians had secretly gathered together to attack the city when its inhabitants were worshipping and all their attention given to piety. It is said that a message from Heaven came to the Saint to tell him of the imminent attack and that, inspired by a divine energy, he spoke to the Indians in Guaraní [the Indian language of

Paraguay] with such vehemence that they gave up their intended attack. Nine thousand Indians, surprised by this miracle, renounced their errors before his celestial voice and begged for baptism.[2]

The eldest son of the President of Paraguay, Don Carlos Antonio López, and his wife Juana Paula Carrillo, la Señora Presidenta, was born on the day of San Francisco Solano, 24 July 1827. As is the Spanish custom, he bore both his parents' names. He had also attained the rank of general and been granted a temporary diplomatic title. He was General Don Francisco Solano López Carrillo, Minister Plenipotentiary of the Republic of Paraguay.

Lust for treasure had taken the first Europeans up the Rio de la Plata* three centuries before, when the conquistadors sailed through what would become Argentina, looking for the silver rumoured to lie in fabulous quantities beyond. The Portuguese went first: seven men who enlisted 2,000 Guaraní Indians to plunder the Inca Empire. The seven were slaughtered but stories of the treasure they sought seeped downriver to the Spanish on the coast.

In 1537, 350 Spaniards sailed 1,000 miles north into the unknown. They took with them seven cows and a bull and when they found a gentle, fertile curve in the river they erected stockades and named the place Nuestra Señora de la Asunción. It became the capital of the Province of Paraguay, the Provincia Gigante de los Indios, of vast size and a coastline of several hundred miles. A Spanish bishop came, then Jesuits. Fortunes were made providing services to a frontier boomtown but the Andes and the Indians defeated too many silver-hunters. Within a generation, those still alive

---

* Literally the 'Silver River', known in English as the River Plate.

began to leave Asunción to the jungle and the Jesuits, for commerce on the coast made more money than chasing elusive Indian ore.

Along the rivers there emerged powerful settlements at Corrientes, Santa Fe, Entre Rios; to the north, Santa Cruz; on the Atlantic coast, Montevideo and the greatest of all, Buenos Aires, founded by sixty-six Paraguayans. Each dismembered the failing Province of Paraguay. In 1616, Paraguay was dispossessed of her coastline by ministers in Madrid and left at the mercy of the infant cities she had spawned, who bullied her with taxes on the wealth she sent downriver as yerba, tobacco and hides. When Buenos Aires asserted independence from Spain in 1811, she looked covetously at the rich *yerbales** of Paraguay, and began to assert a right of reunion. For Paraguay, wrote the Buenos Aires envoy to Asunción, there were only two options: 'incorporation into the (newly constituted) United Provinces of Argentina – or economic asphyxia'[3]. Dictator Rosas of Buenos Aires chose asphyxia and blockaded the river border. Isolated and defensive, Paraguay was closed within her swamp and jungle frontiers until the rivers opened.

The year President Bonaparte became emperor of France, the regime which had dominated the River Plate for twenty years was destroyed and the great estuary city, Buenos Aires, was humiliated by the horsemen of the interior. The Emperor of Brazil paid 500,000 patacones† to the gold-driven warlord General Urquiza, governor of Entre Rios province, to join his forces and depose Dictator Rosas. Urquiza's gauchos galloped south to besiege the city and Dictator Rosas fled aboard a British warship to Southampton. Argentina became a

---

* Plantations of yerba, Paraguayan tea.
† Estimated to be about US$500,000 in today's value.

Confederation of Provinces under General, now President, Urquiza and the capital was transferred 400 miles upriver, to the town of Paraná. The plug had been pulled from the Plate estuary. The great rivers of South America were open and running freely, no longer clogged by the taxes and customs boats of Buenos Aires. The north Argentine provinces could export their corn and cattle and the landlocked Republic of Paraguay to the north, barely known and spoken of as savage, could export its yerba and hides and import arms against the day the river closed again.

Paraguay was governed by the López family, who had inherited a race accustomed to absolute rule. The country was 'but one large farm administered by the President'[4]. Its most profitable crop was yerba. The state – Don Carlos – granted a licence for its cultivation, bought the yield and exported it, duty-free, at an 800 per cent mark-up. Don Carlos frowned upon the term *dictator* and maintained several ministers of government for the sake of appearances but these were 'entirely unimportant, for, with the exception of General López ... none of the so-called Ministers can decide or give an opinion on the most trivial matters without reference to the president who moreover dictates all official Documents for their signature and opens all official communications addressed to them.'[5] The López family owned vast *estancias* (estates). They did not pay taxes. They participated in state monopolies and used the labour of conscripts, state slaves and peons. They sold torn notes at discount to the treasury and were given their full worth in new.

The President and his son knew that Paraguay's unexpected freedom could swiftly end. A united Argentina below and the Empire of Brazil above could crack Paraguay like a flea between two thumbnails but would not do so if there were modern guns along the borders and opposition from the European powers with fleets in South American waters. Thus, before Buenos Aires under a new leader recovered her strength and returned to toll and patrol the rivers, or Brazil quarrelled with her new gaucho allies, or the river provinces of Argentina proved as avaricious as Buenos Aires, Paraguayan borders must be defended from within and guaranteed from without. There must be European merchants in Paraguay, and European consuls in Asunción to represent them, and Paraguayan agents in Buenos Aires, Montevideo, London and Paris to keep Paraguay in the world's eye. Europe must be bound by honour and interest to defend Paraguay against bullying neighbours who would take more notice of Lord Clarendon and the Emperor Napoleon than they did of President López and *el generalito*. In early 1853, while temperatures rose to intolerable heights, British, French and Italian representatives of the new legations to Argentina came slowly up the shifting channels of the River Paraguay to Asunción to negotiate the right of navigation on the River Paraguay in exchange for recognition of Paraguayan sovereignty. The US *Waterwitch* left New York, commissioned to chart Paraguayan waters for the Yankee ships which, when the Yankee treaty was ratified, would be sailing here to trade.

Don Carlos knew the foreign envoys and their compatriots must come and he knew they would make his country stronger, but he wanted them only on his own terms. He loathed and distrusted all foreigners except one dissolute Hungarian colonel in his employ and a few smooth Yankees who had recently settled outside his capital and promised to bring great wealth. That summer, he attempted to trick the British envoy into promising recognition of Paraguay without offering concessions in return and there was an unpleasant month of discussion before:

on the 16th of February, the bases were agreed upon: at least, the President of Paraguay formally promised the Plenipotentiaries that he would accept them.

The terms of the said treaty, which has been signed by the French and English Plenipotentiaries and the Northern American and Sardinian★ Chargés d'Affaires, are more or less as follows:

Free navigation of the rivers granted to the contracting parties.

Individuals of their nations may carry on retail trade [hitherto not permitted to foreigners]. They may visit the towns in the interior and trade there [hitherto they have only been allowed to reside at Assumption]; and, lastly, they may intermarry with the women of Paraguay [which hitherto has not been permitted].[6]

It was signed by the young General.

We hope this treaty [said *The Times*] which will introduce a new legislation into Paraguay, will be but the commencement of a long list of reforms very necessary to be made in that country. Then foreigners may proceed thither with some assurance of safety.[7]

A reception was held. The President remained rudely seated throughout, with his hat on.

Whatever may be the result of these negotiations, we are very glad that foreign Powers are seriously engaged in establishing commercial relations with one of the most charming countries of the world, and in opening its gates

---

★ I.e. Italian, envoy of Victor Emanuel 'King of Sardinia, Cyprus and Jerusalem', whose court was in Turin.

to knowledge and civilization . . . Nevertheless, it may be well to observe, *en passant*, that in our opinion, whatever treaties have been made, or may be made, with the existing Government of Paraguay, will be little more than empty words if they be not supported by forces sufficient to insure their being respected.[8]

A Paraguayan legation had now to visit Europe to ratify these treaties with Victoria of England, Napoleon of France and Victor Emanuel of Italy, place orders for arms and bring Paraguay to the attention of the world. General López was appointed Minister Plenipotentiary. Dr Juan Andrès Gelly, the only Paraguayan with diplomatic experience overseas, was appointed to help him. The two younger brothers, Venancio and Benigno, were made Secretaries to the Legation. The young army officers Paulino Alén and José Maria Aguiar, fervent in their admiration of Francisco, were invited along. Carlos Saguier, descendant of trading Frenchmen, joined them and a small horde of other cousins, officers and friends and packed their bags for Europe, eager to explore the world which Argentine cupidity and Don Carlos' unyielding distrust of all things foreign had kept from them. They left Asunción on 12 June 1853 and sailed to Buenos Aires, Rio de Janeiro and Southampton.

In Paris, no woman remained in the demi-monde without her demi-husband to maintain her. She must move downwards into a poorly paid, respectable job, or sideways into the world of *les lorettes*, the mass of pretty women which fluttered about Notre Dame des Lorettes, awaiting discovery by a rich protector or a theatre manager.

. . . the protector of *une lorette* living, for example, in the rue de Grammont, [wrote *Le Moniteur Universel* in a retrospective of July 1870] could get away with 300 francs a month (for gloves and flowers). In the rue du Helder, it was already more expensive: 400 francs a month (with a groom). In the rue Saint-Lazare and the rue de la Caussée-d'Antin, one had to allow 500 francs a month (a horse and carriage). As for the *lorette* who lived in the faubourg du Roulé (faubourg St-Honoré), she needed a protector who was at least a count, if not a duke. He had to assure her an allowance of 10,000 francs a month, a lodge in an hôtel, two carriages, two horses, a footman and a chef.[9]

A *lorette* was a low-ranking courtesan and a courtesan was the geisha of the Second Empire: hostess and entertainer, depositary and showcase for beautiful objects, gem for precious settings. She sought a protector as companion, status symbol and supplier of money but she did not sell herself like a prostitute – rather, she chose whose offer to accept.

It was to this world that Elisa Lynch's unsuccessful elopement had committed her. In early 1854, she was appearing in a salon run by Madame *la veuve* Dumont on Rue Tronchet, in the 10,000 franc district. Rue Tronchet ran north from the Place de la Madeleine, heart of Second Empire Paris. Lovers sent their servants here to the flower market to pick out blooms for the morning-after bouquet; here was the restaurant Durand, where the deputies had met in the heady days of late 1851 to plot the return of Empire. The courtesans came to the massive new church which dominated the square, dedicated to the first Napoleon's *grande armée*. They worshipped beneath the dim gilt and brown marble among statues of the Magdalen in ecstasy and prayer. More than a thousand people heard Mass here each Sunday, and whispered, caught eyes, exchanged cards and inspected each other's clothes, for the *lorettes* of St-Honoré were famously as elegant as their respectable sisters of St-Germain. Their worlds met here, and along the Champs-Elysées, at the Opéra and in the jewellers' shops of the Rue de la Paix, where the female castes eyed each other curiously and the men who bridged their worlds preserved discretion. The *lorettes* wore the brightest colours, all shades of Napoleonic red and the shrieking greens and vermilions which the dyers had lately learnt to produce. They were the first to embrace the crinoline, which made its grotesque reappearance in 1853; they set the fashion for small, *café-au-lait* horses and po-faced English grooms, the tightest habits, the tiniest hats. Their carriages crowded the Bois de Boulogne. They dragged the longest trains to the Opéra and ordered their lovers to sit on the box so their skirts could fit in the carriage.

'There is no more cosmopolitan city in the world than [Paris],' wrote a young Paraguayan visitor in 1856. It lived in 'a fever of pleasure . . . There, the foreigner is accorded the greatest consideration. To be a foreigner is to be privileged; only allude to your foreignness and all doors are opened to you.'[10] The 'incessant voluptuousness of life' was a revelation to the young foreigners at the embassies and the trading missions and those with the personality and the means made the most of their time there.

It was the General's old schoolmate, Captain Juan José Brizuela, who first prowled the Rue Tronchet and found Madame Dumont and her new Irish 'niece'. Later he returned with the General.

The widow, [Brizuela recalled] judging that conversation between them had already become superfluous, wished to be polite and asked Elisa to play a lively piece on the piano to please the gentlemen. Elisa did not hesitate; she arose swiftly and gracefully, while I approached the General and said to him, in Guaraní, 'follow her'. He got up, offered her his arm and led her to the piano stool. During the whole time *la Lynch* played some part of *Il Trovatore*, the General did not lift his gaze from her. When she finished, the pianist arose like a soldier called to perform a duty and her companion led her back to her seat . . . [López] was sitting between Madame Téofile and his chérie, a true Venus. Between them, he looked like a fly floating in a glass of milk.[11]

What can Elisa Lynch have known of Paraguay, and a Paraguayan general? Paraguay had never been represented in Europe and no Paraguayan goods were sold there. For two decades there had been little intercourse between any of the Plate Republics and Europe and the most visible South Americans in Paris were the Brazilians, slave-owners accustomed to astonishing luxury, as massively rich from their latifundias as were the Russians from their estates. Elisa had only the riches of Brazil on which to base her idea of Paraguay, and these two young men themselves: stiffly uniformed, small and swarthy. The General was shorter than she, bearded and stocky, bandy-legged as were many officers from a life in the saddle, but he had courteous manners and a soft voice and several would speak of his charm.

The musicians began to play lively music. The dance began: Solano López with Elisa and me with my chérie. The Englishwoman, a strong character, had shown herself to be both audacious and witty and the General was immediately infatuated. It was unnecessary to do anything more. When the clock sounded three in the morning, the maid appeared and said to Madame, 'le dîner est servi'. We were invited to go through and sat at table with our respective companions. The musicians continued to play the liveliest pieces of their repertoire during dinner and the diners competed in good humour and conversation. When champagne was served, I toasted the happiness of the new couple, to which Madame replied with wit. We applauded and Madame begged that her new friends should not leave Paris so soon. López completed the round of toasts thanking her for her compliments and expressing his fervent wish for the happiness of Madame and her nieces. We drank another bottle of champagne, sent for the coach and, as the musicians played a farewell, the couples withdrew.[12]

The legation had come to Paris from three months in London, which the General had found distasteful.

Francisco Solano López had been in uniform since the age of thirteen, and a general since that of eighteen. He came from a country where all citizens doffed their hats to members of his family and waited, motionless, until they had passed; where no one spoke the name of Don Carlos, but referred only to *el Supremo Gobierno*.

In the rest of the world, Paraguay was little known and less esteemed. The General's manner did not impress the British Foreign Office, aware of his father's duplicitous conduct towards their envoy in Asunción. On arriving, the General had wished immediately to present his credentials to the Queen but it was September and she was in Scotland. 'The General threatened not to wait [in England] . . .'[13] a Foreign Office memorandum noted, 'but did and was later received by the Queen when she returned to London . . . His own manners were disagreeable and on one occasion, when unavoidably kept waiting for ten minutes at the Foreign Office, he was very impertinent to Lord Clarendon.' The treaty negotiated with little grace in Asunción was ratified. Clarendon agreed to appoint a consul in Asunción to represent British interests and a dour Foreign Office memorandum was drawn up for his guidance. 'You will probably meet with difficulties at the outset,' it advised, in this 'semi-civilised' and 'little-known' state, 'from ignorance on the part of the President of the ordinary usages observed towards the agents of foreign powers.'[14]

The General presented his letter of recall in November and took the boat train to Paris with relief. France had a glamour in South America that no other European country matched. Dashing Napoleon of France was far more to his taste than dumpy Victoria of England and those who knew General López later agreed that Second Empire Paris, where military chic was all-pervasive, was a decisive influence upon him.

> Suddenly emerg[ing] from the semi-barbarism of a remote and almost unknown republic, [he] was dazzled by parade and glitter, the false glory and proud memories of wars and warriors he found around him, and was fired with the ambition of making the brave and devoted people he knew he would one day be called upon to rule, a nation to be feared and courted as the dominant power of South America.[15]

On 22 January 1854, General López was presented to the Emperor Napoleon and gave him one hundred boxes of Paraguayan cigars. For the court, it was one more unremarkable occasion on which foreign envoys queued to bow, murmur to Napoleon, kiss the hand of Eugenie and be processed on. For newcomers to Paris, it was a revelation.

Those to be presented made their way to the Tuileries through a city blazing with light, past bonfires in the Place du Carrousel which illuminated their arrival for the spectators sitting in carriages or pressing their noses to the railings. After presentations in the Salon Louis XIV, the visitors were manoeuvred into a crocodile and marched down the palace corridors, flanked and tactfully herded by officers of the court, glinting and flashing: masters of ceremony in violet, prefects of the palace in amaranth, chamberlains in scarlet, equerries in green, orderlies in pale blue and assorted others in gold and silver. They wore plumes and spurs and epaulettes and dashing boots. The imperial couple went first, Napoleon in white silk tights and Eugenie a mass of expensive spangles, then a gaggle of Bonaparte princes and princesses, the foreign envoys, marshals of France, presidents of the senate and the *corps legislatif* all crossed the Salle du Trône, the Salon d'Apollon and the Salle du Premier Consul. In the Salle des Marechaux, the company sank to the floor as the Emperor and Empress swept past and took their seats on a dais.

The first family of Paraguay had no palace, no court, no court officials, no etiquette, no uniforms beyond the bizarre combination of cocked hat and tailcoat that Don Carlos wore, and no charming empress, for la Presidenta, the General's fat mother, went bare-legged and smoked cigars.

General López took rooms in the Place Vendôme hotel where Napoleon III had lived before his coup. He became a client of Napoleon's shoemaker, from whom he acquired seventy-three pairs of patent leather boots; and of Napoleon's tailor, from whom he commissioned uniforms in red, white and blue, colours adopted in Paris for the Paraguayan flag. He had his portrait painted in uniform and commissioned a tricolour presidential sash. Occasional invitations came from court. One day, he attended a review of the Crimean troops with the Emperor, who ceded brief but glorious command to his American guest. He adored the city, the government and Napoleon and, in the Rue Tronchet, he discovered a companion whose height, fashionable red-gold hair and practised charm were those of Napoleon's empress.

Their relationship was conducted with gallantry and a prodigality of gifts, but discreetly. The couple presumably did all the things a courtesan and her lover were expected to do: attend the Theatre Français and the Salle Ventadour, the Mass at Notre Dame, where the Emperor and the Empress worshipped, and military reviews on the Champs de Mars; go on luxurious picnics, ride in the Bois de Boulogne and spend huge amounts of Paraguayan money on *objets*, champagne, cognac, uniforms for him, jewels for her; descend to the famous sewers and ascend the Arc de Triomphe, attend the races at Longchamps, ride at Meudon and fish at Charenton. Elisa Lynch had found a rich protector and General López had found a guide to Empire life, or one facet of it at least. Perhaps he did not understand Elisa's equivocal position. Perhaps he did not care.

Not all at the Paraguayan legation looked kindly on the General's infatuation. Benigno López, youngest of Don Carlos' three sons, was a young man of wily charm believed to resent his elder brother's status. The name of Elisa Lynch was first heard in Paraguay in a letter from Benigno to his parents, complaining that Francisco was wasting time and money on a woman.

Later assessment of López as a dazzled barbarian bent on warfare was conditioned by hindsight, and unfair. General López' head was turned by Paris but he was a serious and intelligent young man, fiercely aware of the backwardness and defencelessness of his country. He did not doubt that the presidency would be his when Don Carlos died and he was determined to turn Paraguay from an obscure and primitive state into a first-rate South American power. He would build a railway; he wanted an arsenal and a foundry and European methods and materials for his shipyards; he wished young Paraguayans to be instructed in mechanical engineering, medicine and international law; ladies must wear shoes and learn to use forks; there must be inoculation against measles. He sought men who could design defences and manufacture arms to make his country respected. A vital part of his plan for greatness was the creation of a river-navy which would defend Paraguay's borders and break her isolation.

Charles Henderson, appointed British consul after the General's frosty interviews with Lord Clarendon, had sent back a fretful dispatch about the difficulties of reaching Asunción. The commander of the British fleet at Rio would not lend him a gunboat because the shallow waters of the River Paraguay were too dangerous. In Montevideo, he met the Comte de Brayer, newly appointed French consul, similarly frustrated, 'having lost all hope of procuring a conveyance in a Merchant Vessel in consequence of the very limited intercourse between Montevideo and Paraguay'[16]. The two consuls and their wives proceeded to Buenos Aires and came across a third diplomat, US envoy Mr Buckalew, also unable to get to Paraguay. They eventually persuaded a British merchant in Buenos Aires to charter them a boat and left in October.

General López had been instructed by Don Carlos to commission a steamer in Europe and recruit her crew. She would be the first of a fleet of river-boats to connect Asunción to her neighbours. This steamer must be new and splendid, for she would carry the General back via Rio de Janeiro and Buenos Aires, where potential enemies watched. She must be driven by paddles, for these gave optimum manoeuvrability in the shallow waters of the Plate system. When the General visited England, sailing ships filled the Thames basins awaiting conversion to steam, for the Tsar's navy must soon be tackled. A contract was signed with John and Alfred Blyth of Limehead to build a powerful paddle-steamer, named the *Tacuarí* in commemoration of the battle in which Paraguay defeated Argentine invaders in 1811. Her massive wheels, powered by two 130 horsepower engines, could be removed for an ocean passage and re-mounted for river sailing, and she had a top speed of sixteen miles per hour. The Blyths were to recruit her crew and officers; they were also to advertise for, select and engage technical personnel for construction and manufacturing projects in Paraguay.

William Whytehead, one of their own consulting engineers, was a Scotsman living in Streatham with three sisters, commuting to Limehead and leading a life of little adventure. He had already been offered a job in Australia, representing a British firm which sold propellers, when General López offered him the post of Chief State Engineer of Paraguay at £400 per annum, with board, lodging, a servant, two saddle horses and the task of constructing a Paraguayan navy. He chose Paraguay. The General could not have found a better first recruit to introduce into the doubting atmosphere of Asunción: tall, handsome, conscientious and fluent in the essential courtesies of Castilian. George Morice, a retired Royal Navy captain, was engaged to command the *Tacuari* and other Britons contracted to take her to Paraguay and train Paraguayans in the maintenance of her boilers. Advertisements were placed for founders, engineers and masons.

Britain furnished technology but it was in France that the General's vision of a new Paraguay took shape.

Many powerful visitors would come to Second Empire Paris and return with ideas of town planning and public life inspired by Baron Haussman. Great projects covered Paris with dust that year, for the next would bring the Great Exhibition. 'The city of Paris looks like a town that has been bombarded. Whole acres of buildings are cleared away every day . . . Houses that were built not six months ago, according to plans furnished by the government, have been pulled down because they interfere with some new arrangement . . .'[17] Haussman's demolition squads were already at work in the condemned slums of the centre. A vast space outside the Tuileries was scattered with the raw materials of the Louvre. The façade of the Hotel Dieu was obscured by scaffolding.

Across the Bois de Boulogne, ladies and their escorts skirted immense drainage works which would lift Paris from the bogs of the Seine. Such grand public spaces would suit any regime which wished to keep its people happy, impress foreigners and ensure its troops could penetrate every part of a city. Rome was transformed on the model of Paris; so were Madrid, Brussels, Stockholm and Mexico City. General López of Paraguay was among those who left determined to model his own capital on the new Paris just emerging from the old.

As 1854 advanced, the nations of Europe faced each other across the Black Sea. By July, 100,000 French soldiers were gathered at Boulogne, preparing to embark for war. In September, Field Marshal St Arnaud reported that his men were about to enter the Crimea. 'I am full of confidence,' he wrote to his Emperor, 'and full of passion.' A loan of 250 million francs was approved in Paris and an appeal made to the people to back it with their own money. Sixty thousand subscribers answered the call and Napoleon addressed his troops: 'Europe knows that if France draws her sword, it is because she has been compelled.' Soldiers marched through Paris, cheered on their way by the crowds who had paid for their guns.

Elisa was often alone that year, for the General had business elsewhere. In March, he left for the court of King Victor Emanuel in Turin, where his treaty was ratified and he was granted the Sacred and Military Order of the Saints Maurice and Lazarus. Later, he went to Rome to see Cardinal Antonelli. In June, he went away again, to the court of Isabel of Spain. The *Tacuarí* was shortly expected in Bordeaux, crewed by British sailors, with British tradesmen and professionals aboard. Others would come later, on the new twice-monthly steam service from Liverpool to Buenos Aires, then the passenger services the General was to establish between Buenos Aires and Asunción.

The relationship between Elisa Lynch and the General developed. One letter survives, written in Paris on 5 June by Elisa, received in Madrid by Solano López.

> *Cheri*, a thousand thanks my Pancho* for sending me this money so quickly . . . I will send you this evening the letter from my husband . . . farewell, my beloved, do not fail to come soon, your Elisa is waiting for you impatiently and embraces you with all her heart . . .[18]

By the end of July, she was sure of her pregnancy. By October, the General had taken steps to return her to her unmarried status.

There were two ways to make a fresh start as Miss Elisa Lynch, officially unblemished. The Vatican would consider annulments for women whose husbands had proved themselves sexually unfit for marriage because of impotence or kinship; or for women who could put up enough money, preferably accompanied by *raison d'état*, to buy one. A second husband with the pull and the cash to convince the Romans she was a woman wronged might retrieve Elisa's maidenhood.

Xavier de Quatrefages came to Paris in October to attend a meeting with Dr Juan Andrès Gelly of the legation. In exchange for an unrecorded sum of money, he put his name to a cunningly written document, witnessed by HM consul in Paris, which granted Elisa Lynch, 'my wife, residing with me', his permission to regulate independently any possessions or interests she might have outside France. It might be useful in any petition to the Vatican. It would also safeguard property given her by the General, which would otherwise belong to Quatrefages, but it was not a divorce. Elisa remained unmarriageable; Dr Gelly could contrive no more.

---

* Diminutive of Francisco.

It was the ambition of many to make a fortune in the New World, then retire to the Old with cash in the bank. Paris was the city most popular with exiles and absentees – those men who left immense *estancias* in the hands of a manager and moved to Europe; and those others who were ostensibly kicked out in a coup and quietly given a large amount of money to go without a fuss. Ex-President Rosas of Buenos Aires had unaccountably chosen Southampton but Paris was the gilded cage of choice and Elisa, with or without her lover, could expect to return, older and richer. Her Russian was irretrievably lost. Her chance of winning a 10,000 franc keeper was compromised by her pregnancy. The prospect of being mistress to the president-in-waiting of Paraguay was preferable to seeing her value decrease in St-Honoré. That autumn she decided that when the General returned to Paraguay she would go with him.

On 10 November, Elisa left Bordeaux with her lady's maid, Julie, aboard the French passenger steamer *Ville de Marseilles*. On 11 November, the *Tacuari* left behind her, carrying General López, the Paraguayan legation, William Whytehead and two British master founders, one with his infant son. Henri Caston, Parisian hairdresser and cosmeticist was also aboard, and a French cooper called M Chevreux, a few servants and Mr Ouseley, British Minister in the River Plate, to whom López had agreed to give a lift. Captain Morice was in charge of a crew of seventy. His wife Catherine accompanied him. In the hold, there were the boots made by Napoleon's shoemaker, uniforms made by his tailor, the presidential sash, crates of furniture, boxes of repeating rifles and eight steam engines.

They were leaving a continent enmired in war. In December, a second war-loan was approved in Paris and 500 million francs raised by public subscription to pay for a new levy required to join the 581,000 soldiers, 113,000 horses and 62,000 sailors already called up. As the siege of Sebastopol began, the *Ville de Marseilles* reached Buenos Aires. She anchored in the estuary and small sailing boats came to take her passengers to the shallows, where horse-drawn carts drew them on to the hard and customs men waited. The General had been detained in the capitals of Brazil and Uruguay. In Rio, he was received by the Emperor, Dom Pedro. In Montevideo, he met the statesman Dr Lamás and discussed the news in the Plate: the changes in alliance and tendency during his absence and what political system might emerge from the ruins of Rosas' Argentina, divided once more after brief unity into the city-state of Buenos Aires and a Confederation of Provinces. They talked of the threat posed to their own small countries by these and by the Empire of Brazil and the General assured Dr Lamás that, should there be Argentine aggression towards Uruguay in the future as there had been in the past, Paraguay would defend her sister state.

'You bring large political ideas home with you, and large projects,' the Uruguayan remarked.

'No one,' said the General, 'knows what destiny awaits them. If any one thought currently stirs my country, it is the need to count in the politics of the Plate, to be an influence for peace, seeking only that the balance of the powers is preserved and, with it, Paraguay's own life and independence, which will be endangered should ever the old rivals Brazil and Argentina predominate decisively in this region of America.'[19]

The *Tacuarí* carried one man fewer when she left Montevideo, for Juan José Brizuela had disembarked to take up the post of Commercial Agent for the Paraguayan government. Some said this was to preserve discretion about the circumstances in which Elisa met the General. She made Buenos Aires on 3 January 1855, flying the new Paraguayan tricolour, and docked among the other steamers, the brigantines, launches, coal-boats and frigates for Cadiz, La Coruña, Marseilles, Southampton, Bordeaux, Antwerp, Bayonne, London, Genoa, Le Havre, New York, Rio, Montevideo and Australia, *pais del oro*, and a fleet of nineteen Brazilian warships gathering to invade Paraguay.

Chapter Three

In 1493, Pope Alexander VI had granted the Kingdoms of Spain and Portugal the right to seize and occupy all unchristian lands. He suggested the world be divided by a line drawn from pole to pole a hundred leagues west of the Cape Verde Islands. The unchristian world to the east would belong to Portugal; that to the west, to Spain. Both states were pleased with the papal dispensation to conquer and exploit but agreed that the line must be tweaked. In 1494, envoys from the Spanish and Portuguese courts met in the Spanish town of Tordesillas and moved the line 270 leagues further west and six years later, Portuguese sailors landed on the coast of Brazil. With joy they found it was heathen and east of the Tordesillas Line, belonging therefore to King John of Portugal on the authority of the Pope. New World conquests could not be kept quiet and the Spaniards moved in wherever they smelt silver. They smelt it in the South American interior, in unmapped areas where no one knew precisely where the Tordesillas Line fell. The men along the new frontiers fought and three centuries later agreed that the Line of 1494 was not adequate to separate the empires. Representatives of the European crowns met to determine with greater thoroughness the border between

Portuguese Brazil and the Spanish viceroyalty of the Rio de la
Plata. They did so in the Treaty of San Ildefonso, 1777, which
defined the border between Paraguay and Brazil in baffling
terms:

> [the frontier will follow] the Grande de Curitiba otherwise
> known as the Iguazu; following this downstream to its
> debouchment into the Paraná on its eastern bank and
> proceeding thence upstream up the same Paraná until the
> Rio Igurey joins it on its western bank;
> . . . from the mouth or debouchment of the Igurey it will
> follow the course of this river upstream as far as its principal
> source; and from there it will describe a straight line along
> the watershed . . . until it strikes the source or principal
> tributary of the river nearest to the said line, which river
> empties itself into the Paraguay on its eastern bank and will
> perhaps prove to be the one known as the Corrientes. And
> then it will go down the course of this river to its debouch-
> ment into the same Paraguay.

The Treaty of San Ildefonso contained this flaw: it did
not specify which of the hundreds of tributaries along the
Paraguay–Brazilian border was the true River Igurey. When
the lawyers went home, those on the frontiers searched for
streams bearing names which could be twisted to match the
words of the treaty. The Portuguese claimed the Igurey was
the river they knew as the River Garei, which entered the
Paraná below the island of Salta Grande. This would give
them an enviable frontier at the source of the Rio Jujuy which
was, they claimed, in fact the Corrientes. The Spanish said
no, the Igurey was the river they knew as the Yagurei, the
Yoinheima, the Monice and the Ivinheima; the Corrientes,
they said, was not the Jujuy but the Apa. They were still
tussling over the rivers when Madrid lost control of her

colonies and the independent Republic of Paraguay took over defence of the borders.

It was the Apa border to the north which most concerned Brazil, for the River Apa confined the Brazilian Matto Grosso, a vast, rich and mysterious land scarcely settled and full of promise. Communications between Rio and this distant province were difficult. It took a lone horseman one month's hard and dangerous riding to get between them. Transportation of supplies or large numbers of people was possible only up the River Paraguay but no foreigners were welcome on that river, studded with river-forts and guardhouses manned by Don Carlos' soldiers, as unthinkingly hostile to the foreign as their master.

Only Don Carlos had refused to join Brazil and her allies when they attacked Dictator Rosas in 1852, opened the rivers and allowed his legation to Europe. A sly but clumsy Brazilian envoy joined the European envoys negotiating their treaties in Asunción in 1853. His official task was to ensure the river to the Matto Grosso was formally opened to Brazilian ships; his unofficial one was to exclude European influence from these waters. 'He left no stone unturned to thwart and baffle us,' the British envoy wrote; 'he condescended to enter into low intrigues, he endeavoured to influence foreigners, and natives against us.'[1] While the General was in Paris, the Brazilian was accused of dishonesty and expelled. Brazilian troops established a garrison on the disputed border, Paraguayan soldiers forced them back, the disgraced envoy called on Rio to avenge his honour and now a Brazilian admiral was approaching the southern border in the latest attempt to resolve the border dispute, still rancorous four centuries after the Treaty of Tordesillas.

On 13 January, General López and the legation left Buenos

Aires in the *Tacuarí* for Asunción. Elisa Lynch remained behind with a couple of officers and her maid.

The General's arrival in his impressive new ship had been noted in Buenos Aires but there were foreigners enough in port that the presence of the extremely pregnant pretty lady who joined him from the *Ville de Marseilles* was not necessarily remarked upon. Elisa was travelling with a cover story: she was a lady of independent means, travelling abroad in search of amusement and possible New World investment. Her husband (an Austrian colonel) was still in Europe. Her name was no longer Elisa de Quatrefages, but Madame Lynch. This was a neat blend: *Madame* confirmed the existence and foreignness of her husband and her own smart French connections; *Lynch* was just permissible under Spanish custom whereby married ladies added to rather than changed their surname. Her situation was unusual but possible. It was known that the General had recruited several Europeans as consultants and Madame Lynch's husband might have been one of these, detained and sending his wife ahead in the General's care. Already there was one Hungarian officer of dubious reputation in Asunción acting as military consultant to Don Carlos.

The last month of her pregnancy coincided with Carnival. Masked balls continued each night until dawn and few revellers cared for the reports of batteries being built at Paraguayan forts, of ships sunk to block the River Paraguay, of the evacuation of border villages, or the sermons preached by Paraguayan priests to call the nation to arms. The days were steeped in wet heat and the nights were festive. There was little reliable communication with Asunción. No packet sailed regularly between the two cities and news came only from the crew of an occasional yerba boat. Paraguay was the object of hostile, tittering curiosity here. It was said to be a country of serfs and *mestizos**, secret police, backward ways and a monstrous, unpredictable leader. Their first news was unexpected. In February, a US ship brought angry men to Buenos Aires who spoke of insult, honour and compensation.

It had taken Edward Hopkins eight years to ease himself into Don Carlos' confidence, win trade concessions from the old man and set himself up as cigar magnate outside Asunción. He had wheedled and boasted and said the cigars of Don Carlos would rival those of Havana, promoted the riches of Paraguay in Washington and had himself appointed US consul. Don Carlos promised monopolies, slave labour and exemption from duties, for he was to be partner, and these were privileges of a López industry. But when he finally had what he wanted, Don Edward had become less deferential. The Cubans who rolled his cigars and the Yankees who ran his saw-mill did not dismount when a López appeared. Insolence was offered to customs officials. Hopkins spoke warningly of his consular status and Don Carlos' promised participation in profits did not materialise. The Hopkins brothers began to consort less with the López family and more with newly arrived and supercilious Europeans.

One day in November 1853, Don Edward's brother Clement rode out with the wife of the French agent and met two Paraguayan soldiers herding cattle through a wood. They gestured that the riders should pull to one side, but Hopkins galloped among the cows, causing them to panic and run. There was an altercation, a soldier hit Hopkins with the flat of his sword and the large and furious foreigner forced entry into Don Carlos' office to rant of insult. The soldier was flogged 300 times. Hopkins said it was not enough: an apology must be printed in the *Semanario*, Asunción's only newspaper

---

* People of mixed Spanish and Indian blood.

and Don Carlos' mouthpiece. It was too much. Decrees were immediately issued:

1) no servant shall engage in the service of a foreigner without a written agreement or notification given and approved by the government;
2) all meetings of foreigners, except for the ostensible purpose of visiting and innocent diversion, are forbidden, by day and by night.

A defect was found in the sale of the land on which the cigar factory stood; it was confiscated. Hopkins' exequatur as consul was withdrawn. No one spoke to him in the offices of the port and the ministries. His parcels did not arrive. He grew desperate, and stubborn, refusing to send his consular letters of protest in Castilian; Don Carlos returned them unopened and Hopkins was saved from ignominy only by the arrival of the US *Waterwitch*, the ship sent to chart the Paraguayan rivers, whose commander managed to get his consul aboard and away. US sailors manned her cannon as she steamed from port but Hopkins took no compensation for his factory or his land and passed through Buenos Aires swearing the vengeance of Washington.

Meanwhile, the *Waterwitch* ascended the river again to chart the waters of the Paraguayan–Argentine frontier along the River Paraná. The river was divided by a small island, overlooked by the southernmost of the Paraguayan river-forts. To the south of this island, the river was Argentine; to the north, Paraguayan and the *Waterwitch* pilot was unsure of the channel. He steered through southern waters but struck a sand bar. A canoe came from the fort with a letter for the captain but he said he could, or would, read only an English translation, sent it back and took his ship into the northern channel. There were shouts from the fort but the Yankees did not understand them, they said, and kept going. Cannon fired and the *Waterwitch* helmsman toppled: a bullet had ripped through the stern and killed him at the wheel. The *Waterwitch* ground into reverse on one wheel and retreated, returning fire as she went. The Yankees nursed their ship downriver to Buenos Aires, where her commander was now promising that a gunboat would soon be on its way to Asunción.

It was in these circumstances of double threat that Elisa Lynch gave birth to her first son and named him Juan Francisco Lynch de Quatrefages. He would always be known as Panchito. Scant days after his birth, she, her officer escort, the maid Julie, the baby and their servants followed the General north, up the Silver River and beyond, past the frontier fort where the *Waterwitch* had been fired on, past the Brazilian fleet anchored at Tres Bocas and into the American interior.

They passed the estuary island of Martin García and steamed out of *porteño** waters and into those of the Confederation, where General Urquiza governed. Signs of his army's recent siege littered the banks, diminishing as the steamer churned upriver. The province of Entre Rios lay to the right, that of Santa Fe to the left, the size of Scotland and England respectively. The river divided into shifting, shallow channels. It took four days to reach Tres Bocas, the great confluence of the Rivers Paraná and Paraguay. To the east, the Paraná streamed off along the northern border with the Confederation; running due north towards the Andean sierras was the River Paraguay. Here the Brazilian gunboats were anchored, awaiting orders.

Travellers approached Paraguay with a sense of mystery. Beyond the Argentine lay something new and strange, not the

---

* *Porteña/porteño*: belonging to or resident in Buenos Aires.

bastardised Europe of the coast but a different, older America. Across the border, the water deepened, the channels broadened and the vegetation grew thick and gleaming on the eastern bank. It was a landscape with the beauty and brutality of the earliest travellers' tales, scarcely changed since the first treasure-hunters had seen it 300 years before.

They passed the first guardhouse at Cerrito: a viewing platform within a stockade where the men tended mandioca and maize, breaking off to note the names and details of every passenger and cargo entering the country and send them on by horse and canoe to Don Carlos. The midday heat blistered paint from the boards and they came to a hairpin curve in the river. At its apex, on the eastern bank, was the fortress of Humaitá – 'blackstone fort' – the principal Paraguayan defence against invasion. Artillery was going up on the bank. Officials came to confiscate the newspapers brought from *abajo**. A man came aboard to pilot them through the changing channels and a soldier, to prevent those with binoculars from looking at the guardhouses on the bank. *Camalotes* drifted past, free-floating flowered islands torn from the riverbank by winter floods, dense with water hyacinths and wildlife. Jaguars had been trapped on these and carried as far as the port cities, where they scavenged and mauled until they were shot.

Vast expanses of still, muddy water stretched away on either bank: to the west, in the unexplored Chaco from which Indians shot arrows at the infrequent boats; to the east, into cattle-land. For a hundred miles north of the border, there were *lodazales, pantanos, esteros, banados, carizales* – red and green floodplains just below the level of the river, some months dried to grey clay by a withering heat, others still liquid and

---

* 'Below', a term used to refer to Buenos Aires, and then the rest of the world.

dammed by banks where beds of reeds grew six feet high among the palms, colonised by *pata silbador*, whistling duck, and screaming parrots; by whooping frogs, the pampas peewit, spoonbill, turkey-buzzard, snipe and snippet, the delicate mincing ibis, water-hens and lily-trotters which paddled among the *camalotes*; caymen and blunt-nosed water-hogs; *yaguara*, a small freshwater crocodile; agile little deer, jaguar, otter and armadillo. Unseen, but heard at dusk, were monkeys in the high palms.

The only human settlements visible were the chapel villages, *capillas*, established two centuries before by the Jesuits. Superb churches full of their silver and their life-sized painted saints still rose against the sky, around them a plaza of clay and adobe huts below the orange trees. Even in times of peace, this was a landscape barely touched and barely habited. Now, the Brazilians were expected and no one trod the eastern bank but barefoot soldiers from the watchtowers. Their canoes were seen close in by the riverbanks at dusk, carrying the day's reports. By night, they slept on platforms built high, above the mosquitoes.

Ten leagues on, they passed a town, Villa del Pilar. Then the river turned startling red as they neared the River Bermojo, which brought water rich in iron oxide across the Chaco plain from Bolivia to stain the River Paraguay. A day further north, they saw the estuary of the River Tebicuarí, crowded with islets and fig-groves, and the landscape on the east bank changed, the marshes began to drain, the woods to thicken and Paraguay became an orange grove. The hedges were of orange trees and jasmine, laced with creepers. The thatched huts stood each in its group of orange trees. The scent of oranges lapped at the banks. The *esteros* were replaced by red sandstone, the hills were frequent and small villages were visible around inlets. A few stoic individuals still tended their mandioca and their fruit, or squatted in

doorways, sucking their yerba maté* from gourds. The rest
had gone inland.

They passed Villetta, a single square of whitewashed houses
opening onto the river; then the orange port of San Antonio,
where the Yankees' abandoned cigar-factory stood in a recent
clearing. Thick woods lay above, and the city of Asunción:
streets of deep red sand, white houses and more cannon
pointing south. There were low sailing craft in the bay, and
rowing boats with nets.

They stepped from the steamer into boats and from the boats
on to the beach, and up to the cool colonnade of the port
office. Knots of people squatted in the shade of palm trees,
watching. Inside, the port captain took a plaque from the wall
and read aloud.

> *Viva* the republic of Paraguay! *Muera* the filthy and disgust-
> ing tyrant Rosas, so-called President of the Confederation!
> [This was out of date, as the tyrant had retired to
> Southampton.] *Muera* the traitor Urquiza! [Equally out of
> date, as General Urquiza was now the architect of river
> freedom and friend to Paraguay.]
> All foreigners entering the dominions of the Republic
> will observe the following dispositions: 1) hats will be
> respectfully removed whenever passing a soldier of the
> republic. 2) Lanterns must be carried whenever walk-
> ing the streets after dark. 3) No galloping in city streets.
> 4) Should the Supreme Head of the Republic be
> encountered within or without the city, anyone on foot will
> immediately stop and take off his hat; anyone on horseback
> will immediately dismount and perform the same ceremony.
> 5) Fines imposed on all those who contravene these orders

---

*Infusion of yerba sucked through a silver straw.

will be as per rates stated in the Police Station. Signed:
Carlos Antonio López, 1843.

All the glee of a peasant in uniform emerges from accounts of
arrival in Don Carlos' Paraguay. His officials enjoyed making
people wait and spreading their belongings over mucky tables.
They liked to put unnecessarily personal questions in the
interests of national security and make everyone open their
mouths wide and have their tongues examined for disease,
and to confiscate small articles from luggage. No one put
personal questions to Elisa, poked fingers into her Parisian
bags or looked at her tongue, for rumours that *el generalito*
had invited an illustrious lady visitor had already arrived.
Instead, a ceremony of peculiar significance was performed.
It was forbidden that departing foreigners should take out of
Paraguay more than they had declared when entering. Elisa
Lynch declared 500 ounces of gold that day to be her own. If
she left Paraguay, and the General, she would take a golden
pay-off with her.

The General was not at the docks to meet her. He had
arranged that Elisa, Panchito and her servant should spend
their first night in Asunción in a house one block from the
central plaza where he lived. It belonged to the silversmith
Ramón Franco. Franco was a wealthy and important man but
he was a merchant, not a gentleman; not a diplomat or an
officer of the government or army, not a cleric or a landowner
or a member of the small cosmopolitan section of Asunceno*
society which occasionally received important foreign visitors
with a letter of introduction.

The city was desolate. Heat haze and red dust overhung
the streets, empty but for barefoot soldiers. The treasury, the
great silver ornaments of the cathedral and the powder in the

---

* *Asuncena/Asunceno*: belonging to or resident in Asunción.

arsenal had been dragged away in ox-carts and hidden in villages. The inhabitants had gone and their houses were shuttered. Soldiers bivouacked in the plazas. When a golden-haired vision appeared in a carriage sent by the General, officers' voices faded mid-order and the men let their guns droop. Hats were whipped off in the unthinking deference to any manifestation of the López family which characterised the population of Paraguay. Some of the young men who saw her that day asked their officers if she came from a different world.[2]

Her officer escort introduced Elisa to her hostess, Doña Tomasa de Franco. This lady spoke neither French nor English and possibly little Spanish. When the officers departed to report to the General, Elisa, Julie and the baby were alone with this incomprehensible, barefoot woman who smoked small cigars. Just before nine, the silence of an empty city was broken by drums in the Plaza del Gobierno, beating the day's retreat. At nine precisely, the cathedral bells rang the *queda*, a thunderous peal which ordered silence. Those still in the city shut themselves behind thick walls of bedrooms furnished simply: 'a wooden bed, a mattress, a pillow without a cover, a cotton bedspread'[3]. Utter quiet was interrupted only by whispering soldiers on patrol and those few whom necessity obliged to break the curfew, carrying their lanterns.

General López was in a difficult position. He might not yet have told Elisa what everyone else knew: that he already had a long-term mistress living in Asunción with their ten-year-old son Emiliano and eight-year-old daughter Adelina. The lady was Juana Pesoa, whom he had met in Villa del Pilar when eighteen and newly a general; she was a few years older. Their liaison had been interrupted by his trip to Europe but he had no intention of ending it. Many of the crates loaded on to the *Tacuarí* in Bordeaux had been unpacked in Juana Pesoa's house by the time Elisa Lynch was shown into Señora de Franco's spare room.

Doña Tomasa can have found the evening little easier than her guest. It was she, unused to the soft endings of French, who first addressed Elisa as *Madama*. It was the name by which she would be most often known in Paraguay.

The General could devote little time to Elisa and Panchito. He had ordered the return of an envoy sent by Don Carlos to parley with the Brazilian admiral on the border and spent most of February at Humaitá fort, supervising the construction of emergency defences. On 15 March, the admiral arrived in Asunción on his flagship. He and the General met day after day in the *casa de gobierno*★ by the river, making proposal and counter-proposal for the borders ill-defined by San Ildefonso. They reached no agreement but signed a treaty of friendship, navigation and commerce which recognised the right of Brazilian ships to sail to the Matto Grosso. A twenty-one-gun salute to the admiral's ship assuaged the wounded honour of the Empire and the Asuncenos came back. Valuables returned on carts, the silver statues of the cathedral were replaced in their niches and the market women returned to the squares.

It was a small city, squeezed between the riverbank and the woods, of red, rutted streets and intense light. In the early morning, when the air was still cool, men sat on the steps before their houses and brewed yerba maté, that narcotic, aromatic, dreamy tea which the whole nation drank at every hour. The women began to arrive from the fields, barefoot and in single file, each with hair loose and dark down her back, square in a fringe across her forehead, a basket or water jar on her head and a cigar in her mouth. They colonised the docks, the cathedral colonnade and the market square, 'seated upon the ground, encircled by fruits, vegetables and an eager crowd of buyers'[4]; or pounding maize, two or three

---

★ Government house.

standing to strike rapidly in a wooden mortar. Slaves came from the dim houses to shop and ask if they had seen the General or his *querida*★ and the baby. No one spoke of Don Carlos for the *piragües* were everywhere, the 'feather-footed ones' who lived, and had always lived, among Paraguayans like the household gods of tribes: tolerated, placated, fed and feared.

There were two principal plazas, wide dusty spaces of grass hummocks and earth, with buildings arranged irregularly round them and views of open country between the gaps: Mercado Guazú†, where the General lived; and the Plaza del Gobierno a block below, fronting on to the sandy rivershore with a view across to the flatlands. Here was the new cathedral, sturdy and neoclassical, with porticos where the women sold their fruit and bread; Don Carlos' house, filling half one side of the plaza; and the *casa de gobierno*, where congress occasionally sat, part balconied palazzo, part building site. Three different corps of guards stood duty, presenting their arms periodically to the shouts of their officers. They wore the new colours imported from France, their crimson blouse and blue kepi bright against tawny dust. Priests fluttered between the cathedral and the seminary behind. Occasionally the reverend figure of Padre Maiz was seen, grave and square-faced, a fast riser in the Paraguayan church via tutorship of the López boys to directorship of the seminary, close and constant adviser to Don Carlos. Ministers of government trotted between the President's house and the *casa de gobierno* with their trains of slaves, clerks and private secretaries, young canny men who had caught the President's eye from their benches in the seminary or the Escuela de Matemáticas.

★ *Querida/querido*: sweetheart.
† *Guazú*: 'big' in Guaraní.

The only carriage used in Asunción came once or twice a day from stables behind Don Carlos' house. The scene was observed by a newcomer. 'Three ministers of state hung out of a window sucking oranges'[5], waiting for movement so they could run to their houses, put on a hat and be ready to take it off again as Don Carlos appeared. If his own hat was white, he was in a good temper. If it was black, he was not and this was a code all Asunción understood. His carriage was drawn by three pairs of horses but had no coachman, for his dignity was infringed by a back turned to him from the coachman's seat. The horses were steered by three soldiers, each mounted on the left-hand horse with his sword on his shoulder, the foremost brandishing a terrific whip. Trumpeters struck up the national hymn when the President appeared and he shouted for silence, cursing them and their instruments as he heaved his great body into the seat. Those who had no hat hid behind pillars. The coach would jog off to the docks, the house of la Presidenta or the Mercado Guazú, where Don Carlos would motion for silence and shuffle through the corridors to his son's office as swiftly as his bulk allowed, for he liked to burst in without warning on this clever, wilful son and see what he was doing.

The city filled with naked children, smoking. There were mulatto and Negro slaves. At the docks, the Payagua Indians sold their pathetic few items in the plaza in front of the customs house and drank *caña** until they slept. High-sided ox-carts bumped among and between them, bringing yerba in tight, ox-skin bales for shipment to Buenos Aires. Where the city dissolved into fields and red tracks to the east, soldiers trained outside the city garrison on Plaza San Francisco and chain gangs of negroes, convicts and state-owned slaves shuffled to the brick works.

---

* Rum.

Along the unpaved streets of clay, the houses were low and Pompeian, 'decorated with pilasters in low relief and coloured a delicate buff or violet, the wide and lofty doorway . . . showing the pillared courtyard beyond'[6]. Their brick roofs, lintels and window frames all followed the meandering inclines of the streets, up or down with the accident of the ground. Their rooms were dim and cool within dark plastered walls a yard thick, with brick floors and wooden furniture – a couple of painted wooden chairs against the wall, a table. In front of each house, a section of pillared verandah cast shade and protected the adobe walls from the torrential rains of summer. Women paced below them with water jars on their heads, dressed in the white drapes of the *tipoi*, a loose, belted smock which left most of the shoulders bare. Naked small girls carried smaller jars behind. Ladies of status spent their lives in the *sala*, waited on by slaves, dozing and dreaming, telling their rosaries, sitting at the small, glassless windows which gave on to the road, unseen in the dimness within and watching as life went by; or snoozing in hammocks by the orange trees in the yard, waiting for the slaves to come from market with news of the city, the General and the woman he had brought from Paris.

Visitors to Asunción were few and the ladies of the city eager to call upon them. In this season of great heat, their visits began at dawn, when they dressed themselves in the heavy, unnatural dress of the European and forced shoes upon their feet to walk slowly with their slaves along the streets. Flowers were received and given, a younger caller would tell an older lady 'I dreamed of you last night'[7] to express respect. Yerba maté was drunk and cigars rolled and smoked. Each morning, Madame waited in Doña Tomasa's sala but no ladies called, only the officers sent with flowers from the General, or a few merchants sniffing new money. By midday, the ladies had withdrawn to their houses and returned to lighter dress and bare feet. The midsummer heat was unbearable and nothing stirred except the red-faced, sandy-haired foreigners at the docks and the *piragües*, who converged in the Plaza del Gobierno with their reports.

When the light faded, the market women put their baskets on their heads and filed away to the fields, the leader carrying a torch from which to light and re-light their cigars. The foreigners left the docks and Madame, escorted by officers, went riding on one of the General's horses, along the riverbank or to the sugarloaf hill at Lambaré on the green edge of the city. A peal of bells was rung at dusk, shutters came back across the windows and bats awoke and arose from the roofs of reed and earth. Then there was nothing but the *queda*, and the shuffle of teenage soldiers, and the spies. The General was busy. None seemed willing to offer friendship. Newspapers came infrequently from Buenos Aires and the European steamers on which these depended for European news were fewer, for Britain and France were requisitioning ships for the fight against the Tsar. Sometimes, in the evening, the General or Paulino Alén would come to visit. Thus her days passed in tedium.

Until the General told Elisa his father wished to see her.

Don Carlos was a mound of autocratic flesh beneath a great, pear-shaped head, topped always by a huge hat. British visitors remarked on his strange likeness to George IV. He had never left his country and did not wish to. He regarded the foreign professionals imported by his son with grudging respect, for they were necessary to the development of Paraguay and such men were not yet to be found at home. His respect was not extended to Elisa. When news came of her arrival, he had referred to her as Francisco's *hembra*, an aggressively coarse term for a woman, and his remark at the end of their brief interview was discouraging.

'Statesmen,' he told her, 'are not made for love. Francisco has great responsibilities; he may be called on to replace me at any time. Those who bear such responsibilities bear corresponding obligations. Officially, we do not know you.'[8]

Elisa Lynch had already made her way in two difficult milieux: garrison wife in Algeria and courtesan on Rue Tronchet. In Algeria, she was protected by the might of French empire and her status as married woman. In Paris, she had been the native guide and the General always the visitor. In Paraguay, the roles were reversed and the bewildering hostility which met her from all sides left Elisa dependent on her ability to retain his esteem and affection.

She was not invited to the celebrations following the conclusion of the Brazilian treaty. Juana Pesoa did not go either. It was clear that the General would attend state functions as a bachelor, leaving both his women at home. One small victory was gained. She would be the only person in Asunción, other than Don Carlos, to have a carriage. How the General persuaded his father to allow one to this woman when he ordered all others to lock their carriages away in sheds is unknown, but Elisa got her carriage. It was a symbol of independence and defiance.

By winter, the influx of foreigners into Asunción was visible and exciting. They worked hard, putting in twelve-hour days Monday to Friday and a half-day on Saturday. A foreign ship would arrive in the bay every week or so, bringing more flushed, hard-drinking Englishmen or Scots, a few with wives and children, or crates of industrial equipment from Limehead, Liverpool and Bordeaux. The Paraguayans stared at the newcomers in their strange and uncomfortable layers of cloth, the absurd crinolines which would not go through doors and the tight little shoes which hurt their feet. The newcomers stared back at dark-skinned graceful women

49

glinting with gold, unconfined by their *tipoi*, and men in white kilt and poncho, barefoot below heavy silver spurs. All seemed to be performing their role in the transformation of Paraguay. The consuls were sending home reports on the possibilities of commerce and manufacture. Engineer Whytehead, who had made a most favourable impression, was working on the first steamer to be produced in a Paraguayan shipyard. Master Founder Richardson had overseen an acceleration in production at Ybicui foundry outside Asunción. At Humaitá, the 'London Battery', equipped with British guns, was being built by conscripts under foreign direction. Captain Morice was training a Paraguayan crew to replace the sailors and boilermen who brought the *Tacuarí* from Europe. Other foreigners were arriving on each ship in, engaged by the Blyths as 'mechanics', 'artisans', 'engineers' and 'machinists'. They moved into bachelor quarters provided for them by the government in a house by the river known as *el Castillo*, the castle, because it had two storeys. They were the advance party in what would be the largest and most homogenous corps of foreign experts ever introduced into a Spanish American state. Only Madame Lynch's role in the transformation was unclear. There were no precedents in Paraguay for a lady in her position. The concept of *maîtresse en titre* did not exist here; nor did the demi-monde, nor the society in which such ideas could have meaning. Her salon skills could not be set to work to transform a society which had no salons.

Madame had maintained her cover story on the steamer which brought her upriver to Asunción. It would protect her until more satisfactory marital arrangements were made and she had decided whether or not she wanted to stay. However, Benigno López, the General's youngest brother, and the other members of the legation were already here, Benigno expanding on his letters home about Francisco's woman, other members of the legation who might have been polite to her face as the General's companion, not so complimentary when telling their stories of Europe to friends and relatives. Nor was she the first of López' European recruits to reach Paraguay, for Ildefonso Bermejo and his Spanish bride, Doña Purificación, had already come off the Liverpool–Buenos Aires steamer and made their way upriver. They were staying in the General's house until their own was ready.

Ildefonso Bermejo, in exile from Spain for some political miscalculation, had presented himself in Paris. He seemed a man for the new Paraguay: he could write plays, direct plays, establish a theatre company, teach, translate and run a school, he said. The General did not meet his bride, then fiancée, but this lady claimed noble descent and had a fearsome idea of her own worth. Disregarding her position as guest in the General's house and her husband's as an employee of Don Carlos, she was sending forth tongues of fire as Elisa stepped from the boat.

'She has sold her body,' said Doña Pura, 'in every brothel in Paris and now . . . for money . . . she has come to be a despot's concubine.'[9] Since Madame abandoned her husband, Doña Pura told all who would listen, she had flaunted herself at the spas of Baden Baden with an English lord; she had been in Madrid, enrapturing and humiliating a Spanish lover; she had then moved to London, where she exploited and ruined a banker; she had even, Doña Pura said slanderously, captivated Cardinal Antonelli in Rome before sinking her hooks into the young General. Her stories stormed the patios of Asunción, already buzzing with the excitement of the General's return. The reaction of the General's mother was much enjoyed. 'That woman,' she was reported to have said, 'will never enter my house.'[10] When Madame arrived with her baby and her uniformed escort, where she sought friendship, she found pious rejection.

Twenty thousand people lived in Asunción. Society numbered perhaps one hundred families, the foreign community fewer than twenty and the principal ladies of both had decided Madame was wicked, immoral, greedy and spiteful. They snubbed her in the street and refused to return the cards left by her servants. Hostile spaces were left around her when she entered a shop on Calle Palma or attended Mass. Skirts were held away from her crinoline.

The social season of Asunción in the cooler months was lively, in a sedate and provincial way, but the General would not flout convention by escorting his mistress to any function attended by his female relatives. She could attend public celebrations, with her maid or an officer as escort, but it was more difficult to gain an entrée to private houses, including the General's own. She had noticed, however, that la Presidenta and her two daughters left parties at midnight. This, she allowed to be understood, happened to be the correct hour to arrive at any reception in Paris. The midnight entrance was one of the first fashions she set in Paraguay.

In the first year of her new life, Elisa hovered miserably between the public and the private. She had none of the social life she had known in Paris, for there was none of the infrastructure created by and for women in her position. There were no restaurants in Asunción. There was no theatre, opera house or concert hall. There were no pleasure gardens, no carriage drives, no gaming or dance halls or tea shops or shopping arcades, dressmakers' salons or amusement parks and if there had been, there was no woman with whom to share them except her maid. Only occasional horse racing by the river was offered but the General would not escort her, for his family might be present. But if social life were denied her, so was any private life, for every detail of her relationship with the General was leaked to the city by spies and the gossip of the market outside.

The venom against Madame was new and specific, for all the López sons kept acknowledged mistresses, some – like Juana Pesoa – of respectable family, and these women did not attract the same hatred. Juana was the sister-in-law of a wealthy Asunción merchant. She continued to live with her family, apparently no less regarded for having borne López illegitimate children. The other López brothers, too, took their principal mistresses from families of name and property, who continued to go about and be received. Madame was different in startling ways from these women. She was married, and the other mistresses were not. She had a sexual past. She was foreign – visibly, stunningly so – and thus a symbol of how much the General had moved away from his own. It was said that he was infatuated and under 'the Englishwoman's' thumb. It was said that she could persuade him to any scheme she wished and was turning him against his own. The degree of her influence over him was unnatural and dangerous.

There was one young and much-respected lady in Asunción, proud of her pure Spanish blood, whose name had been linked with the General's before he went abroad. It appears he had attempted to climb into her room one night. Some said he had been bent on vicious rape; others thought this was a youthful prank and he intended no harm. Either way, he was rebuffed and left shortly afterwards for Europe. When he returned with Elisa, Pancha Garmendia was relieved – some said – for she had dreaded a renewal of his attentions; or enraged – said others – because she had held out for marriage, not concubinage, and this was now unlikely. Even had Pancha herself been indifferent to the General's loss, he had been the best *parti* in Paraguay and Elisa's presence frustrated the plans of many mamas.

Elisa would regain both privacy and a public role only by creating around her a society which resembled the one she had inhabited in Paris: one where she would be less isolated in private and less visible in public and for this, her own household was essential. The General was already building himself a new house on the Mercado Guazú and another for Madame on the other side of the square, in a street named Calle Fábrica de Balas – Bullet Factory Street. It was a defiant location, yards from the Plaza del Gobierno, the cathedral and Don Carlos' house, in the heart of the city, surrounded by watchers and whisperers. As her carriage came from the stables at the back, the *piragües* knew it. Her destination was common knowledge, with her purchases, the graciousness of her reception, her dress and the colour of her parasol. The spies knew the contents of each crate of European marvels delivered to her back door from a ship in the bay. They knew each time the General visited, and how long he stayed. They knew when one of his aides was sent to the lady with flowers and the General's regrets. They knew what she ate and drank, how often her slaves washed her sheets, what she said to Henri Caston when he did her hair each morning and what she said to Julie when she took it down each night. They knew the General kept his own *piragües* in her household.

Elisa's house was paid for by the General out of his vast income and its function reflected his own status which, like Elisa's, was an amalgam of public and private. The house on Calle Fábrica de Balas was furnished in a way Asunción had never seen, at massive expense, and would host some of the functions elsewhere held in royal or government palaces, for Don Carlos and la Presidenta had neither talent nor inclination for entertaining. Elisa's house was designed to show off its owner but also to show off the new Paraguay.

It caused talk in Asunción, and beyond.

Chapter Four

Madame Lynch was one of two foreign experiments in Paraguay which attracted the attention of a newspaper editor in Buenos Aires. *La Tribuna*, recently established and forward-thinking, had given the General a warm welcome home from Europe, wishing prosperity to his 'young and lovely republic'. Its editor was Hector Varela, Uruguayan by birth, *porteño* by adoption, previously Argentine representative in Madrid, Turin and Barcelona, a man of letters with a high opinion of all he stood for and a lascivious eye for the ladies. He noted the foreign ships docking in Buenos Aires that year bearing professionals, equipment and matériale for Paraguay. He saw shipping companies had begun placing advertisements in his *Marittima* column for freight and passenger services to Asunción. He had remarked on three ships of French colonists who had stopped in Buenos Aires in April, June and July en route to Paraguay and had heard the rumours which crept out in the gossip of seamen that they were unhappy.

In September, he embarked with a lady companion and sailed north. The captain of the ship had met Elisa. 'Be very careful,' he warned them, 'about what you say and who you speak to. There are those in Asunción who are jealous of Madame Lynch. Do not believe half what they say. She is an excellent lady, kind and charming to everyone . . . Asunción is full of spies.'[1]

The riverbank network was swifter than the steamer and a list of all aboard had already reached the port office when Varela docked. Captain Aguiar, formerly of the legation to Europe, was waiting to take him to the General's new house. Don Carlos was uninterested in this visitor: he belonged to the tiresome world of *abajo*, to which his eldest son was go-between. The two men did not know each other well and both were anxious to make a good impression. Varela saw 'a young man, short rather than tall, elegant, with easy manners and a pleasant and expressive face'. He was struck by the General's easy mention of Elisa in their conversation. When he left the house, he observed Captain Aguiar carrying flowers to the house on Calle Fábrica de Balas.

Varela and his lady companion were guests of distinguished Paraguayan acquaintances. Those Varela might expect to meet in the *sala* of Señora de Jovellanos were patricians. They began to arrive at seven in the morning, with flowers and best wishes. Ladies were shown in by slaves, yerba maté was served in silver gourds, cigars lit and then the conversation turned to the topic which fascinated the city.

'The first name which rose to their lips,' Varela wrote, 'to curse it, was that of Elisa Lynch . . . the favourite subject of conversation was the life which Elisa Lynch led there: her beauty, her elegance, the luxury she enjoyed, her ability to seduce and enchant . . .'[2] They told him the López ladies refused to receive her and all decent women turned their faces should they meet her in the street. The General ate from her bewitching hand, they said, and she took revenge on those who snubbed her by turning him against them.

'She is *una malvada*, a wicked woman,' said a lady of the Gil family. 'It will be a great misfortune to us if she stays here after the President's death, we will be *muy desgraciadas*.'[3]

Doña Pura de Bermejo came, tightly laced, begloved, enraged. She told Varela all her stories of Madame's Parisian days, of the banker, the English lord and the cardinal.

Since she came, [she told Varela] she has sought me out, she has visited me, she has sent me gifts, she has humiliated herself trying to seek my friendship. I have been firm, even rude, in resisting her. If she came to my house, my servants said I was out; if she sent me a gift, I returned it; if I met her by chance in some public place, I would not let my eyes meet hers . . .[4]

When the ladies retired, the men began to speak up. Every foreigner in town, they told him, called on Madame Lynch, and many important Paraguayans, but no ladies. That bridge which connected the demi-monde of St-Honoré with the *monde* of St-Germain, two-way for men and one only for women, had already sprung up between Calle Fábrica de Balas and old Asunción. The men were fascinated by the General's *querida* but their conversations were brief and low, because of the spies. When a message came from Madame, asking Varela to call, they gave wary congratulations, for this was a sign of favour from the General. He went alone, for it was unthinkable his lady friend should enter that house. When a uniformed lackey opened the door on Calle Fábrica de Balas, he understood the sensation Madame had caused, for Asunción was left at the door.

Luxury, elegance, *caprice*, distinction: all these were to be seen . . . a Frenchman would have said that house 'stank of Paris'. Everything was tasteful: the furniture, the bowls, the curtains, the pictures, the bronze and porcelain *objets* which lay on the tables, the books in beautiful covers, the Aubusson carpets . . .[5]

It was the Rue Tronchet in Asunción. The footman conducted him to a sumptuous, empty room where he sneaked a look at the bronze bowl full of calling cards from visiting foreigners. He looked up to see Elisa approaching.

'If there exist women who, for their combination of grace, beauty and distinction; for their proud and regal carriage, for the . . . riches with which nature has endowed them; for the mysterious power of their glance, which cannot be met without yielding to tenderness; if there exist women who possess the privilege of *imposing themselves* from the first instant at which one lays eyes on them – then, I declare, Elisa Lynch seemed to me one of these women as, graceful and elegant, she entered the salon . . .'[6]

What, asked the sophisticates of Buenos Aires, represented in the person of Hector Varela, now rising to his feet to kiss the hand of this vision, was she doing in Asunción? And with the son of that wily *mestizo* who kept the nation she graced in semi-slavery?

He and Madame circled each other on that and later occasions in agreeably flirtatious conversation, speaking French. Pleasantries were exchanged about the beauty of the countryside; guarded questions put and guarded answers given as to the visitor's standing with Francisco's mother. Madame would send for refreshments and a magnificent golden tray be brought, with a decanter and glasses of monogrammed crystal: a medallion encircling a delicate arrangement of her initials in gold. The decanter contained Pale Ale, a delicacy ordered direct from England and poured for favoured guests by Madame's own hand. The servant who brought it would retreat to one corner but did not leave the room for he was one of the perpetual, omnipresent spies of old Paraguay, and he worked for the General.

Varela was left fascinated and bemused.

Don Carlos was displeased by his son's project for the wild Chaco bank, the second of the General's 'experiments' to attract Varela's attention.

During his year in Europe, the General had decided to follow the example of Argentina and Uruguay. Both had been starved of immigration during the twenty-year violence of Dictator Rosas' regime but were now eagerly inviting groups of European 'colonists' to populate their countries. Varela's newspaper was an enthusiastic promoter of such schemes for he believed that European immigration was what had made the great republic in North America so much stronger and more stable than the republics of the South. General López had contacted an immigration agent in Bordeaux and arranged for the recruitment of 1,000 French Basques to begin the settlement of the Chaco wastelands.

I — who am — years of age, healthy and head of a family composed of — undertake in my name and in that of the aforementioned family, to leave the port of Bordeaux on the ship — bound for the Republic of Paraguay.

As soon as I arrive at this destination, I undertake to work and fertilise the soil which will be transferred to my ownership but which will not belong to me absolutely until I have reimbursed the Government of the Republic of Paraguay with a part of the produce of my harvests, the cost of my passage evaluated at 56 pesos, seeds, tools and livestock as well as any other expense which the Government may incur on my behalf.

In order to embark, I must have a passport for Paraguay, a residence certificate from the Mayor which must also attest my morality and the good conduct of my family; I must have sufficient clothes and take with me the sum of at least 100 francs and a certificate of baptism.

I hereby declare that, from the time of my arrival, I recognise no other authority than that of the Republic of Paraguay.[7]

That year 1,013 put their names to this contract and arrived in Paraguay.

The colony was to be called Nueva Burdeos – New Bordeaux. Land had been set aside twelve miles upriver from Asunción on the Chaco bank and the French consul, Comte de Brayer, was taken to inspect it. 'At present,' he told his colleague Henderson, it was 'uninhabitable and at times haunted by Tribes of uncivilised Indians' but the government had promised 'to take efficient measures of Protection'[8]. A large garrison was to be established there under Lieutenant-Colonel Vicente Barrios, latterly of the Paraguayan legation, fiancé of the General's sister Inocencia. The soil appeared good. The first 150 colonists arrived in April, were 'well-welcomed, well lodged and well fed' and sailed upriver with General López to inaugurate the colony on the day of San Francisco Solano, 24 July, with much celebration. Everyone was 'happy and hopeful'. They set about erecting houses and a church while waiting for their seed and animals.

'It is said,' wrote the French Minister in Buenos Aires, 'that General López acted in this matter without the authorisation of his father: this is possible and, knowing the feelings of the President of Paraguay, one may doubt whether he was happy to receive such a large number of foreigners.'[9] He was not. The General had gone too far on his own initiative, bringing back from Europe not only consuls, engineers and a warship but the blonde cocotte in her insolent carriage and now these one thousand French with their ideas of citizenship. Don Carlos did not want more foreigners on his land; he wanted his borders with Brazil guaranteed, ships and a railway built, and the river kept open for the transportation out of yerba, and in of guns. These needs, in Don Carlos' view, were the only justification for their presence.

Don Carlos' dissatisfaction took the form of sabotage and the colony was in trouble even before the second shipload of settlers arrived in June, having plagued the Paraguayan agent in Buenos Aires with requests and complaints en route. The winter was cold but the shelter, fuel and medical aid promised by the Paraguayan government were slow to materialise. The land had not been cleared; the fields which should have produced a first crop that spring were deep in jungle roots. Tools did not arrive, or arrived broken, or late. The oxen were wild and could not be backed into a yoke. Some fields were ten miles from the village, where all colonists were obliged to live and to which they had to return each night, on foot. No provision had been made to travel into Asunción and if any colonists wanted to see their consul, or use their hundred francs to buy the tools and food Don Carlos was failing to provide, they had to walk through alien country where Indians, crocodiles, snakes and an infinity of poisonous insects lived; or build a hardwood canoe to paddle downriver. Worse than the natural hazards was the garrison of hostile soldiers sent, supposedly, to protect them against Indians and in fact to ensure they did not leave the village, for Don Carlos would not have fraternisation. They accompanied the men into the fields, locked up their tools each night and patrolled the streets. Communication was difficult. Lieutenant-Colonel Barrios might have spoken some French. The other soldiers spoke only Guaraní and a little Castilian, the emigrants only French and Basque. These were the first complaints made by the French.

Then came tales of beatings and arbitrary confinements and Consul de Brayer was 'called upon to appeal against the rigour with which these colonists are treated'[10]. In July, several attempted 'escape into the vast Desert which lies beyond the Colony [to] face the Wild Beasts and Savage Indians of the Chaco, rather than submit to the hardships they were made to suffer'[11]. The whole colony was punished and Don Carlos announced that future escapers would be sentenced to death. Consul de Brayer protested. In September, a further seven escaped, of whom five were retaken by Barrios' cat-eyed soldiers, and sentenced to death. Don Carlos refused to commute the sentence.

Despite Don Carlos' truculence and the colonists' desire to go home, the General was concerned that Varela should take back to Buenos Aires a good impression of Paraguay's first foreign colony. The government had bought the merchant steamer which brought the first French settlers and renamed her the *Rio Blanco*, a belligerent reference to one of the border rivers whose ownership was disputed with Brazil. An expedition aboard was to be organised for Varela, his lady companion, the Argentine consul, Adolfo Soler, and a few friends. This chattering group embarked early one morning in anticipation of their treat.

There was unbroken prettiness on either bank and the air was fresh, the scent of oranges discernible. The languorous beauty of Paraguay worked its charm. For an hour, the guests exclaimed and approved and walked the decks, then turned to see Captain Mesa and the officers bowing with great deference to a lady who had just emerged from the cabin, dressed with 'the most exquisite elegance in a silk dress of apple-green, with boots and a hat of the same colour. A nurse came out of the cabin with her, also beautifully dressed and holding a baby boy about a year old in her arms. The white clothes he wore were of such richness they could have belonged to the heir to the crown

of England when he played in the palaces of Windsor and St
James as an infant . . .'[12] Behind the nurse were two manservants
in livery and the General's spy.

There was a rustle of whispered fury among the guests, for
no one had been told Madame would be aboard. Madame,
used to maintaining dignity before such a reaction, directed
the servants to offer food and drink to her guests. Seeing
Varela looking sheepishly in her direction, she bid one of her
men take a tray to the woman who accompanied him, who
did not trouble to lower her voice or hide her disgust. 'If I had
known that wicked woman was coming,' she said, 'I would
never have come myself . . . what insolence that that English
prostitute should flaunt herself . . . I refuse even to look at
her . . .' and turned her back.

The servants stood rigid in astonishment. 'I have rarely
experienced a more disagreeable moment,' Varela wrote. Elisa
beckoned him over.

'Is this lady from Buenos Aires?' she asked.

'Yes.'

'I thought so; I have never met prouder women and now I
see they are not only proud, but ill-mannered too.'

'I would be grateful if we did not talk about this incident,'
said Varela. 'I am very sorry it happened and I do not approve;
however, I respect the principles which might impel any
woman to do certain things.'[13]

This piece of piety was unpleasant from a man who had
spent cosy hours in Madame's drawing room, drinking her
Pale Ale and enjoying her wit.

'Elisa Lynch arose and called the three servants, who were
standing as still as statues. They approached her, she said a
few words and they threw the entire contents of the three
trays over the side and into the river . . .'[14]

The passengers stood mute and furious, watching their
lunch float away.

The colonists of Nueva Burdeos had heard the thunder of wheels and come to the riverside. They were thin and wary, taking off their hats as Madame disembarked with her little suite, followed at a pointed distance by the Argentine lady and her embarrassed companions. The colonists knew and recognised Elisa, and greeted her with deference, for they knew she was a conduit by which their grievances might reach a powerful ear. In other circumstances, Elisa Lynch would have been a perfect patron of this new village, populated by her semi-compatriots.

They had come at a moment of crisis. A twenty-year-old Parisienne had contracted typhoid and there was no medical practitioner and no medicine in the colony. When Varela was told of this, he entered the girl's hut to take charge but Madame had already arranged for her to go on board the *Rio Blanco* and return to Asunción. Elisa, a priest and Varela sat with the girl, laid on two mattresses on the saloon table, and bathed her face while the steamer thundered back downriver. The priest hinted so many people might distress the patient and Elisa left; Varela could not conceive himself superfluous. As they carried the girl from the dock to the house on Calle Fábrica de Balas, she died.

Despite this distressing episode, Varela left with a good opinion of Paraguay and its new colony. In *La Tribuna*, he wrote of the 'courteous and attentive treatment we received in Asunción, where we were accorded every consideration'[15]. He defended the General and Don Carlos against complaints made by the French which he said were exaggerated, or groundless; French colonists, he reminded his readers, were notorious for complaining. His less complimentary opinions of Madame and the Paraguayan government's treatment of the French were saved until much later, when he wrote a flawed and dishonest book which contradicted what he had said in 1856.

In November, four of the Nueva Burdeos colonists crept away in the night, leaving their hutmate, Dorignac, asleep. He was interrogated, beaten and immersed in cold water by Barrios' men until he lost consciousness. Consul de Brayer made a formal protest to the Minister for Foreign Affairs. Don Carlos' reply came on 29 November in the new Asunción newspaper the *Eco* and was a personal attack on the consul himself. It was followed by a letter, calculated to infuriate, which denied the torture of Dorignac, denied maltreatment of other colonists and requested that Brayer cease bothering the government with his complaints.

On 26 December 1855, Don Carlos took the steamer upriver to hear the grievances of Nueva Burdeos. One Frenchman spoke. They were sick, he said, because there were no doctors; they were isolated, because the garrison would not let them leave; they were hungry, because the land would not yield; they had suffered first drought, then heavy rain. Don Carlos listened and replied, disdaining all points except the last. 'I am not Joshua,' he said, 'to halt the course of the sun, nor a prophet to predict great things in the future.' All who wished to leave could write their names on a list and were free to go. The colony was dissolved. There was jubilation. Delivieries of food, Don Carlos continued, would cease immediately and those departing the country had fifty days to pay their debt to the government. Even this did not damp the excitement of the first few hours of freedom but later, after the party, they realised Don Carlos had set an impossible task: he was demanding they pay the entire cost of passage out, as well as the (supposed) cost of tools, clearance, seed and livestock. It would take years to save such an amount.

Ildefonso Bermejo was sorely overworked and Doña Pura had decided this was entirely due to Madame.

'*Ella sola*', she insisted, 'she alone is the origin of all the humiliations that poor man is suffering . . .'[16] It was revenge, Doña Pura said, for her own refusal to return Madame's attempts at friendship. 'She knows I would rather die before humiliating myself by keeping company with vice and corruption.'[17] Her claim was nonsense: Ildefonso Bermejo worked for Don Carlos and Don Carlos did not take his cue from Madame.

Within a month of his arrival, Bermejo had established Asunción's second newspaper, the *Eco*. It was a four-sheet thrice-weekly journal which carried news of Paraguay, the Plate and, when he could get it, Europe. This was the first modern newspaper Asunción had, for the *Semanario* was a close-printed and wholly eccentric gazette, outlet for Don Carlos' tirades. Bermejo's paper carried advertisements for household and luxury goods, a domestic column (apparently written by Doña Pura) in which hints were given for keeping flies off horses and away from cheese and a social column in which ladies were mentioned coyly by initials and complimented on their charm.

Running the newspaper was only one of his tasks. Don Carlos had long been interested in the provision of education for boys. Most villages had a primary school and the rate of male illiteracy was the lowest in the Plate. He had already experimented in the capital with an Escuela de Matemáticas for a selected group of bright boys, taught by Pierre Dupuy, a French musician who had come to Paraguay some years earlier. He now wished those same boys to progress in their studies and either he, or Bermejo, decided that the next stage in their education must be an Escuela Nacional for one year and then an Escuela de Filosofía for two. It was Bermejo's task to devise and teach the curricula of both, reporting constantly and in detail to Don Carlos on his pupils' progress. The first months were difficult, for the boys who had already done one year in the Escuela de Matemáticas felt they were being forced to start again from the beginning in Don Ildefonso's different method. Bermejo went to Don Carlos and his pupils were soon a dozen fewer. The ringleaders had been pressed into the navy.

'The 49 pupils Your Excellency was good enough to entrust to me for tuition in philosophy' were taught a strict and full curriculum. First of all, the 'adulterations' in their spoken and written Castilian were corrected and instruction given in the fiendish grammar of that language. Then 'work is assigned as follows':

Monday: logic in the morning; rectification of errors in the afternoon

Tuesday: grammar in the morning; rectification of errors in the afternoon ·

Wednesday: geography in the morning; rectification of errors in the afternoon

Thursday: arithmetic, practical and theoretical, in the morning; no class in the afternoon

Friday: history in the morning; rectification of errors in the afternoon.[18]

Bermejo was the only tutor.

His next task was self-appointed. Like the other foreign workers, the Bermejos had been given a house but provision of domestic service had not been discussed. He wrote to the General, who sent him two teenage slaves from *la ranchería*, a pool of about 1,500 state-owned slaves kept on a farm outside the city. The girl spoke only Guaraní so they sent her back but the boy, Manuel, spoke Castilian and seemed an intelligent child. Very soon, Bermejo had begun to instruct him in reading, writing and the elements of the Christian faith.

When not teaching, translating, writing editorials, running the newspaper office or appeasing Doña Pura, Bermejo devoted himself to the formation and training of the first state theatre company of Paraguay, for this was the task which most fired his enthusiasm. He had been giving hints of the delights to come since establishing the *Eco*. In mid-June, auditions began for the first production.

Elisa Lynch was a lover of the theatre. In Paris, frequent attendance was compulsory for those who wished to remain in the public eye. She had a passion for amateur dramatics, played the piano competently and would have been a natural and enthusiastic patron of Bermejo's theatre company, but was excluded, for the theatre was considered a suitable occupation for respectable young ladies and gentlemen. Clustered about the virtuous Doña Pura, they left no room for Elisa Lynch.

French and Spanish theatre dominated taste in the Plate. The plays of Molière and Dumas were popular but for musical entertainment, the public inclined towards the *zarzuela*, a Madrileño form of operetta. *El Valle de Andorra* was playing in Buenos Aires and this was what Bermejo chose for his opening night. Roles were cast, orchestral instruments came upriver and the orchestra fingered them uncertainly in rehearsals with Maître Dupuy, released from the Escuela de Matemáticas by Bermejo's arrival. A party of ladies marshalled by Doña Pura cut and stitched and measured and produced the costumes.

Their greatest handicap was lack of a theatre but construction or conversion began that winter near the plot occupied by the Escuela Normal, in the street which led from Calle Fábrica de Balas to the Plaza del Gobierno. It was probably built, as were other public works, by convict and slave labour.

It was decided that the theatre company would debut as part of the festivities on Don Carlos' birthday.

From eight in the evening on Saturday 4 November 1855, San Carlos' Day, the public were arriving. The central box was reserved for the presidential family, the great body of Don Carlos accommodated by a large, velvet-lined seat. 'One rarely sees,' wrote Varela, observing from another box, 'a more impressive sight than this great tidal wave of human flesh.'[19] The young Juan Crisóstomo Centurión, one of Bermejo's pupils, stood behind him. Don Carlos' wife and two daughters sat alongside. In a separate box beside Don Carlos, where cowardice met discretion, was the General. And in a box of her own, bang in the middle of the theatre where no one could miss her, was Elisa Lynch, sparkling defiantly, laden with jewels, dressed in silk, groomed by Henri and powdered by Julie, perfectly poised and elegant.

The President gestured his readiness. Centurión rang a bell. The curtain went up and Bermejo took the stage.

'The opening of the national theatre,' he announced, 'has opened a new epoch in Paraguay.' There were speeches to the President from the students of the conservatoire. There were *vivas*. Pierre Dupuy's orchestra played an overture and then the curtains drew back to show a shepherd on a mountain top. '*Ah!*' he sang, '*del valle. El alba asoma! Ah! del valle. Ya despunta el nueva día, ya amaneció.*' A policeman appeared to join him in his hymn to morning, the inevitable story of love, jealousy, confusion and joy followed and the hero and his maiden went off to thunderous applause. 'During the entire performance, the President ostentatiously wore an enormous, atrocious hat,' Varela noted, more interested in the presidential circle than the shepherds on stage; 'during the evening, I watched [Don Carlos] for a sign of any impression produced upon him by witnessing a play for the first time in his life. It was like watching a stone in the field.'[20] As the curtain came down, the audience joined in the hymn to San Carlos. 'Without any display of either approval or disapproval, the old monarch of the jungle glared momentarily at Madame Lynch and rose and left.'[21] The theatre emptied behind him. The López family and their circle attended the ball given late that night in honour of la Presidenta. Elisa Lynch drove the few yards to her house on Calle Fábrica de Balas, alone in her carriage.

Chapter Five

The first hungry French were seen begging in Asunción when Elisa Lynch conceived her second child. News of her pregnancy went round the markets and malicious eyes gathered on her belly. Her early pregnancy coincided with the torpid months of summer.

The wealthy of Asunción spent their summers in *quintas*, country houses surrounded by large, private gardens along the long, straight road which connected the city to the hamlet of La Trinidad. Quadrangle after quadrangle could be placed together or set corner to corner to extend as far as a growing family and its servants required. Their colonnades enclosed gardens, watered by a well or the buckets carried from the river by trotting peons. There were exotic birds and lizards and monkeys kept as children's pets. High square rooms led off the cool colonnades. It was here that the General bought or built a second house for Madame. For the watchers and spies and prognosticators, the *quinta* was proof that the General remained devoted and Madame was not going home.

The General was absent for long periods during this second pregnancy, for the persistent clouds of San Ildefonso were gathering again. The Emperor of Brazil had refused to ratify the treaty concluded with the Brazilian admiral because it had not settled the borders. Coal was being stockpiled by eager merchants in Montevideo, sure the Brazilian fleet would soon be fuelling on its way back to Paraguay.

Pedro de Alcantara João Carlos Leopoldo Salvador Bibiano Francisco Xavier de Paula Leocadia Miguel Gabriel Rafael Gonzaga Braganza of Brazil, known as Dom Pedro, was two years older than General López and had been emperor of eight million souls since the age of six. His vast territory was the fruit of Portuguese persistence over centuries. Already it dominated the South American continent, from Belém to Rio Grande, from the ocean to the Matto Grosso, but many Brazilians believed it should extend further, to the Empire's 'natural frontiers', the River Plate and the River Paraná. The *banda oriental,* the 'eastern strip' which tore itself from Brazil's flank in 1825 and became Uruguay, denied the Empire access to the Plate estuary; Paraguay sat square and infuriating along the river to the Matto Grosso. Slowly, these obstacles must be removed.

The masterly Brazilian diplomat José Maria da Silva Paranhos came to Asunción in April 1856. On his way upriver, he called at the palace of General President Urquiza, the most venal man in Argentina. They talked of the affairs of the Plate and the navigation of the rivers and, when Paranhos embarked for Asunción, he left behind a present of 300,000 patacones★.

The treaty concluded in Asunción that winter failed, like the previous ones, to settle the borders, stating only that arbiters would be appointed to solve this question in six years' time. The right of Brazil to sail the River Paraguay, however, was extended. Brazil could now send two warships upriver and an unlimited number of merchantmen. These would not

---

★ Approximately US$300,000 today.

stop at the police guardhouses below Asunción; their passengers would pay no visa fees and Paraguayan authorities had no right to ask information about their cargoes. The river must be kept open for other nations who might wish to trade with the Matto Grosso and the principle be acknowledged that Paraguay, despite owning both banks of the river, did not have sole right of regulating shipping on it. Don Carlos salvaged only the small victory of making the Brazilian envoy wait thirty-eight days for ratification.

Few foreign observers could muster personal sympathy for Don Carlos, but most strongly disapproved Brazil's tactics. 'Thinking men,' went a report by the British consulate, 'do not consider it rash to assert that the pretension of Brazil is to send up to Matto Grosso a respectable naval force and all the armament and forces which Brazil might wish to station in that province with a view to back by force all the demands which Brazil may wish to make on Paraguay.'[1] If anything had been needed further to persuade the General and Don Carlos that Paraguay must strengthen her position, it was provided by this treaty, which transparently allowed Brazil to transport arms along Paraguayan waters.

The General's response was a military one. The garrison at Humaitá was increased. Twelve sixty-eight-pound guns were acquired from the Blyths and brought in aboard a British steamer. Construction of a second new battery began. Upriver from Asunción, floating batteries and armament depots were established and the garrison at the river-port of Concepción was reinforced.

Don Carlos preferred to play war games than go to war; always he favoured sabotage over the clash of swords. His first decrees came as Paranhos left: all foreign vessels must carry a Paraguayan pilot between Asunción and the Matto Grosso and the Paraguayan government would henceforth levy taxes on foreign shipping in her waters. Others came later: two of the four fuel depots north of Asunción were placed out of bounds; foreign cargoes in Brazilian ships would be treated as contraband. Treaty-wrecking was an old game.

Madame's second baby was born in August 1856 and all Asunción knew it, and knew the General acknowledged paternity. Madame was not to be seen in those winter months after the birth but the General was, for the expansion of his family coincided with two triumphant moments on the docks. One month before the baby girl was born, the steamer *Ypora* was launched, the second Paraguayan-built ship produced at Whytehead's yard; three days before Madame gave birth, foundations were laid for an arsenal.

They called the baby Corinne Adelaide. Her surname was Lynch.

Summer approached and change was smelt. In November, the interior was flurried by Don Carlos' sudden call for a congress. Deputies left their *yerbales* to ride along the dry gullies which served as roads, across the plains and cordilleras, fording rivers, sleeping in the houses of police chiefs. Don Carlos wanted ratification of changes to the electoral law. The age at which a citizen was eligible for the presidency was to be reduced from forty-five to thirty, the age just attained by the General. There was no debate. No questions were asked. Don Carlos hauled himself to his feet, surveyed the deputies with contempt and 'express[ed] his determination to resign at the end of the term for which he last accepted office which will be at the end of March 1857'.

'Why did he make us come so far to do something so simple?' one deputy asked another, and was overheard by Don Carlos.

'Who has the impertinence to speak?' the President yelled. 'Get out, animal!'[2]

The deputy slunk away.

Congress was to reconvene that month. General López was 'generally designated as His Excellency's successor'[3].

The resignation threat was an old song in a dictator's repertoire. The expected response was a formal expression of the people's wish not to abandon them to anarchy. Ex-Dictator Rosas of Buenos Aires had used this ploy routinely and been astonished when General Urquiza pretended to take him seriously, accepted his resignation in 1852 and went to war against him when he said he had not meant it.

The deputies journeyed back to their towns and villages and the matter was discussed there. It was talked of at the docks and on the patios, in the markets, the foreign merchants' shops and the *quintas* of Trinidad. A lady of the Gil family had told Varela that it would be a great misfortune if Madame were still in the country when the President died. Now it seemed death would be preceded by resignation and the *malvada* would be launched to power even faster than feared. She had defied their attempts to hurt and depose her. She had accumulated wealth and the General's infatuation had not diminished. He was firmly in Madame's camp and old Asunción's chances of luring him back to his own seemed low. The topic buzzed around the country as the summer temperatures rose.

Corinne Adelaide was taken ill when she was five months old, and the days were steeped in wet heat. She died of an obscure fever in the soaring heat of February and could not be left unburied. The same afternoon, a tiny funeral procession stood in La Recoleta cemetery, heard the service and saw the little body lowered into the ground. Even here there were those who watched and reported. They said Madame had wrapped her daughter's body in white and sewn gauze wings on her back so she went into the ground dressed as an angel. They said neither of Francisco's parents, nor his sisters, nor his brother Benigno were present. Only Venancio, the middle brother, represented the López family. The stone was engraved in English:

> To the sacred memory
> Of
> CORINNE ADELAIDE LYNCH
> Born August 6th 1856
> Died February 14th 1857
> Ere sin could blight or sorrow jade
> Death came with friendly care
> The lovely bud to heaven conveyed
> And made it blossom there.

There were spelling mistakes; 'blight' had become 'blithe', and 'bud', 'but'.

Madame went into mourning. Asunción watched and speculated.

Congress met four weeks after the baby's death and Don Carlos duly resigned. No, no, the deputies cried, but with less conviction than he had expected.

'It appears,' wrote Consul Henderson afterwards, 'that on the President declining to accept his re-election, General López, his son, was at once unanimously elected, and that it was only upon his positively refusing to accept the Presidency, that the President was urged and consented to accept his re-election . . . I believe it to have been the wish not only of the Congress but of the Country, that the General should become President, a hope being entertained that he would carry out a more liberal and beneficial Policy for the country and of a more friendly character towards other nations . . . General López [felt] no doubt that as President he would either be thwarted in his attempts to alter the established state of things or would . . . be obliged to follow on with the present system . . .'[4]

General López may well have suspected his father's wish to relinquish power was insincere. A fight between father and son would cut lasting schisms into his own family and the General's relations with his mother and sisters were affectionate. He knew Don Carlos would sabotage any scheme he did not care for and that his own embryonic power-base would not be sufficiently strong to prevent this. Barrios at Nueva Burdeos was an example: he was a fellow-officer, of the General's generation, who had travelled to London and Paris and shared the legation's exposure to different ways. Nonetheless, at Nueva Burdeos, he had implicitly sided with Don Carlos against the General and the deep Paraguayan distrust of the foreign had swamped European memories. Deputies, provincial priests, judges and all the others whose allegiance to Don Carlos had not wavered in eleven years would continue, like Barrios, to defer automatically to the old man's wishes.

Relations with the French consul were worsening. When Don Carlos announced that those colonists in debt to the Paraguayan state would be put to forced labour, Brayer requested instructions from Paris. They were slow in arriving, for the river was low and the gunboat *Flambeau* unable to reach Asunción. She delivered dispatches to the Post Office on 14 June, where officials copied their contents to Don Carlos. The following day, he absolved all remaining of their debts. France had made its imperial muscle felt.

In the Argentine, French communities were collecting funds. The French Minister in Buenos Aires, Viscount Bécourt, was besieged by compatriots from the failed settlement, demanding the Emperor Napoleon send a fleet to enforce respect and compensation. Dorignac was brought to his house and set to 'simple tasks'[5], for the man had been 'reduced almost to imbecility' and no other work could be found for him. Even these proved too much, however, and he was repatriated to Bordeaux, where his family would have to assume responsibility for this sadly reduced brother or son, returning from his New World adventure. Weekly anguished letters came from Consul de Brayer in Asunción, sick and desperate to be relieved of his post.

> I believe, [the Viscount wrote to Paris] that M de Brayer cannot remain much longer in Asunción and any replacement could only be made after it has been brought home to López that no government [even one protected by] the double guarantee of insignificance and distance, will go unpunished if it forgets what is due to the subjects and the agents of the Emperor [Napoleon] . . .[6]

During a prolonged stay with Urquiza in Entre Rios that winter, however, amid weekly news of groundings, Bécourt realised navigation of these rivers was too tricky for such an expedition.

> Although there is a depot of wood in Santa Fe for the regular steamer, combustion of the wood there does not give enough pressure to make passage safe and rapid [he wrote in a later dispatch]. One cannot deny that the difficulties of navigating the Paraná and the Paraguay during 8 or nearly 9 months of the year are a great encouragement for President López and a very effective defence against the European powers, whose displeasure he does not fear to incur.[7]

In November 1856, a French gunboat came to take off Consul and Comtesse de Brayer and the British consulate assumed temporary responsibility for the French community. It was a humiliation for the General. His name was on the treaties arranged in celebration of the opening of the rivers.

No representative had yet arrived from Victor Emanuel of Sardinia. Relations had cooled with the representative of Victoria of Britain. The treaty with the United States was battered, the treaties signed with Brazil had not secured the borders and relations with the envoy of Napoleon III, whom the General admired most, had broken down entirely.

General Urquiza, President of the Argentine Confederation, hosted another Brazilian envoy in his Entre Rios palace that year and signed another treaty. It stipulated that 'the merchant shipping and men of war of Brazil are at liberty to operate in Paraguay and Uruguay. In the event of a Paraguayan–Brazilian war, the unrestricted transit and supply of the Imperial [Brazilian] fleet along the River Paraná will be permitted.'[8] *La diplomacia del patacón* – the diplomacy of Brazilian gold – was at work.

The summer of 1857 was kind neither to Elisa nor the General. Panchito was two when his sister died and both his parents adored him. It may have been that the love story which kept her in Paraguay after the death of her daughter was not with the General but with his son, for no one left Paraguay without permission from the López'.

One mourned six months. When Madame resumed her life as the General's companion, she found her isolation diminished, for during her pregnancy, her second motherhood and her grief, more foreigners had arrived and some were eager to extend friendship. The Crimean War was over and military professionals were looking for jobs in South America.

In the late 1850s, only Paraguay and Brazil seemed to offer peace and security on a seething and belligerent continent. To the south, the latest in a ceaseless cycle of Uruguayan governments had just been overthrown. Those ousted engaged Italian mercenaries and raided from Buenos Aires. News came to Asunción of their defeat and of reprisals, the hunting down for sport of prisoners stripped naked and told to run, the spearings, disembowellings, bayonetings and slitting of throats with cattle knives. Weary Uruguayan farmers and merchants waited for the increased taxes and spoil of another war. When Montevideo urged General Urquiza to join forces and attack Buenos Aires, which had aided the latest raiders, war seemed inevitable in Argentina too.

It was well known that the Paraguayan government was eccentric, Don Carlos was a coarse and dreadful old man and it was sometimes best for foreigners to avert their eyes but, compared to the democratic republics of the Plate, with their liberal constitutions, their free press, their political parties and their continual bloody feuds, Paraguay was a delightful place to be – particularly for the British. 'Everything,' wrote Viscount Bécourt, 'revolves around the English [by which he meant the British] up to and including the heart of the heir presumptive.'[9]

Dr William Stewart was one of three brothers from Galashiels. One brother, George, was an arms and yerba trader in Buenos Aires. The other, Robert, had remained in Scotland and worked in a bank. William had been a military surgeon at Scutari. When the war ended, he joined a colony for British ex-servicemen in the Argentine, which swiftly collapsed. He looked east and south to chaos and bloodshed, then north to where foreign professionals earned good wages. In March 1857, aged about thirty-five, he became Surgeon to the Republic of Paraguay with a fabulous salary and the honorary rank of colonel. Two British doctors were already there but Dr Stewart's brief was specifically military. He was to establish an army medical corps. A couple of months later, he was joined by Dr John Fox of Southampton. In Chile, George Paddison, Chief Assistant Engineer of the Santiago-Valparaíso railway, was looking for new work. He, too, looked to the peace and prosperity of Paraguay, brought his wife with him and became Chief State Engineer of Paraguay. Just behind Paddison came an extraordinary young Englishman, George Thompson, aged about eighteen, multi-talented, multi-lingual and already an experienced South America hand. All these were soon enthusiastic guests at Elisa's supper parties and whist drives.

About two dozen more arsenal and foundry technicians arrived that year from Britain. William Newton came with his wife to take over the foundry outside the capital at Ybicui, for Master Founder Richardson had succumbed to 'tropical fever'. Newton loved the place; within months he had learnt Spanish and was signing himself *Guillermo Nuton*. Master Mason Alonso Taylor came from supervising road-gangs in the Crimea to oversee the construction of the arsenal. He joined forces with Alessandro Ravizza, a recently recruited Italian architect, and another British mason, John Moynihan. They had been brought to create a new, imposing city.

Paraguay was in renaissance. Bermejo's sixteen brightest students were sent on government grants to Europe to study mechanical engineering, languages and law. They left with Captain Morice aboard the *Rio Blanco*, the first ship ever to go directly from Paraguay to Europe. They took an embalmed *yacaré*, a Paraguayan alligator, for the Museum of Natural History in London, but it was swept overboard in a storm off the Azores.

Miners were prospecting for minerals near Ybicui and laying a canal to connect the deposits to the foundry. Tram lines were going down across Asunción. Materials for a railway leading east to Luque, Aregua and Paraguarí had been brought from England and lay in piles where soldiers dug out the embankments. The vast apparatus of scaffolding blocked the roads. Mule trains and slaves hauled crates of building materials east from the docks. The city lived to the sound of metal on stone as a railway station, a post office, a customs house, a theatre based on La Scala, an unloading dock in the bay on which the garrison band played every Sunday, a new church at Ivirai and the vast new 'erecting-shops' of the arsenal, where the first Paraguayan-made artillery was fired in 1858, were all being built. Inocencia López, now married to Colonel Barrios, wanted a grand new house; so did the brothers Venancio and Benigno; so would the younger López daughter, Rafaela, and her trader fiancé Saturnino Bedoya when they married. New houses spread across the city. They did not have the small glassless windows of old Asunción, which kept the houses cool and dark, but the large, glazed spaces of the house on Calle Fábrica de Balas, designed to allow those in the street to admire the family's expensive and foreign possessions. Elisa was still a silent presence in the city but her fashions had entered where she could not.

The railway was crawling eastwards, towards the hills and the lake of Ipacaraí, said to have been formed when the heathen refused the Jesuits' offer of baptism and the waters swept them away until the 'good fathers' sprinkled holy water upon them. It was a favourite spot for those seeking cool and rest outside the city. One travelling foreigner spoke nostalgically of the 'beautiful lake of Ipacaraí, about four leagues in length by one in breadth, its ripples washing the stems of the palms which crowded the shore, and breaking up the deep shadow from their feathery foliage which, ever restless, swung in the light breeze.'[10] On the hills around the lake, country houses of all sizes were just seen through the green covering, with 'white walls and a thatched roof'; beyond 'rose more palms, then cedars and lofty forest trees, hung with bright, flowered orchids and brown rope-like creepers, wave after wave to the very hilltops . . .'[11] It was here that Elisa acquired her third house, Patiño-Cué, 'charmingly situated at the foot of a wooded hill, with a full view of the lake and orange plantations on either side'[12]. The advancing railroad halted obediently close by for, in aristocratic manner, a small station to serve Patiño-Cué had been programmed into its route. The more senior newcomers were soon seen at Elisa's houses and some of them brought wives and daughters with them. If Mrs Henderson, Doña Pura and the ladies of Asunción still snubbed Elisa, these young women were less mindful of the danger she posed to their morals. Doubtless there were ribald comments at the docks when incoming workers saw the General's beautiful companion for the first time, but on the whole they disregarded her irregular status and some clearly relished the opportunity to be friends with the most glamorous woman in Asunción. There was little for the women to do here. Their men were out at work all day; few could speak Spanish or had any entrée to Paraguayan life. They had more time and money in Paraguay than at home. Elsewhere, these might have been spent in shops, theatres and lecture and concert halls but Asunción did not have these. Their place was taken by two or three shopping streets and Elisa Lynch's houses.

By now, there were more activities in the city to keep the ladies amused. The little merchant community in Calle Palma had grown, for more people envied Madame's style than wanted to know her. One dressmaker worked full time for Madame and one or two others had premises in town, copying the fashions she introduced and diffusing them among the bolder Paraguayan ladies. Ships coming to Asunción had begun to bring Indian muslin, lace, velvet and satin, perfumed gloves, sandalwood fans, gauzy parasols and straw hats to be dressed with flowers, for all these were paraded by Madame and imitated by those who watched the house on Calle Fábrica de Balas. *Coiffure*, until recently quite unknown in Paraguay, brought its own accessories and its own small businesses. Paraguayan women had used to 'dress their hair in two long plaits, sometimes worn wreath-like around the head, or else simply rolled at the back, and fastened by a large tortoiseshell comb, heavy with gold and jewels'[13], or a rose behind an ear, with sometimes a couple of fireflies caught to it, and a candle passed the length of their hair for shine and grip but such simple arrangements would no longer do at society affairs. Costume jewellery made to wear in the hair came upriver and the first cosmetics: 'making-up pomades' and 'essences' with which to achieve the loops, curls and complexion of Madame.

One of the expatriate wives' favourite occupations was to attend sewing bees at Madame's house, reading magazines from Buenos Aires and Europe, working with her dressmaker to recreate the models in them, sending for samples from the shops near the docks and sitting round a table sewing seams and trimming hats to match. Madame offered other entertainments. There were no shops or libraries in the city where foreign newspapers could be read, for circulation of these was strictly controlled. Madame's house, the General's apartments and the British consulate – when its dispatch bag was not broken into – were reading rooms for those who wanted news of the outside world. In the evenings, when the menfolk joined them, they played whist. Madame had what may have been the only grand piano in Asunción. She invited local musicians to give recitals in her houses and, now she had more friends available, indulged in extravagant amateur dramatics. Plays were staged in her houses on Calle Fábrica de Balas and the road to Trinidad. It gave the women something to do while the men were at work and the men something to look at when they came home.

In the evenings, she and her guests sat for dinner unlike that served anywhere else in Asunción, with up to eight courses of French cooking eaten from foreign china, drunk from foreign glasses. Madame herself occasionally took a hand for she could cook an accomplished *budín**. Her speciality was orange *budín*: a mixture of Paraguayan fruit and Irish stodge which the General particularly liked.

It was a strange thing for the Parisianised Irishwoman with her salon ways and her powerful protector to seek friendship from the wives of 'mechanics' and entertainment among the baking trays. Asunción was changing but life must still have been dreadfully dull.

The López ladies and their circle continued to ignore her.

Most foreign observers who passed through Paraguay in the time of *los López* commented upon its rampant 'immorality'. Cohabitation, one foreigner explained, 'was a common practice in Paraguay . . . So many obstacles have been placed in the way of marriage that, as an institution, it is disappearing in the country. However, at the same time men and women live happily together as husband and wife and the women are notably faithful when they enter into this relationship. A large number of families live in such a way; in fact, this is completely usual in Paraguay.'[14] The paranoid bachelor Dr Francia, Don Carlos' predecessor, had done everything in his power to diminish the hold of the church on his masses and marriage was rare outside the tiny propertied class.

There was a numerous class of women in Paraguay, perhaps the most numerous – called the *kyguá-vera*, the shining combs. They were 'free women, who worked as peddlers in the market and the streets of Asunción. They . . . sold sweets, cigarettes, *chipá*,† clothes, baskets, hats.'[15] A traveller said they wore their treasure on their backs: their fingers were covered with rings . . . they had earrings of precious stones, rosaries and necklaces around their throats. They wore clean and tempting

---

* Hispanicisation of 'pudding'.
† A sort of maize bread with cheese.

tipois, which flared above starched petticoats; they covered their shoulders with multicoloured, embroidered shawls and went barefoot. Wonderful dancers, they were the delight of popular fiestas. They chose a lover as they wished and held him only as long as love and pleasure lasted because they were happy to bring up their children in splendid and dignified matriarchy. . .'[16] These were the women who filled the streets and are depicted in pictures of the docks and the market, those to whom the squabbles of society were nothing and their concern for legitimacy laughable. Most foreigners in Paraguay assumed the basic work of these women to be prostitution, unable to comprehend their 'dignified matriarchy' and indifference to the sacraments. Only one Italian traveller left a more perceptive comment: 'nowhere,' he wrote, 'are women as happy as they are here, free as the birds.'[17]

Elisa did not yet seek the good opinion of the *kyguá-vera* and the *populacho**, except casually. That they cared little about her unsanctified union cannot have been of great importance to her but it provided the only opportunity to indulge in a pleasure officially denied her, that of appearing with the General in public. Elisa's social life with General López took place exclusively in her own houses. Invitations were sent out in her name which all knew to have the General's suggestion or acquiescence behind them. Still no one else ran salons in which the couple could be sheltered; still they lived in a demi-monde of two. The only entertainments at which they might lose themselves in the crowd were those of the *populacho*, for the young General enjoyed enormous popularity among his people and his companion was accepted with a graciousness lacking in the upper classes.

The entertainments of the people were exotic to a European. There were mass spectator events during the cool

---

*Common people.

months to which rich and poor and both sexes went, the wealthier in their boxes and the poorer standing behind them. There were bull-fights, horse races, music and *la sortija*, a Moorish game in which horsemen tilted at a ring suspended from a ribbon and bore it away on a lance. There were great feasts, fuelled with roast oxen and *caña*.

The Paraguayans were lauded by their few visitors as exceptionally graceful dancers. Dances, in public squares or the yards of private homes, were frequent. 'Next to smoking and sipping yerba, the great amusement, one may almost say business of the Paraguayans, is dancing – I never met with people who devoted themselves so thoroughly to its enjoyment.'[18] At the end of the dance, when dawn came, maté would be brought, and cigars and then the slaves or peons of the host would tumble into the yard dressed as *camba rangha* – black images – 'grotesque maskers who danced and played absurd antics'[19] in the costume of tigers, lions, tapirs and devils.

Elisa enjoyed dancing but was taller than Francisco and – when the General felt on show – obliged to dance with other men. When they went out with other officers, she did not lack for partners. At other times, she had to wait for the bolder of the men to approach, ask permission of the General and take her away to the strange and fleeting intimacy of a dance. The people at these affairs called her la Señora Madama, struggled to express themselves in Spanish and showed her the admiration and respect the Hispanics of old Asunción denied her. It was from her attendance at these popular entertainments that a new dance emerged, called the 'London *carapé*'.

Evita would speak of her affection for her *cabezitas negras*, the 'little dark ones' who showed her devotion when the haughty of Buenos Aires shut their doors. Elisa Lynch found something similar among the *mestizo* Paraguayans who regarded her as the General's lady, kind and beautiful, and did not care for what she was before.

*

In January 1858, the sly Brazilian diplomat José Maria da Silva Paranhos came again to Asunción and Elisa Lynch conceived her third child.

Paranhos came upriver on the summer floods from Entre Rios, where he had just agreed another treaty with General President Urquiza, declaring the Rivers Uruguay, Paraná and Paraguay open to shipping of all nations. In February, General López added his name to the signatories and a Brazilian steamer service was established. The *Marqués do Olinda* would make eight round trips of 4,000 miles each year between Rio and the Matto Grosso.

Enrique Venancio Lynch López was born on 2 August. He was named after his two uncles: Elisa's brother, Henry, and Venancio López, the only member of that family to deal courteously with Elisa. The question of baptism arose.

Panchito, now three, had been born and baptised outside Paraguay, ostensibly as the son of a European officer and a respectably married mother. Corinne Adelaide is thought to have been baptised quietly in a church in the interior, although all Asunción knew of her presence and her paternity. Madame did not want her second son to have the same clandestine baptism her dead daughter had been given, for Enrique's baptism would be scrutinised to reveal how the General regarded the liaison and its offspring. She wanted it performed by a priest whose standing in the church would reflect the General's in society.

The Reverend Fidel Maíz was an august and imposing figure, square-faced, hawk-nosed, grim-mouthed, with something of the look of a North American Indian about him. He was second in the church hierarchy to the aged and infirm Bishop Urbieta, confidant of Don Carlos, with whom he conferred 'almost daily'. The bishopric, when its present incumbent died, would fall naturally to him.

'La señora Elisa Lynch,' he recalled much later in his self-serving book, 'sent to tell me she wished me to baptise one of her sons, which I promised most willingly to do.' However, 'when the day came, she notified me that she expected me to bring the entire corps of seminarists, to perform a solemn baptism in her private house. Such a message surprised me, and I could but ask her to excuse me, since I was not able to do so in her home unless the child were gravely ill.'[20] A cathedral baptism would have been the most triumphant proof that the General considered the children borne by Elisa Lynch to be his family, as legitimate as their mother's marital situation allowed. Standing about the font as parents was as near as they could come to standing at the altar as bride and groom and it was probably the General, therefore, who vetoed the cathedral. Always cautious in the public acknowledgement of Madame, he would never go so abruptly against convention. A baptism in the luxurious surroundings of her own *quinta* was not so good, but certainly better than creeping incognita into a humble country church.

In Villetta, the riverbank hamlet south of Asunción, there was a priest called Manuel Antonio Palacios, of about the same age as the General, a little younger than Padre Maíz. He was slovenly, lazy and sly. A messenger came from Madame to his house among the orange groves of Villetta and he was requested to present himself in the city. There, an agreement was made, coldly. Padre Palacios would baptise Enrique Venancio as Madame wished, with all the ritual of *la Santa Iglesia*; in return, her influence would be used in transferring him to a different position, with more money.

The baby's godfather was Dr Stewart of Galashiels. Padre Palacios became Dean of Asunción Cathedral.

'A short time ago,' Consul Henderson wrote at the end of November 1858, 'it became known here that the American

Congress had authorised the government to adopt such measures and use such force as might be necessary for obtaining Compensation and satisfaction from the Government of Paraguay.'[21] A fleet of US gunboats was on its way to the River Plate to obtain compensation for the death of the *Waterwitch* helmsman and the factory owned by Edward Hopkins and his lout of a brother. The tirades of Don Carlos began in the *Semanario*. His editorials spoke in incontinent prose of conspiracy. The commander of the *Waterwitch*, he said, had deliberately sought a rupture 'in accordance with the views of annexation of their government'. President Buchanan was a terrorist. Other South American countries must wake from their lethargy and watch for Yankee designs. Paraguay would appeal to its European 'friends' for intervention and 'resist to the last against aggression'[22].

Christmas celebrations were interrupted and General López, the Hungarian Colonel Morgernstern, military adviser to Don Carlos, and other officers took a steamer to Humaitá to direct operations against the Yankees as they had done five years ago against the Brazilians. In Asunción, Don Carlos was contacted by various eager foreigners offering mediation in return for support in some scheme of their own. Viscount Bécourt came from Buenos Aires to open the rivers again to French commerce. The Brazilians sent an envoy. General Urquiza, who was once again considering an attack on Buenos Aires and wanted Don Carlos' army on his side, presented himself personally and with information.

Urquiza had obtained a copy of the Americans' secret instructions while the fleet was in Montevideo: the US ships were allowed to go into action only if Don Carlos refused to accept future arbitration of the Hopkins affair. Urquiza 'took a special steamer and, hurrying to Paraguay, advised López to haggle for the least amount possible; not to deny liability but finally, if he could not induce the expedition to depart without too large a payment, to await the offer of arbitration and . . . trust to duplicity and corruption to secure a favourable result'[23]. He, General Urquiza, would mediate. Urquiza may have picked up another rumour in Montevideo: that the extravagant expense to which the United States had gone in sending such a large fleet to such an insignificant country was 'a pretext for withdrawing from the forts and arsenals of the North [of the US] all the munitions of war, thus leaving them unprovided with arms whenever the plans for the great Rebellion should be matured,' for the States were on the brink of civil war and this, too, must have weighed on Don Carlos' 'cunning, Jesuitical mind'[24]. Many in that fleet wanted to go home.

On 1 February, an agreement was signed with the Yankee mediator as Urquiza had suggested. A formal expression of regret for the death of the *Waterwitch* mariner was made, payment of $10,000 compensation to his family agreed and the Hopkins case deferred for arbitration in Washington. The Americans had won on every point but, in deference to Don Carlos' wishes, the expression of regret and the payment of $10,000 remained unpublished. As soon as the fleet had left his waters, Don Carlos began his decrees. No foreigner would henceforth be admitted to Paraguay unless he could show a 'lawful object'. All seamen transshipping in Asunción must obtain a passport from the chief of police at a cost of six dollars. They were published in the *Semanario* under the headline 'Foreign Intrigues' and Paraguayans, unaware of the real agreement, thought the old man had outwitted the Yankees again.

Urquiza's envoy came in May, and again in June, on the secret mission whose object everyone knew. 'All that President López has resolved to do in this matter,' Henderson wrote, 'although he had led General Urquiza to entertain hopes of assistance from him, has been to offer his mediation'[25] to the two Argentine governments now squaring up for the next round in their interminable battle.

In the River Plate, trusting to duplicity and corruption seemed a workable strategy.

Chapter Six

Buenos Aires and the Confederation were at war again, without Don Carlos' army. On 23 October 1859, the armies of General President Mitre of Buenos Aires and General Urquiza of the Confederation met in battle at Cepeda, a few miles outside Buenos Aires. On the evening of 23 October, the government of Buenos Aires struggled to prevent Urquiza's victorious troops from marching on the city. A third party must be found to mediate an armistice and peace treaty and they called on General López of Paraguay. It was a commission of great prestige. He left aboard the *Tacuarí*.

The diplomatic commission steamed past the banks of the lower Plate, now held by Urquiza's men, with the white flag of parley and disembarked in Buenos Aires. For five days, the General talked with President Mitre and his ministers and persuaded the *porteños* to save their city and rejoin the Confederation. Paraguay guaranteed their pledge and the *Tacuarí* under Captain Morice took the proposal north to Urquiza's camp with the request for an armistice. He agreed. 'No more unitarians,' he declared, 'and no more federalists.'[1] His soldiers began embarking troop ships which would take them north to Entre Rios and plans were made in Buenos Aires to celebrate peace and General López for bringing it. The General was owed 'a sincere and burning vote of gratitude,' said *La Tribuna*. 'His conduct throughout could not have been more dignified, more cultured, more circumspect ... the entire country regards General Don Francisco Solano López today with respect and admiration and gives him heartfelt thanks for his generous efforts to preserve the tranquility of the Argentine Republic.'[2] The foreign community began subscriptions to present the General with costly gifts. Albums were richly bound and inscribed with words of thanks:

> we present Your Excellency with our most sincere thanks and congratulations for the Peace which, obtained through your benign influence and diligence, will re-open in better conditions for the progression of well-being and growing prosperity.[3]

A *Gran Polka Militar* was named the '10 de noviembre' in celebration of the treaty and dedicated to the General. Banquets were given and a Te Deum celebrated. When General López toured the city in an open carriage, flowers were thrown and women ran to kiss him. *Porteño* bands played Paraguayan music and the General was a hero. No one knew that the representatives of Great Britain had decided to take advantage of his presence in Buenos Aires, for there was a British subject in one of Don Carlos' gaols who had been the subject of profuse correspondence and, just before the battle of Cepeda, the recall of Consul Henderson.

Santiago, or James, Canstat had been among those who supplied Hector Varela with gossip during his trip to Asunción in 1855. He was a lively and indiscreet young man, engaged in the yerba trade, whose loose talk, laughing disrespect and unwise friendships had landed him in trouble. It was said in early 1859 that a conspiracy had been discovered against the life of Don Carlos and a dozen Paraguayans, and Santiago Canstat, were arrested. 'Conspiracy' was the term generally used for disagreement and it is impossible to know whether any serious plan to overturn the government had been entertained; it is more likely that a few men who disliked the López family for its low origins, or its refusal to allow private enterprise, muttered discontentedly and were overheard by *piragües*. At the time of the arrests, no one was aware that Canstat's father had been Scottish and he was therefore entitled to claim British nationality. Consul Henderson took immediate action, bombarding Don Carlos with letters, demanding to know why charges had not been brought, what they would be, what was the evidence and who were the witnesses. Don Carlos was deeply reluctant to back down. Not only was hostility to foreigners a fixed principle of his government, but if he released one of the 'conspirators', his continued detention of the others would be suspect. There was much bluffing and blustering. The prisoners lay in irons, starving and sick, while the fight went on above their heads. It was thought by the foreigners in the city that Don Carlos hoped they would die before the fight with Consul Henderson came to a conclusion.

There was another dirty side to this quarrel, equally difficult to disentangle from suspicion and slander, that involved the General. It was said that the fiancée of one of the men arrested, Carlos Decoud, had been the object of his attentions and that he had urged his father to find some pretext for Decoud's arrest in revenge for having been slighted. There may have been some lingering disagreement between General López and Carlos Decoud, for the Decouds were of old and European blood and the tight little inner ring of families to which they belonged despised the *mestizo* blood of the presidential family. The General was a philanderer and perhaps did make some clumsy pass at Carmelita, Decoud's fiancée. Whatever the truth behind the General's involvement in the affair, the unexpected nationality of Santiago Canstat became its most important feature. When Don Carlos refused to release him, Henderson was recalled from his post. In August, he sailed for Montevideo, where he talked to Admiral Lushington of the British fleet and the Honourable Edward Thornton, Her Majesty's representative in the Plate and Henderson's superior.

On 29 November, the General and his companions rode smiling through crowds to the docks of Buenos Aires and went aboard the *Tacuarí*. Cannon fired; national anthems were played and she steamed gently away just before one. They were still in city waters when cannon fired across her bow and Captain Morice saw a British gunboat on either side. He ordered immediate reverse. The General appeared on the bridge and ordered fire be returned but for Morice to fire on one of Her Majesty's ships was treason. He asked the General to return to port, put all Britons ashore and put a Paraguayan officer in command. Given the threatening presence on either side, the General had no more choice than Captain Morice and granting permission to the British to go ashore gave him an excuse to withdraw from an engagement he could not win. The *Tacuarí* returned to dock. She would be held hostage until Santiago Canstat was released from gaol and compensated. Triumph had become humiliation.

The British in Asunción were deeply alarmed when this astonishing news came up the river. They wanted no quarrel with London to interfere with their lives. In Buenos Aires, the authorities which had just fêted the General sent an official protest to Admiral Lushington but they had no fleet of their own to escort the *Tacuarí* north and would not risk bad relations with the British over an insult to Paraguay. Their best offer was an overland escort and this the General was forced to accept, leaving the *Tacuarí* under British guard in Buenos Aires.

He did not come straight back, however, but consoled himself in Villa del Pilar where, by the end of December, Juana Pesoa was pregnant with their third child. Then he returned to Asunción, where Elisa Lynch had recently found she was expecting their fourth.

Federico Lloyd Lynch López was born in 1860 in Asunción. A couple of months later, José Felix Pesoa López arrived in Villa del Pilar.

'An institution is hereby founded which will be called the Club Nacional, whose objective will be to offer its members a meeting point where they can enjoy honest entertainments, such as a reading room, recreational games and dances.'[4]

The Club Nacional was not only a place of entertainment but also a replacement for some of the functions of the Plaza del Gobierno, where public business was transacted, in the manner of ancient Rome, in open-air *corredores* which fronted its buildings. The Club Nacional would allow those who had previously muttered among the colonnades to discuss their affairs discreetly, on sofas, with liqueurs in their hands and a billiard table nearby as gentlemen did in London, Paris, New York and Buenos Aires. It was more civilised but not as discreet as those not yet accustomed to the espionage of Paraguay might have hoped, for the *piragües* moved in with the furniture and never moved out.

The club was housed in a large building on Calle Palma, the busiest street of the city, which ran from Mercado Guazú towards the docks. Along Calle Palma, or just off it, were the warehouses of the principal foreign merchants of new Asunción. Italian Antonio Rebaudi, Uruguayan Nin Reyes, the French Duprat-Lasserre family, the Spanish stationer Dionisio Lirio, the French importer of pomades Jules Henry, yerba trader and part-time Argentine consul Adolfo Soler, the immensely rich Genovese steamer-captain Simon Fidanza; and their Paraguayan colleagues, most related by blood or interest to the López family: Carlos Saguier, formerly of the legation, and his brother Fernando; yerba trader and future López in-law Saturnino Bedoya. All these were among the 126 eager founding members of the Club Nacional, along with the three López sons; Vicente Barrios, husband of Inocencia López; army officers and every diplomat in town. Even Don Carlos approved this venture.

The merchants who signed the act of foundation had found not only a recreational space but a large order book. The club was decorated in European style. It had a grand piano in the ballroom and large, glazed windows onto Calle Palma, carpets, sofas and curtains in European fabrics and a continuous supply of liquor. The López boys had introduced the Parisian habit of drinking champagne at dinner and brandy afterwards and the Italians and French had brought with them their own preferences for aperitifs, digestifs and table wines. All these had to be brought over in ships, stored in warehouses and sold in shops. All traders benefited from the Club Nacional and the fashions it spread among those who frequented it, admired its furnishings and menus, and wanted the same at home.

The Club was open to ladies in the mornings, at lunchtime and for the evening dances. The rest of the time it was a gentleman's club, open late for Benigno López and his cronies to play cards, for Venancio López to drink, for the foreigners to discuss prices and freight. The influence of Madame was present everywhere. The choice of furniture, the music played on the grand piano and by the little orchestra, the London *carapé* and the waltzes she had introduced into her own parties which found their way across the plaza to the Club, the menu and wine list all directly reflected Fábrica de Balas, but the lady herself was seldom seen. The General still did not allow her to attend functions where his mother and sisters were present and these ladies were assiduous frequenters of the Club. La Presidenta and Don Carlos would retire at midnight, however, and then someone would be sent to tell Madame that the coast was clear, and she would come from her beautiful house, fresh and sparkling, to greet those who would speak to her and ignore those who would not.

In November, a self-important personage arrived in the port. He was Charles Ames Washburn, appointed Commissioner by President Lincoln to settle the tired case of Edward Hopkins' company.

José Berges, a distinguished and intelligent man in Don Carlos' service, had already visited Washington, as agreed when the US fleet came to call. His fluent English and mild manner had impressed the arbitration board there and, away from the shrill belligerence of Don Carlos and the presence of armed men, the affair was arranged with courtesy. The board had decided that Paraguay was not liable in any way for Hopkins' losses. When this decision was relayed to the government department which had convened the board, it was overturned. The arbiters were told their instructions had been not to decide whether or not Paraguay was liable but how that liability should be calculated in dollars. Berges' trip had been a waste of time.

Charles Washburn cut an unusual figure in Asunción in his wide-brimmed hat and cowboy boots, the slim-cut trousers and short-tail coat of the Yankee gentleman. He spoke no word of Spanish and did not impress Don Carlos, who considered the Hopkins affair to be settled and saw no reason to be polite to the envoy of a president being whipped by General Lee.

Washburn's first official interviews were an exercise in humiliation – one of Don Carlos' favourite tricks was to place a slave behind him who, at a signal, would whip off the white hat and replace it with the black to keep his guests permanently ill at ease – and he remained in Paraguay only because there was no guarantee his own country would exist by the time he returned to New York. He took trouble to create for himself a pleasant life in Asunción, where he was graciously accepted. He ingratiated himself early with Don Carlos' wife and daughters; he became a member of the Club Nacional and was soon on terms of cordiality with the López sons, the Saguiers, Barrios, Bedoya and the rest. He was friendly, despite the circumstances, with Minister Berges; and with Benigno López, with whom he played cards and snooker and talked of women. He did not form the same friendship with the General, whom he found reserved. He was soon a frequent guest at Madame's house. After one pleasant evening in her house, he wrote effusive words in her album:

> it has been an occasion of intimate pleasure to me to have known a lady of such erudite culture, enlightenment and good taste, with whom I have often been able to recall in conversation the classics of the English language and exchange ideas about the literature of our times.[5]

One of his fellow guests, also newly arrived in Paraguay, was George Masterman of Croydon, engaged by the Blyths as apothecary to the military hospitals being established by Dr Stewart. Masterman was an insatiably curious young man, a bachelor like Washburn, and an avid knower and meeter. He toured the villages of the cordillera, staying in private houses on the grounds of tenuous acquaintanceship, cataloguing beetles and photographing Indians. He, too, joined the Club

Nacional, sniffed out the gossip of the capital and swiftly found his way onto Madame's guest list.

Masterman's initial impression of Madame was markedly different from that of Hector Varela six years before. He found her 'a tall, stout and remarkably handsome woman, although age and the rearing of many children had somewhat impaired her beauty' and was more enthused by her hospitality than her looks. 'She gave capital dinner parties,' he wrote, adding, 'she could drink more champagne without being affected by it than any one I have ever met.'[6]

Elisa's dinner parties were now an established feature of Asunción life. It was accepted that visits on official business to Paraguay which involved dealings with the General also included a meeting with Madame Lynch. The Brazilian envoy Silva da Paranhos danced with her in 1859. It was said that General Urquiza sent her thoroughbred horses after his visit to Asunción the same year. Governor Pujol of Corrientes was in frequent contact with her. Her guest list was almost entirely non-Paraguayan, except for a few of the officers who had known her in Paris. Paraguayan ladies still hesitated to enter her house but there had been a change in their relationship with Madame. Her position was substantially different in 1861 than it had been in 1855. She was established as a wealthy and influential woman. She had borne four children to the General and maintained a transcendent influence over his way of life and political opinions which none of his other women achieved. She managed him, Masterman noted, 'with admirable tact', treating him 'apparently with the utmost deference and respect, whilst she could really do with him as she pleased'.[7]

Masterman, a recent arrival and acute observer, put a different construction on the unwillingness shown by upper-class Paraguayans to attend Madame's parties. In his view, it was due as much to timidity as hostility. Many families, he thought, particularly those who spent most of their time on their *estancias* and little in Asunción, were ill at ease with her European manners. 'The mode of eating amongst the men,' he explained, 'is very primitive, forks having only been very recently introduced and still somewhat awkwardly handled.'[8] No one would wish to expose themselves to the humiliation of dropping a potato in the lap, particularly under the sardonic eye of Madame Lynch. 'The correct way of eating beef,' he explained, having been instructed in this on one of his tours, 'is to seize as much as your mouth will hold between your teeth, and then cut it off close to your lips with a long, keen knife. Of course, the young ladies did not follow this fashion in public, but I strongly suspect they did so when at home, for they were always very shy of eating in the presence of foreigners.'[9]

The European veneer was still thin. Masterman was struck by the fact that one might see 'the wife of a colonel at a Club ball, dressed in last year's Paris fashion', and, visiting her the next day find her 'in the midst of her family, clad in a very scanty cotton gown, and without shoes or stockings, sitting in the midst of her slaves with disheveled hair, and scolding them in uncouth Guaraní',[10] while naked children ran and played among goats and chickens. He could not understand why ladies such as this one had not seen the error of their Paraguayan ways. There was also the question of conversation. Although Madame spoke fluent and correct Spanish, as well as competent Guaraní, the language in which she entertained continued to be French, with concessions to monoglot Yankees, English and Scotsmen. In a country which possessed not even the rudiments of an education system for females, few ladies spoke a foreign language.

In April 1862, Edward Thornton came from his home in Buenos Aires to pour oil on the waves caused by the kidnap of the *Tacuarí*. When the talks were done, no invitation was extended by Don Carlos or la Presidenta to some concluding social affair. The invitation from Madame filled the gap. The General, Charles Washburn and Colonel Morgernstern were all there; so were George Masterman, William Whytehead and a solid corps of the General's foreigners.

The ladies of Asunción no longer mattered to Madame when the Honourable Edward Thornton, representative of Victoria of Britain, sat at her left and Charles Ames Washburn, envoy of the United States, sat at her right.

In 1860, William Whytehead returned for some months to Britain, entrusted by the General with ordering industrial equipment from London, Liverpool and Manchester, all meticulously described in letters sent back to Asunción. He had bought 'a copper improved still of 120 imperial gallons with brass vacuum safety valve, flanged Cap Screws, Discharge pipe & Gun; a drilling machine Class A; Patent Railway Cable-Fencing; a self-acting Sawbench with Timber carriage and Carts'[11] and many other expensive and incomprehensible items. He also brought home specifications for war-steamers, drawn up in the Liverpool shipyards.

Elisa Lynch had given him her own commission. He returned with the first two sewing machines in Paraguay.

Whytehead moved out of *el Castillo* on his return. With more than one hundred foreigners now in residence round the docks, many of them young, boisterous bachelors, it was a less congenial place. He rented a *quinta* instead, on the road where Madame had her own, and dedicated much time to gardening. He had a shrubbery and an orchard. In the yard, there were pigs, cows, chickens and ostriches. His sisters in Streatham sent him seeds for his flower garden. In November 1861, a glum entry was made in his notebook: 'portion of fence in garden has been maliciously pulled down and cattle driven in. To Mrs Lynch in evening.'[12]

The flower garden was an interest he shared with Madame, who was creating another at her own *quinta* and becoming as frequent a visitor at Whytehead's homestead as he was at her house. They had known each other now for several years and Whytehead had been a constant and courteous guest from the earliest of Madame's difficult parties. He was intelligent and well-read, a humanist and astrologer, a gentle man of many interests who offered companionship markedly different to that of the army officers with whom she spent so much time. They would exchange seeds and cuttings and he would present her with home-grown fruit and vegetables. Madame was one of many who sought him out. Dr Stewart and his Paraguayan fiancée Venancia spent much time at the *quinta*, George Paddison, 'a man of very extensive reading and very liberal, cosmopolitan views'[13] visited often; so did the consular couple sent from France when relations had been patched up over Nueva Burdeos, although never when Madame was there, for they refused to know her. George Masterman and Charles Washburn soon became friends. Washburn was an unpublished and hopeful novelist and brought his manuscripts to Whytehead for criticism. The two were sometimes joined by George Thompson and would go off on long walks in the country, shooting jungle partridge and returning by moonlight. Soon Whytehead's *quinta*, like Madame's salon, was a meeting place for the European and North American élite but with an easier atmosphere and fewer *piragües* and without the General's sometimes subduing presence.

There was gossip in Asunción the year that Charles Washburn arrived, for news had got about that the General had taken another mistress.

The sexual liaisons of General López were numerous. Many claimed – and continue to claim – kinship with him because of the seduction of a servant maid or one of the women who lived around the garrisons but none of these casual liaisons had rocked his two principal households. He now had three sons with Elisa Lynch and three children with Juana Pesoa. His eldest son, Emiliano, was soon to be sent overseas to study and acquire the polish of Europe. The daughter, Adelina, was approaching her teens and José Felix was an infant. The General did not spend as much time with Juana's children as he did with Elisa's but his paternity was acknowledged and they received regular visits during his trips to Humaitá, twelve miles from their home in Villa del Pilar.

Little is known of the General's third principal mistress. She was the daughter of Pedro Burgos, judge of the village of Luque, and therefore a woman of some social standing. She was 'tall and rather fine-looking'[14] and began her visits to the General's house on Mercado Guazú during Madame's fifth pregnancy. These continued after the baby, Carlos Honorio Lynch López, was born, a fourth son in a household which had lost its only daughter three years earlier.

Despite the General's liaisons with *la Pesoa* and *la Burgos*, Elisa Lynch was 'understood to be the favourite'.[15] Any hopes she had had of an annulment of the Quatrefages marriage had been disappointed. It was unlikely she would ever make the General her husband. When she mentioned him in public, she referred to him as 'His Excellency' on all occasions except when obliged to speak of him in connection with herself. Then, he was 'the father of my children' and this circumlocution was significant. The General was known to dote upon Panchito, now seven, who dressed in miniature uniforms and accompanied his father to review the troops and inspect the arsenal. Emiliano Pesoa López was older and had a Paraguayan mother, but it was Panchito Lynch who was dauphin and Elisa who was prospective mother of the king. Those such as Washburn who observed the movements on the market square presumed that the presence of Señorita Burgos in the General's bed was a slight to Madame. Madame, however, had borne him five children in six years: the heir, the three spares and the dead daughter. She may have looked upon her 'rival' with relief, for her services provided liberation from constant pregnancy.

Nevertheless, *la Burgos* did not entirely replace Elisa, or replaced her only gradually, for in 1862, Elisa gave birth to another boy, Leopoldo Antonio Lynch López. He was a sickly infant.

The General had two acknowledged illegitimate daughters, apart from the dead baby in La Recoleta. One was Adelina Pesoa. The other was a small girl called Rosita Carreras who lived with la Presidenta in Trinidad – some said as a loved granddaughter; others, as a servant. The General had paid her mother off or she had died, and the López family had taken the baby in. The General was a frequent visitor to Trinidad, where both his mother and his sister Rafaela had *quintas*, and knew the child well. He took her from his mother's house and installed her in Elisa's. A substitute for Corinne Adelaide? A consolation for yet another son? An instant daughter to circumvent the draining lottery of childbirth? Whatever her status in la Presidenta's household, in Elisa's she was brought up as a member of the family. The fondness of the General and Elisa Lynch for small children was well known.

Chapter Seven

At dawn on 10 September 1862, a dolorous group stood about the bed in the house on the Plaza del Gobierno. La Presidenta, Venancio, Inocencia and Rafaela were crying. Don Carlos' young and favourite secretary, Silvestre Aveiro, was there. Francisco was leaning against a wall in the shadows and Benigno was holding his father in his arms, for the old man was dying.

The General had been in Humaitá, engaged on his constant task of creating a super-fortress on the river, when he was told that his father was gravely ill. He arrived in Asunción in cold mid-August and went to the house by the cathedral, where Don Carlos dictated his wishes for the succession.

'We, Carlos Antonio López, President of the Republic of Paraguay . . . appoint as vice president of the Republic the Brigadier General citizen Francisco Solano López, Minister of War and Marine . . .' The document was given to Silvestro Aveiro, just named State Archivist by the dying man. Only he, Don Carlos and the General knew of it.

Under the constitution of 1844, the General was empowered to act as interim president until congress met to confirm him in the post, or elect another man to it. The weeks of waiting began. Hay went down in the streets on either side of Don Carlos' house. There was a rare silence in the streets and the markets.

Late in the afternoon, Don Carlos called Francisco nearer. 'Many matters remain to be resolved,' he said. 'Resolve them with the pen, and not the sword.'

Padre Maíz administered the last rites. He died at dusk.

'Is he dead?' Francisco asked and Dr Stewart nodded.

Bishop Urbieta was too ill to celebrate the funeral and Padre Maíz officiated.

It was the greatest state occasion in nearly twenty years. Don Carlos had been the nation's judge, governor, arbiter and employer. He was to be buried in the new church at Trinidad, near his wife's *quinta*, and all Asunción turned out to see the cortège. They lined the streets in silence, wearing the black bands of mourning. La Presidenta and her daughters rode behind the coffin in its French hearse as it left the Plaza del Gobierno and made its slow way to the church of Trinidad. An escort of a hundred army and navy officers followed. The railway had been requisitioned for guests attending the funeral; horse-drawn carriages unused in nearly two decades were taken from sheds and brought to Trinidad station, from where they would convey guests to the church. For Carlos Saguier, it was an important day, for he was the government's Master of Ceremonies and he would ensure the day passed off with solemnity. To him fell the arrangements for seating and transport and these were delicate tasks. After some unknown process of proposition, threat and per- suasion in which the unfortunate Saguier was go-between, the mistresses and children of Francisco and Venancio were found seats at the ceremony but la Presidenta cannot have looked kindly on their presence.

The service was grand and solemn; many wept before the altar where statues of Saints Carlo Borromeo and Antonio

faced those of John the Baptist and Paul. A choir sang behind
them, stationed in the gallery over the dark-wood door.

General López wore the presidential sash he had brought
for his father from Paris and medals from the courts of Brazil,
France and Italy. At his side were Venancio, in the uniform of
a colonel, his brother-in-law Vicente Barrios, also in uniform,
and Benigno. The General had personally requested Padre
Maíz to take charge of the funeral service. 'I then enjoyed,'
wrote Maíz much later, 'the best and friendliest of social
relations with the General.'[1] If he really believed this at the
time, he was naïve. To have passed him over without some
compelling reason would alarm those who would shortly be
convening to confirm the General's presidency. Maíz gave
the oration. He 'deplored the loss of that great citizen, the
most diligent and patriotic governor, who raised the name of
Paraguay to that of the greatest power in this region of
America for its progress and wealth . . .'[2]

Then Carlos Saguier escorted la Presidenta and her
daughters from the church, put them in their carriage and
saw that Venancio's mistress was awaiting transport herself.
Madame's carriage stood near; he ushered the girl inside
and she trotted off. The supporters of Saguier claimed
afterwards that this was a mistake: he had thought it was
merely one empty carriage among several, he had thought it
would be back in time to receive Madame as she came from
the church, but who, after the years in which Asunción saw
only two carriages in the streets, would mistake one of them?
Perhaps Saguier had had his arm too painfully twisted in the
matter of seating and this was the pay-back. Scarcely had
her carriage gone than Madame appeared, her children
around her and demanded to know 'why she had been thus
insulted'. She refused his explanations and accused him of
lying.

★

There was an interregnum of five weeks between Don Carlos' death and the meeting of congress to elect a successor. People noted an increased military presence in Asunción, reinforcing the corps in the Plaza del Gobierno and the garrison in Plaza San Francisco under the command of Colonel Venancio.

The impending election dominated gossip in the Club Nacional. They whispered that the General had forced his sick father to write the decree of 15 August, naming him as interim successor. They reported that Padre Maíz believed that Don Carlos intended Benigno López to convoke congress, not Francisco, and had written an earlier decree to this effect which the General had torn up. Nonetheless, they said, Benigno had 400 highly placed supporters and the General's election to the presidency was not a foregone conclusion. Captain Fernandez of the police went to Madame one evening with a report from a spy in the Club Nacional. A certain Riveros, drunk and talkative, had been heard speaking of Benigno's plans to steal the presidency from his brother. Riveros was gaoled that evening but for General López to move openly against the people he had named would be folly, causing only alarm and a rush to support Benigno's candidacy. He waited.

There was espionage elsewhere. 'The priest Palacios,' Maíz would claim, 'established a secret spy network to watch my doings in the Seminary and it was brought to [the General's] knowledge that I wanted a new constitution to replace that of 1844, which gave the president extraordinary and dictatorial powers.'[3] These reports were laid aside with the others; the General took no action yet.

Congress met on 16 October, surrounded by a triple ring of soldiers, commanded by the General's old friend, Paulino Alén. Washburn's informants believed it to have been packed: 'the judges, police chiefs and *curas* [priests] in various districts outside the capital, who had enjoyed more of the respect and confidence of the late President than was pleasing to his successor, were displaced, and men on whom he could entirely rely were substituted for them'[4]. The only points before the deputies were the election of a new president and the duration of his mandate. Padre Justo Roman stood in the hot and crowded room from which the soldiers' feet outside were clearly heard and proposed the candidature of Citizen Francisco Solano López as President of the Republic for ten years. Only one man rose to question the proposal. If any concerted manifestation of opposition had been agreed upon, the unsmiling presence of the General inside and his troops outside had squashed it before it began. The man on his feet, hideously exposed, was Deputy José Varela★.

'*Señores diputados*, the constitution forbids nepotism, that is, government by relatives, and as the candidate proposed by Padre Roman is the son of the recently deceased President, I do not see how that his election can be consistent with the constitution of 1844.'

Awed silence continued for a few seconds, then Minister Vasquez and Padre Roman rose and spoke simultaneously.

'I absolve you!' cried the priest, absurdly.

The other spoke with less excitement.

'The reservations expressed by Deputy Varela are correct,' he said. 'In Paraguay, direct inheritance of power is not permitted. However, such is not the case in this session. The candidate will not *inherit* power, rather we will *elect him to it*, we, the Deputies elected and convoked to that effect.'

Varela made a last attempt in the vast, echoing auditorium.

'Deputy Vazquez has entirely persuaded me. I therefore withdraw my concern. I take this opportunity to state that I

★ No relation to Hector Varela.

intervened for legal reasons, in order to facilitate the election of the proposed candidate, whom I too, from this moment, support.'

The largest supper ever held in the Club Nacional took place to celebrate the election 'by general acclamation' to the presidency of Citizen General Francisco Solano López Carrillo. Three hundred people sat to dinner. There was not enough china in the club's pantries and through the afternoon a stream of servants trotted back and forth between the club and Elisa's house to borrow her silver. Bells rang all evening in celebration. 'For how many,' said Padre Maíz, unaware he was already a marked man, 'will those bells shortly be tolling?'

There were few immediate changes to government. Don Carlos' old friend Mariano Gonzalez stayed in the Hacienda*; José Berges was appointed Minister of Foreign Affairs; and the elderly and inoffensive Francisco Sanchez became Vice-President and Minister of the Interior. The Ministry of War and the Marine, vacated by the new President, was passed to Venancio López. Benigno got nothing.

The news of General López' accession to the presidency was formally relayed to the rest of the world. Answers came from friendly nations.

January 10 1863, the Palace of the Tuileries
I was gratified to receive the private letter you wrote to me and by the affectionate memory you have of your stay in my Imperial court. Believe me when I say I, too, retain this memory and my appreciation of the noble qualities which distinguish you, and thus congratulate your country on the election which has raised you to your destiny. It gave me pleasure to follow, with a friendly eye, the tangible progress

---

* Treasury.

made by Paraguay under the illustrious leadership of your late father. I do not doubt that under your own wise leadership, your country will continue to move rapidly along the road of civilisation. With best wishes for your personal happiness and for the glory of your Presidency, allow me to offer you my esteem and my friendship. General, I pray God keep you in his holy care.

Your good friend,

Napoleon[5]

For some time, the rumour mills in the Club Nacional, the consulates and the gentlemen's clubs of the Plate had been grinding out an extraordinary idea: the President of Paraguay was about to declare himself Emperor.

In March 1863, a stranger arrived in Asunción. He was a Frenchman, identified in British dispatches as *Dr S*, travelling under cover of being a scientific explorer. George Masterman accompanied him into the interior and was struck by his lack of knowledge in any branch of science. He and Charles Washburn supposed him to be 'a political emissary of the Emperor Napoleon', one of many whose presence was 'suspected in the mushroom republics of Central America'[6].

The year that the first shouts of '*Hail Francisco Primero!*' were reported in Paraguay, Napoleon III was about to embark on the creation of a New World Empire thousands of miles to the north. At the start of the Civil War, he had already expressed interest in assembling the southern states of North America into a French Empire but had been dissuaded from intervention on behalf of slavers. Now, he was looking a little futher south.

When the first Napoleon marched across Europe at the beginning of the century and the king of Spain fled his throne, Mexico declared its independence. Since then, the country had enjoyed scarcely a year where its crops had not been trampled by the troops of a general, warlord-priest or bandit. General Santa Ana had survived longest and called himself the Napoleon of the West, accumulating fabulous wealth. When he failed to prevent the United States from taking one third of his territory, he fled to a Caribbean island with his harem and his fighting cocks and lived in luxury. The 1850s saw the rise of his replacement, the incorruptible and ruthless Benito Juárez.

Juárez was a silent and self-educated Indian of extraordinary brilliance. He was driven by hatred of a church which had become fabulously corrupt, charging for the administration of sacraments, levying arbitrary taxes, abusing both sexes and all ages with impunity. Under Juárez, the day of that church was over. It lost its lands, its monasteries and its private courts and the income which passed to Juárez' regime by this expropriation went to pay the war-debts of decades. It was not enough; in 1861, Juárez declared that no interest would be paid for two years on loans contracted with European bankers. Foreigners were attacked in the streets and ports; a silver-train carrying treasure destined for European ships was held up by soldiers. Britain, Spain and France sent in a combined force but when Spain and Britain reached settlement and withdrew, the French army stayed, for Napoleon and Eugenie had been caught in the net of Mexican schemers who were trawling the courts of Europe for a crowned head to spare. When the French army drove Juárez from Mexico City, the French general convened a 'supreme council' and, in the name of the Mexican people, begged Napoleon's protégé, Archduke Maximilian of Austria, to take the throne of Mexico.

The interests of Napoleon III would naturally be engaged by the creation of a French-friendly empire in the Plate; Washburn said the General had told him himself that Napoleon had promised his recognition of the Empire of Paraguay.

★

Juan Crisóstomo Centurión was one of the students who had been sent abroad to study at government expense. In February 1863, he returned from five years in London and Paris, his ship passing that aboard which Ildefonso Bermejo was returning to Spain. Bermejo's last months in Asunción had been painful, for there had been rumours that Doña Pura had been caught *in flagrante* with one of his ex-pupils, Natalicio Talavera, editor of the *Semanario* and great friend of Centurión. Centurión did not confirm or deny the rumour in his book; the affair, if such there had been, had taken place during his absence. In Montevideo, he went aboard a Paraguayan state steamer commanded by another old friend, and asked for news of Paraguay under the new General President.

'Our country at the moment resembles an empire more than a republic,' he was told. 'Wherever you turn your gaze, you will see nothing but military display – in theatres, at balls, in the streets, everywhere, exactly as you do in France. You must be very careful because you are bringing back customs acquired in a free country . . . it is the opposite here among us, the situation is very delicate. If you want to get along well, you have to pay court to *esa grandísima puta*, that great whore who goes everywhere with the President. Now she has come out into the open. Until recently, she did not appear in public but today she does so shamelessly: she even gives speeches at banquets!'[7]

Elisa Lynch was at the heart of the new regime. Opinions differed on how great her influence was on the General's political ideas. Masterman thought she was 'the real ruler of Paraguay'. Secretary Aveiro disagreed. Nevertheless, it was Elisa who controlled informal access to the new President and it was soon known that promotions, concessions, contracts and other favours could be more easily achieved in the informal surroundings of Elisa's *sala* than in an office in the *casa de gobierno*. Not only did Elisa now have the ear of the

President, rather than the President's son, she also had a wider field in which to work. Don Carlos had not underestimated the use of the military and had kept it well supplied with the tools of its trade but he had not held military rank himself and had not used the armed forces to popularise or enforce his rule. His eldest son had a different vision. Paraguay was militarised under the new President not only along its borders but in the *salas* and receptions of the capital. To gain a place in the inner circle, or one of the circles which radiated from that, it was necessary to have some contact with the armed forces and squirming into that inner circle was made easier by an acquaintanceship with Elisa. It was known that a promotion, a transfer or a contract to supply the forces with food, horses, livestock or clothes was more likely if Elisa gave it her support. Her patronage is impossible to trace precisely, for it took place in private conversation, not public speech, and in friendships and sympathies sometimes known only to the people involved. Gifts and donations were discreet. The threads which led to the promotion of officers, or the concession of lucrative contracts to merchants, or the approval of a tricky property purchase or trading permit, cannot be neatly unravelled to a couch in Elisa's drawing room, but those who attended Elisa's parties were those who did well in the new administration.

The role of facilitator was not the only one Elisa played. The origins of her independent wealth in Paraguay are shadowy. She arrived with 500 ounces of the General's gold and an unknown but probably trivial quantity of her own. Within a decade, she was a rich woman, possessing three houses bought for her by the General, and acquiring in her own right both real estate and shares in the export of several commodities. Not enough documents survive to date these activities, or to know how they were initiated, but within two years of the

General's accession, she had moved from arranging favours to being a partner in their rewards, for she had a stake in several businesses supplying the army's needs. She had also become a moneylender, using the services of Lieutenant Francisco Fernandez, army officer, government official and the General's own 'right hand man in all his business matters'[8], proof in itself of her intimate access to the machinery of state. On 18 March 1863, Lieutenant Fernandez administered the contract with one Citizen Rafael Zavala, who borrowed the sum of 6,663 pesos from 'Madama Lynch', putting up a house in Asunción as security. The period of the loan was two years. Interest was charged at eight per cent, two per cent more than the rate charged by the state[9].

There was another person at the centre of the new regime.

Six weeks after the General's accession, a letter left for the Vatican, addressing the issue of who should succeed Bishop Urbieta when he died. Under Don Carlos, Padre Maíz would have been considered the obvious candidate, but the man suggested for the post in November 1862 was 'Dean of the Cathedral, born in the Republic of good parents and of legitimate marriage, deserving for his well-known good moral conduct and holy discipline, observant of Holy Law and subject of Your Holiness'[10], the man who baptised Enrique Lynch López and whose 'sermons were the baldest blasphemy, and entirely devoted to the praise of López, and to instructing the people in their duties towards him.[11]

Shortly before Bishop Urbieta died, a pamphlet was issued in Palacios' name and distributed in the interior. It was based on the work produced by the Spanish church in the wake of the last Inca insurrection and was a catechism of absolute obedience.

Q   May the supreme magistrate impose laws on his vassals?
A   Yes, for God has given him legislative power over them.

Q What [must the vassal do] if the law seems burdensome?
A Obey; and humbly prefer his petition.
Q Is it a sin to murmur against or speak evil of the supreme magistrate?
A Yes, for God says, 'thou shalt not murmur against thy Gods, nor curse the Prince of thy people.'[12]

'I knew the character of General López intimately,' said Padre Maíz, 'and the omnipotence which he would give himself once elected President of the Republic. This is why I wanted a constitution which would deny him absolute power and would put a brake on arbitrary rule . . . I also knew how he had been groomed for power from the earliest age . . . my desire for a new Constitution which would establish the independence of the legislative, the judiciary and the executive was interpreted malignly.'[13] Many shared the priest's concern but if there was any international unease over the General's election to office, his first diplomatic acts were reassuring. In January 1863, an agreement was signed with Britain which ended long-running disputes. In March, relations with France were improved when the General President signed a treaty of friendship with Viscount Bécourt. Don Carlos would have approved his son's first foray into international relations.

Foreigners continued to arrive. An ambitious inoculation programme was underway. Railway sleepers, steam engines and cotton gins were unloaded in the bay. A military academy was to be established in Asunción, run by French officers, and M le Baron Bourgeois, then commander of the gendarmerie at Bougie, Algeria, had accepted the post of director. He would be accompanied by his brother-in-law, a military doctor offered the role of Médécin de l'Ecole Militaire. Mr Treuenfeld, a German engineer, had been engaged to lay telegraph lines connecting the capital with the river garrisons.

The consulates received letters from foreigners who saw Paraguay as a golden opportunity. One Señor Castellano wrote to the new French consul from his existing, not very profitable, business in Rosario, for advice on opening a Spanish–French academy. He had been told, he said, that there were no teachers in Paraguay, could the consul confirm this? Adding that he used to grow cotton in Africa, did the consul think there might be interest in this instead? Roger Fils & Co. of Meules à Moulins & Carreaux (Windmills and Carriages), with houses in Paris, London and New York wrote to ask whether Asunción, in the consul's opinion, might be a profitable next outlet. Consul Cocholet was also dealing with a request from M le Baron Bourgeois' brother-in-law to know his chances of establishing a 'lucrative and rapid' private practice and whether Asunción had sufficient wealthy families to secure him an ambitious income of 20,000 francs.[14]

The *Semanario*, brought in by the yerba boats, was read by the editors of Buenos Aires. The comments at *La Tribuna* that autumn were brief:

April 13: *absolutamente nada de nuevo* – absolutely no news.

May 12: *nada de nuevo* – no news.

Then in June, there was a small stir of curiosity. A 'revolution in Paraguay'[15] had been reported. Padre Maíz, Benigno López, Deputy José Varela and others had been tried by a secret court for 'conspiracy'.

Padre Maíz had been arrested soon after the election, when the reports of the seminary spies were brought out. It would have been unwise to prosecute him for discussing the merits of the constitution, for this was not an offence. He was therefore accused vaguely of conspiracy and specifically of having taught heretical doctrines to the seminarists. Stories were leaked that Maíz had confessed 'that for many years he had been given up to debauchery and had been the first to lead astray scores of innocent young women'[16]. It was put about that he had led a life of 'the deepest hypocrisy and lewdness'[17]. He waited, in irons, for his case to be brought before first a criminal and then an ecclesiastical court.

The blanket word *conspiracy* was also used against Benigno López and the *populacho* was duly alarmed by the spectre of civil war, such as wrecked the Argentine provinces. He was sentenced to five years' exile in the interior, forbidden to re-enter the capital until 1867. 'An extraordinary number of arrests were made at this time by the police,' Masterman recalled. 'On two occasions, returning to my quarters late at night, I saw a group [of police] with fixed bayonets hurrying respectably dressed men to prison . . . the exact charges against political prisoners, and their sentence, was rarely known; the evidence, the names of the denouncer or witnesses – never; and their families and friends were shunned as if plague-stricken, for to be suspected was to be condemned; and seldom did one fall into disgrace without dragging half his relatives with him.'[18]

In August, Padre Maíz was taken from his cell in irons to be tried. His judge was Colonel Robles, the most senior officer in the army after the General himself. Silvestre Aveiro was secretary to the court. They took his statements of unease as proof of guilt and passed him to the jurisdiction of the Bishop's palace, where Palacios waited greedily. In the ecclesiastical court, Maíz was accused of being a Protestant, for a picture of Luther had been found in his desk as well as books of Victor Hugo, Voltaire, Rousseau and 'other dissidents from Catholicism'[19]. Palacios brought the trial to an end by remarking on the strange fact that Maíz had gained weight in his cell.

'Are you without shame,' he said, 'that you are growing fat

as a pig, when you should be crying over your crimes against *la patria?*'

'*Illustrisimo Señor*,' replied Maíz, 'I have never been greedy, still less so now in prison, I do not know how to explain the fact that I have put on a little weight, except that it may be by the tranquil resignation with which I bear my misfortune. I deplore from my heart the fact that you compare me to a dirty pig . . '[20] and in this surreal atmosphere of farmyard squabble, Padre Maíz was sentenced to five years' imprisonment.

Four months of fiesta now linked the two most important dates in the national calendar: the birthday of the General President on 24 July and the anniversary of his accession to the Presidency on 16 October. The great ball of 24 July 1863 to open the season was 'intended to be the grandest affair of the kind ever known in Paraguay'[21].

A request had gone to Gregorio Benítez, Paraguayan chargé d'affaires in Paris, to procure and forward 'an almanac containing the etiquette governing attendance by the various bodies of the [French] court, secular and religious, on ceremonial days'. One end of the Club Nacional ballroom was revamped before the celebrations of July. Workmen appeared with sketches for a new piece of furniture. They erected a dais, and a series of steps by which to reach it. They covered this edifice in lengths of thick fabric, carefully pinned to the back of each step to prevent farcical tumbles, and smoothed across the platform. In the centre, they placed a massive gilt chair, 'gorgeously trimmed in damask and gold'[22], backed and shrouded by a canopy of velvet. Word went out that year that 'no one was ever to sit in the presence of His Excellency when he was himself standing'[23]. A further new disposition governed the balls of 1863. Dancers standing for quadrilles must form themselves in sets stretched diagonally across the room, for it was not now 'proper for anyone to turn his back on the President'[24].

It had been customary for many years for representatives of the principal families of Asunción to call on the General and his mother on his birthday. Flowers would be brought and a formal expression of best wishes and loyalty be made. Although the power of Elisa Lynch over the General had eclipsed that of his mother many years ago, the General's sensitivity had always meant his companion's house was not included in these ritual visits. That changed this year and it was Elisa who engineered the change, for the General still clung to appearances. She put out the suggestion, conveyed to society by acquaintances who bridged the two worlds, that after their visit to the General, the ladies should call upon her also.

It was also Elisa who managed the festivities. The new craze that year was for fancy dress and she decided that the General's birthday ball should follow the fashion. She had 'almost unlimited direction'[25] and dictated the dress for all. Some said she chose, with malicious pleasure, the costumes least suited to the weight and grace of the guests she held in disfavour, 'assigning the garb of a Swiss shepherdess for one, an Italian fruit-seller for another, and prescribing for each some peculiar style of costume'[26]. The General appeared in gala uniform, eschewing fancy dress, but Elisa had chosen a costume of marked significance, 'arraying herself in the gorgeous style of Queen Elizabeth'[27].

Carlos Saguier was still Master of Ceremonies, despite his gaffe at Don Carlos' funeral. Dashing between his office, his *yerbales* and Elisa's house to discuss arrangements, he decided to use the ball to make a public gesture of apology. When Queen Elizabeth entered the Club Nacional to applause from some and gnashing of teeth from others, Saguier was right behind her, dressed as the Doge of Venice. 'The affair passed off so well,' said Washburn, 'that he seemed to regain the favor he had lost, both with the favorite and the President.'[28] The ball was in some ways a triumph for Elisa. She had conceived it, organised it, given it its style, setting and *ton*; she was known to be the companion and adviser to its guest of honour. Still, however, she went unacknowledged for even on this occasion she was not 'permitted to enter the royal set' and López, wrote Washburn, 'did not venture to insult the foreign guests by bringing her face to face with them in so public a manner'[29]. When the ladies' choice was announced, only Inocencia López, the elder of the General's sisters, was regarded as of sufficiently high status to lead him out.

The ball of 24 July was one of many that winter, for several communities threw some party in the President's honour, at their own expense. The foreign merchants subsidised several receptions in homage; the ladies of the city organised their own balls, so did the ladies of nearby villages, 'civil employees of the Administration, garrison officers and naval officers, artisans of the Arsenal'[30] and merchants. At each, the General made his subtly more formal appearance. At each, the appraising eye of Madame was behind the menu, speeches, gifts and costume but never did the couple arrive together, nor meet on the floor to dance, nor intimate in any way that, after the party, they would be sharing a bed.

There was a more sinister aspect to this show. The constant receptions were a means to keep the wealthy in the capital instead of making possible trouble on their *estancias*, some of which bordered nations whose leaders would lend a happy ear to disaffection. The General and his advisers knew that not all the dissidents among the deputies had been eliminated; they knew his election to the presidency had not been well regarded by some who had hoped for a more liberal regime. Forced expenditure was a tactic rulers had used for centuries. The display of luxury, alien to Paraguayans, intrinsic to regimes such as the imperial court of France, was one of the principal means by which the wealthy were parted from money they might otherwise use on nefarious causes.

'The new queen of fashion,' wrote Washburn, 'set an example of extravagance that the more wealthy tried to imitate and they, in turn, dragged their poorer neighbors along the same road of folly. It was no longer proper to appear in the same dress at two balls. Poor as many of the families were, the young ladies must not only go, but they must observe the new order of things, that required the observance of a custom which, being the rule at the courts of Europe, the court of Paraguay could not ignore. Very likely the expense to which this rule subjected them obliged them to scrimp themselves in many other things . . . yet the state balls must be worthy of a court and shortcomings would, sooner or later, be followed by severe penalties.'[31] The merchants grew rich.

It was as important to keep the *populacho* happy as to keep the wealthy under surveillance and 'a continual series of balls, excursions by river, excursions by railroad, bullfights, fire-works and everything that is calculated to dazzle and please the multitude'[32] was on offer that winter. There were street parties: a triumphal arch was erected and 'an immense saloon of wood and canvas' put up in the Plaza de Gobierno for which subscriptions were invited from 'wealthy natives'[33]. A great bullring was built on the sand at the river's edge, unroofed, and large enough for several thousand people. Canvas decorated with flowers and the branches of palms was affixed at an angle to its rim, to shade the spectators. To one side was the bull corral; to the other, a 'row of boxes draped with scarlet cloth and muslin curtains, the centre one for the President and officers of state, the others for the élite of Asunción, while the rest of the space was thrown open freely to the people, who swarmed and clustered from the barriers to the top-most beam'[34]. There were bull-fights, horse-races, music and *la sortija*. Wine and *caña* were distributed free. As darkness came, the *camba rangha* appeared in the ring. Later still, when the revellers left the bullring and went to the saloon in the Plaza del Gobierno, they danced to the 'heavy throb' of the Indian drum, 'beaten in turn by hundreds of willing hands . . . [pulsating] louder and quicker'[35]; more dancers crammed into the room, and left only at dawn. In Calle Fábrica de Balas and the Mercado Guazú, Madame Lynch and the General were surrounded by the celebrations of their people.

Chapter Eight

Uruguay was the other battered American child of Tordesillas, trapped between two large and acquisitive states, fought over by Spanish and Portuguese, Argentine and Brazilian; invaded, betrayed, divided, invaded again. A series of horseman generals had taken command of Montevideo since independence, claiming they brought liberation. The Thirty-Three Immortals of Lavalleja, the Farrapos and the Caballeros Orientales all defeated their enemies then turned against their comrades. Some fled to exile in Buenos Aires or Rio or were garrotted, beheaded, bayoneted, dragged naked behind horses until their skin was flayed by the thorns of the pampas or tied to four posts and left to die in the sun; others were proclaimed liberators, protectors and patriots. In 1835, politics in Uruguay had been defined by two rival generals in words which, mutating constantly, still underlie Plate politics: *blancos* and *colorados*. The general in power, Manuel Oribe, told his supporters to wear a white sash to the polls. They were *los blancos*. Supporters of his rival, General Riveras, ran to the dye works to tint their sashes bright blue, the other colour of the Uruguayan flag, but they had little dye and the sashes were too indeterminate and various to bear the name of any specific colour. They became known simply as *los colorados*.

When General Oribe was ousted by General Riveras, he sailed to exile to Buenos Aires and planned his return, with Dictator Rosas' forces behind him. The siege of Montevideo by Oribe's *colorado* forces, aided by the troops of Buenos Aires, lasted nine years; then skeletons opened the city gates and General Oribe was back in power. His rivals went to their own protector, the Emperor of Brazil, who bribed General Urquiza and sent in the massive army which defeated Oribe in 1851, then crossed the estuary to tumble Dictator Rosas from his throne in 1852. Uruguay was in ruins from a nine-year war, with a debt to Brazil.

The 1850s had opened with civil war but under the leadership of moderate men of both parties by 1853 'all seemed to promise well and the country appeared to be entering on a course of peace and consequent prosperity'[1]. Then, in July 1853, a group of extreme *colorados* rose in rebellion and among them was Colonel Venancio Flores. 'Crafty, cruel and ignorant, all his tastes and instincts found true indulgence as a leader of banditti,'[2] wrote Charles Washburn. The government chose not to raise arms against them but to invite them into the administration, hoping to absorb and moderate them. Flores was made Minister of War. The gamble did not work. The moderate President who had given him the post was soon forced to flee for his life. A junta composed of Flores and two men of fame but great age were left. Both soon died and Flores was alone in power; but when he allowed elections in 1855, the country voted for his replacement by another moderate, Dr Lamás.

When Flores, defeated, left for Buenos Aires, 'the country soon assumed a condition of peace and quiet entirely unprecedented', but he and other extreme *colorados* were already planning their violent return, with the governor of Buenos

Aires 'notoriously in sympathy with the filibusters'[3]. When elections approached in 1858, they seized the moment. Flores went to make a diversion in the north and his colleague General Díaz landed in Montevideo to stage the *colorado* comeback. The panic-stricken government put a young and fanatical *blanco* in charge of national defence. With extraordinary energy, this man, Antonio de la Carreras, raised an army, chased Díaz from the city, surrounded him at a spot named Quinteros and slaughtered his remaining forces, some in battle, some in cold blood after their surrender.

Revenge for the slaughter of Quinteros became a rallying cry for *colorados* everywhere and there was a price on the head of Carrefas. General Flores and his men returned to Buenos Aires to wait.

Over the previous twenty years, the *colorado* and *blanco* divisions of infant Uruguay had mutated beyond recognition under the influence of personal loyalties. They had crossed the rivers and bled profusely into the politics of the Argentine. 'The colour of Argentine passions seeped into the Uruguayan soul and the hatreds of the Uruguayans were those of the Argentines'[4], so much so that Americans on both sides of the border now identified themselves by the colours chosen by squabbling generals in 1835. The manifesto of the Argentine Confederation, challenging the centralisation of power in Buenos Aires, had become the greatest call to the *blanco* flag. The cause of Buenos Aires, subduing the provinces and gathering the wealth of the old viceroyalty to the estuary, became that of the *colorados*. Paraguay fell naturally to the *blanco* side of the party line; more so each time Buenos Aires emerged victorious over the Confederation in their interminable wars and made again her sinister threat of 'incorporation or economic asphyxia'. Both sides spoke routinely of the other as tyrannical; both claimed to uphold the cause of liberty.

The peace in Argentina negotiated by General López in

1859 lasted less than two years. General Mitre had signed the treaty with his fingers crossed and began re-arming as soon as Urquiza's troops returned to the provinces. In 1861, he found an excuse for war in the assassination of a provincial governor and the bloody reprisal which followed. The National Congress in Paraná, capital of the Confederation, refused to accept deputies sent by Buenos Aires and demanded new elections. Buenos Aires refused in her turn and was declared a rebel province. Urquiza's army prepared to attack the city for the third time in a decade. Don Carlos refused, again, to intervene and Paraguay watched as Argentina went to war.

The president of Uruguay in 1861, the *blanco* President Berro, had come to power determined to break his country's 'disastrous intimacy'[5] with Argentine politics. When the *blanco* horsemen of Uruguay rose to join Urquiza's army, he dissuaded them. Venancio Flores had no such scruples about interference. He and his forces were there beside Mitre when they met and defeated Urquiza at Pavón in September 1861 and reversed the result of Cepeda. Buenos Aires was once again the seat of government, Argentina was again precariously united.

Mitre wrote personally to President Berro to thank him for restraining his supporters from joining the Argentine war. But he was in equal debt to Berro's enemy, Venancio Flores, who reminded him each day of the *colorado* exiles who wanted to go home to Uruguay. Since 1858, he had been an officer in Mitre's army, living in anticipation of the moment he would cross the estuary and take revenge for the dead of Quinteros.

On 12 October, Mitre was elected president of Argentina. He addressed the nation in an editorial.

'Perhaps,' he said, 'we are destined to reconstruct the great work which has been destroyed by local passions, returning the American nationalities to their status they enjoyed before the events which reduced them to their current state.'[6] Some thought he referred only to the Confederation of Argentine Provinces; others knew his gaze fell beyond the rivers.

On 1 March 1863 the mandate of President Berro of Uruguay expired and, a week later, Flores resigned his Argentine commission. He had been among the Uruguayan Immortals who first defied Brazil with their declaration of independence thirty-five years before and his life since then had been spent in the saddle, fighting. His methods were vicious. His men were not held back from torture and rape. His prisoners were executed for sport. He had no formal alliance with General Mitre, for that tactician would not give Urquiza another opportunity to march on Buenos Aires with the support of the Uruguayan *blancos* and reverse the defeat of Pavón. Nevertheless, when Flores and three men crossed the river to Uruguay on the night of 19 April 1863, they were in a boat lent them by the Argentine fleet, waved from the dock by the Argentine Minister of War and funded by money given them during a meeting in President Mitre's house.

They landed at Rincón de las Gallinas on the Uruguayan bank and struck out across the countryside. By dawn, they were tens, by midday, scores; by the time they besieged the first *blanco* garrison, they were hundreds. The government in Montevideo did not own enough horses to relieve its border garrisons. They fell swiftly to Flores' men, with cruelty and much delight in death. The *porteño* press hailed him as a liberator. 'American nations,' wrote *La Nación Argentina*, 'must tend towards expansion, for this is the law of nature . . . the fusion of nationalities who have interests and a past in common, united by geography in the reciprocal annexation of neighbouring republics . . .'[7] Few can have understood what *reciprocal annexation* meant but enthusiastic gun-running began in its support. Protests were immediately made by the *blanco* government in Montevideo and the diplomatic corps of the Plate. Mitre replied with fabulous insincerity. His government in no way supported Flores, he said; Buenos Aires adhered strictly to a policy of neutrality.

At the beginning of June, Uruguayan authorities discovered arms and munitions aboard a merchant vessel in a Uruguayan port. The skipper said they were the property of the Argentine government, the port authorities confiscated them, Buenos Aires seized a Uruguayan ship in retaliation and the two countries were on the brink of war. All that prevented Mitre sending in the troops of Buenos Aires was the old fear of General Urquiza.

Flores had friends not only in Buenos Aires. Forty thousand Brazilian 'outlanders' worked cattle lands which straddled the border with Rio Grande do Sul, the easternmost province of the Empire of Brazil, from which Uruguay had been torn in 1835. They lived from contraband and the transfer of vast herds from one side of the border to another without payment of duties. The *blancos* had made consistent efforts to impose the taxes and authority of Montevideo upon them and the outlanders had been sending tall tales to Rio for many years of imposition, persecution and atrocity committed by officers from Montevideo, intent on breaking their 'rights'. General Netto, honorary chief of the outlanders, talked with Flores. It was agreed that the *colorado* government, when it came, would be more tolerant.

Montevideo, pressed and harassed by Flores' army, now sent out envoys on parallel missions. Dr Lapido left for Asunción to engage the protection of the powerful army of Paraguay. Dr Lamás, the Uruguayan statesman who had heard General López' 'large ideas' on his return from Europe, was sent to Buenos Aires to persuade President Mitre to observe the neutrality he claimed. His arrival coincided with that of an envoy from Rio, also sent to request Mitre's neutrality and bring the civil war in Uruguay to a swift end, for the interests of Brazil were badly affected, he said, by the marauding bands which crossed the outlanders' land with impunity, trampling crops and stealing to feed their men and mounts.

News of the *colorado* invasion of Uruguay, subsidised by Buenos Aires, came upriver to Asunción as the city entered its season of celebration in 1863. Dr Lapido was given a cordial reception. General López listened closely to his flattering request for protection and his argument that Buenos Aires would not stop at the conquest of Uruguay but would next look north to Paraguay. He made no promise to intervene, but the Uruguayan was an honoured guest at official receptions that winter.

The hot season passed in festivity in Paraguay, bloodshed in the Uruguayan pampas and growing fear in Montevideo, where the *blanco* government sent urgent dispatches to Dr Lapido, urging him to persuade General López into action. The Paraguayan and Uruguayan navies must join forces and occupy the island of Martin García in the Plate estuary. This would send a clear signal to the ships on the Argentine shore that they could no longer sail insolently and bearing *colorado* arms into Uruguayan waters.

On 6 September, López sent a note to the Argentine government asking 'friendly explanations' of Mitre's participation in the recent events in Uruguay and the truth of Lapido's denunciations of Argentine complicity. The concern of Paraguay, said the note, was to maintain the 'balance of power in the Plate'. From Uruguay, the government sent letter after letter to Buenos Aires, asking similar explanations for their acts in transparent support of Flores' troops. The occasional replies from Mitre's ministers to both Montevideo and Asunción were brief and barely polite. They listened to the representations of Dom Pedro's envoy with greater respect.

General López, wounded in pride, concerned by the cynical

spread of Argentine force, now agreed to some of Dr Lapido's suggestions and Lapido shot back to Montevideo to announce his mission had been successful: the President of Paraguay had offered himself as arbiter between the two sides with the most powerful army in the Plate behind him. In Buenos Aires, meanwhile, Dr Lamás had brought the Argentines and the Brazilian envoy together and made a skilful deal. Hours after Dr Lapido's triumphant arrival in Montevideo a junior diplomat dispatched by Dr Lamás came in with his own good news from Buenos Aires: Argentina had agreed to remain neutral and Dom Pedro of Brazil had agreed to be arbiter. It was an immensely tricky situation. Accepting the arbitration of Dom Pedro meant Uruguay was dangerously dependent on the goodwill of the Emperor, who would take advantage to press his claims on its eastern border. Accepting the offer from General López would annoy Dom Pedro, and this could be equally dangerous. The government in Montevideo hesitated, discussed, procrastinated and decided rashly to shelve the Brazilian offer and trust to the diplomatic – and, they hoped, military – guarantees of Paraguay. Dr Lamás was incandescent.

By this sacrifice, [he wrote] we continued the misunderstanding with the Argentine government. We abandoned a neutrality legalised, effective, definite. We alienated the sympathy of Brazil. We acquiesced, incredible as it may seem, in the abandonment of arbitration, our most important conquest, as a means of solving our international conflicts. Finally, we deprived ourselves of the beneficial co-operation of the united action of Argentina and Brazil in quenching, as soon as we would, the internecine war.

The consequences were immediate – the civil war continued – the prohibition to us of the military use of our own waters . . . ended by weakening the action of the

Uruguayan Government – and the relations of the latter with that of Brazil gradually assumed another character. And such immense sacrifices were made on the altar of the *amour propre* of the Paraguayan President.[8]

A rumour flowed with the Plate as the end of that turbulent year approached. In the *salas* of Asunción it was whispered that the New Year would see a coup: the man who had ringed the senate with troops when it elected him president would soon declare himself emperor.

In November 1863, the General sent for Henry Burrell and Percy Volpy, English engineers recently sent by the Blyths to work on the Paraguayan railways. He had a new project for them: the construction of a vast new palace on a riverbank plot between the docks and the Plaza del Gobierno from which the huts of the poor had recently been cleared. It was to be enormous and formidably European, foursquare and turreted, quite different to the low, colonnaded house he inhabited on the market square. It was to house a royal dynasty, for General López had asked the hand in marriage of the Princess Isabel of Brazil, younger daughter of Dom Pedro and aged seventeen, bearer of Braganza blood and incontestably royal.

These were not the first rumours of the General's marriage to some eligible virgin to reach Elisa since she had arrived in Asunción seven years previously to tales of infidelity, illegitimate children and ambitious families. Who knows what role the General intended for Elisa and their sons within a Paraguayan Empire ruled by the new dynasty? He may have considered retaining Panchito as heir apparent, or in some military role traditional to a royal bastard. Madame, if she stayed, would have to step sideways, into the role of *maîtresse en titre*.

Madame had no intention of going home, for she had been

buying up vast amounts of real estate around the plot where the General intended to build his palace. Some of this she intended for commercial use, for modern buildings of two storeys interspersed with arcades of shops on the Parisian model. She had drawn up plans for these and begun to import materials for their construction. Had her scheme been realised, this would have been the largest building project in Asunción. Her project for elegant squares and streets, linking the new customs house to the new theatre, skimming the planned oratory opposite the Club Nacional and the improved market outside the General's old house, leading to the new railway station, would have changed the face of the city. This was not the only purpose of her property purchases. If the General was going to have his vast new palace (and install a Brazilian princess there) then so was Madame. While rumours built of the General's matrimonial projects, she 'openly talked of building another [palace] equally magnificent, for herself'[9].

The same month the General called in the engineers to discuss his palace, forty-one armed men in the pay of Buenos Aires were discovered attempting to land on islands in the River Uruguay and taken prisoner. An outrageous riposte came from Buenos Aires: one of the islands was adjacent to Argentine territory, the arrest was therefore illegal, Uruguay had violated Argentine sovereignty and must release the men and pay compensation. There were belligerent articles in every *porteño* newspaper. It had all happened before many times; what was different in November 1863 was that Brazil no longer appeared anxious to press for Argentine neutrality.

The Empire had been much put out by Montevideo's bad faith in asking Brazilian help, then accepting Paraguayan mediation, but had continued to restrain the 40,000 trouble-some Brazilian 'outlanders' from joining Flores' rebel army. But when the Brazilian Chamber of Deputies reconvened in Rio de Janeiro in January, it was with a change of ministry and a change of mood. The new deputies were young men; they wanted participation in great events; they called for action. An outlander magnate stood in the Chamber and talked again of the 'atrocities' committed by the *blanco* government on decent Brazilians along the border. Privately, he reminded them that Rio Grande do Sul had already seceded once from the Empire. He mentioned the fact that Buenos Aires, geographically nearer the outlanders' estates, was sympathetic to the outlander cause. Alarmed and newly hawkish, the deputies considered his claims. In April, they voted to demand compensation from the *blanco* government for damages to Brazilian subjects. Envoy Saraiva was appointed to visit Montevideo, backed, as was the Brazilian way, by a fleet to blockade the city. He was authorised to speak soothingly to the outlanders, sternly to the besieged government in Montevideo and amicably to Buenos Aires, the traditional enemy whose interests in Uruguay now appeared to be coinciding with Brazil's own.

Two men in Asunción acted on fears that many expressed in whispers: a great war was coming and the new General President would not, like his father, remain aloof from his neighbours' squabbles. Carlos and Fernando Saguier secretly sold their assets and went to visit relatives in Buenos Aires. They did not come back.

No one in Asunción could fail to see another increase in military activity in early 1864. Some thought the new General President was merely stamping his style on the regime; others, like the Saguiers, feared he was squaring up for a fight.

In January, he established a new training camp at Cerro León, thirty miles east of Asunción in the hills, near Patiño-Cué. The railway was to be extended to service the new garrison. In March, orders went to the chargé d'affaires in London to buy modern arms and commission ironclads. At the end of that month, the President and his *état-major* moved to Cerro León. He left correspondence with his many, pressing foreign envoys in the hands of Chancellor José Berges, the gentle and erudite man who had settled the Hopkins affair in Washington, although not a word of Berges' letters was allowed to go unchecked: messengers whizzed between capital and camp with draft, correction, second draft and final approved version for Berges to sign and send. In April, army officer Pedro Duarte went recruiting along the southern border and assembled a force of 10,000 men in case the President should give the order to march into Rio Grande do Sul. In May, two more Uruguayan envoys arrived in Paraguay and were closeted with López for many hours. Rodríguez Larreta and Vásquez Sagastume had been told by their masters in Montevideo to force a written promise of support from Paraguay for so far, the General had offered *puras palabras*, nothing but words. In July, they were joined by Antonio de la Carreras, the Uruguayan who had ordered the massacre of Flores' men at Quinteros. In Montevideo, the government was divided between those who pinned their hopes on Paraguayan support and those who wanted to come to an agreement with Envoy Saraiva and trust to Brazil to enforce Argentine neutrality. On 18 June, Envoy Saraiva met Venancio Flores and the Argentine Chancellor to sign a pact by which they agreed limited joint measures against the *blanco* government of Montevideo.

In Asunción, the war dominated everyone's thoughts. The trains were full of soldiers. Recruits were seen drilling in public squares and that winter's celebrations took place against a 'St Vitus' Dance' of war fever. The usual horse races were held; there was the *sortija* and dances in the plazas for the *populacho* but Asunción lived in anticipation of war. The usual invitation was sent to important families to attend the Mass of Thanksgiving 'in just celebration of the joyous birthday of the

Excelentisimo Señor Don Francisco Solano López, President of the Republic and General in Chief of the Armed Forces'[10]. Sagastume and Larreta were guests at the balls and banquets organised by Elisa. They attended the great reception in July to celebrate the opening of San Francisco railway station, when the upper salon was decorated with chandeliers and the Club Nacional sent food for hundreds of guests. The Brazilian envoy, Vianna de Lima, and his wife were among them but they left when Elisa entered, with ostentatious disgust.

At the beginning of August, Envoy Saraiva presented the *blanco* government with an ultimatum, demanding compensation for 'atrocities' committed along the border and threatening reprisals from the Brazilian fleet if this were not paid. In Rio, a congressman stood to ask whether the borders of the Empire should not be extended to take in the whole of Uruguay and in Asunción, José Berges presented the Brazilian consul with the General's protest against this ultimatum. Paraguay, the General warned, would never accept the Brazilian occupation of Uruguay. A contemptuous reply was returned: the Brazilian Emperor would not be prevented from protecting his subjects.

Elisa had been making her own preparations for war. Among the foreign merchants resident in Asunción whom she knew well was one Don Sinforoso Cáceres, a native of Corrientes, who traded between Asunción, Buenos Aires, Montevideo and the Argentine cities. As the Paraguayan armed forces expanded, Cáceres and Elisa went into partnership and were granted the rich concession on supplying the troops with cattle.

Saraiva's absurd ultimatum was inevitably rejected by Montevideo and the Brazilians moved smoothly to the next step, planned three months previously, signing a prepared treaty with Argentina. It agreed 'joint intervention in any possible events in the River Plate caused by the Uruguayan question'. On 30 August, Berges sent a note to the Brazilian consul to tell him Paraguay regretted being forced into the situation where her threat against occupation of Uruguay must be made effective, but Paraguay had already been sidelined. The two ancient enemies of the smaller Plate republics were in agreement. Paraguay must be prevented from interfering while they acted as they wished in Uruguay. When word of the Paraguayan protest reached Buenos Aires, coverage was spiteful and editorials vicious: 'by what right does Paraguay, from that corner of the world in which it lies, cut off from the light of civilisation, prevent a sovereign and independent nation claiming reparation from another, equally independent?'[11] They continued for three days, increasingly nasty. 'The man who calls on the balance of powers in the Plate is a risible dwarf, a Quijote who, when the day comes, will be given a sharp lesson to teach him that he cannot continue to test the patience of civilised governments.'[12]

On 16 October, as the grand ball to celebrate López' accession to the presidency was taking place in Asunción, 12,000 Brazilians crossed the Uruguayan border and made their first killings at Villa del Salto. The ultimatum López had delivered was put to the test. Would his famous army be put into action and march to stop the Brazilians from taking Montevideo? López made no move.

There was an immediate chorus of contempt in the Buenos Aires press. 'After the first declarations from Paraguay, everyone expected that when news arrived there of the events at Villa del Salto, the promise would immediately have been fulfilled – but no' . . . 'Soon even schoolboys will be laughing at López' . . . 'Paraguay will never emerge from her chrysalis'[13]. The words of López were 'empty boasts'.

On the evening of 10 November 1864, the Brazilian steamer *Marquês do Olinda* put in to refuel at Asunción on her way to the Matto Grosso. She carried mail, the troops' pay and the new provincial governor sent from Rio. She also brought newspapers and correspondence from her various ports of call, which were sent to the General in Cerro León. He opened them to find news from Juan José Brizuela of the sufferings in Montevideo and the actions of Brazilian troops whose command in Rio had taken no notice of a Paraguayan threat. His pretensions as statesman were brutally caricatured in editorials and cartoons. Later, it was said that it was these insults which tipped him into his first open hostility against Brazil, but Charles Washburn dined with the General a couple of days later and remembered another letter brought ashore from the *Marquês*. It was from Dom Pedro, to his 'great and good friend' President López and it reported, in careful language, the betrothal of his two daughters to European princes.[14]

Washburn thought that the Emperor's concern for his daughter weighed as much as politics in this dynastic game. 'Knowing,' he wrote, that 'any person whom for state or ambitious purposes [López] might take to share his throne would hold but the second place in his regard, and be in reality but the servant and captive of his mistress'[15], he declined the offer of dynastic fusion. Madame's powerful presence might have made life wretched for the teenage princess but a marital alliance with Paraguay might not have met with Dom Pedro's disapproval in other circumstances. Marriage was a step towards the amalgamation of the two states and princesses were traditional down payments in such agreements, expected to do their duty. Whatever his earlier deliberations, however, events in the Plate that year had made the marriage of a Brazilian princess to a Paraguayan president impossible.

Within hours of receiving news of events in Uruguay and Brazil, the General had sent an aide by express train to Asunción with orders for his brother Venancio at the city garrison: he was to send the *Tacuarí* after the *Marquês* and take her by whatever means necessary. He would threaten the closure of the rivers to the Matto Grosso. Ten hours later, a shipload of alarmed Brazilians entered Asunción bay, escorted by the *Tacuarí*, and were surrounded by gunboats. Equipment, official correspondence, passengers' belongings and stores were taken off and searched and Captain Mesa of the *Tacuarí* set up an impromptu tribunal. The Brazilian captain was asked why he was in Paraguayan waters when Paraguay and Brazil were at war following the Brazilian note of 30 August. He replied emphatically that there had been no declaration of war. Captain Mesa ended the audience officially by declaring him, his crew and passengers to be prisoners of war. Unofficially, he ended it by turning to the new governor of Mato Grosso and saying quietly: 'What can we do? These are government affairs, be patient.'

News that the *Marquês* was held in the bay had raced around the city and there were already people in the streets shouting '*muera el emperador!*' – 'death to the emperor!' – and sending up *vivas* outside the General's house. The immediate popular reaction was of overwheming enthusiasm. They had always known that *los macacos, la camba, los negros* – all insulting terms for the Brazilian 'baboons' – were the enemy.

Forty-two members of the *Marquês'* crew were allowed downriver out of Paraguay. The rest, with the new governor of the Matto Grosso and the passengers, were detained. Some were sent to *estancias* in the interior, 'no one knew where'; others were housed 'in a barn on the docks'[16]. Two thousand muskets were found aboard, proof that Brazil had been using the steamer line to transport arms to the Matto Grosso. Four hundred thousand Brazilian dollars, intended to pay the troops, were seized. The rest of the cargo and stores were sold by public auction at the docks and the money raised was given to the government. The flag of the *Marquês* was made into a rug for López' office.

The foreigners who had come to Paraguay to make money, and the Paraguayans who had entered into business with them, were dismayed by this sudden, violent turn of events. They had had twelve years of tranquility and increasing prosperity in Asunción, whose citizens were learning to covet and spend and dress and show, while the rest of the River Plate fought its eternal battles. Don Carlos had taken them close to the edge more than once, but had backed down, choosing to pay or negotiate his way out of international difficulties. Now the young General, not yet two years in office, had led the country into war with its biggest neighbour.

The Brazilian special envoy in Asunción was greatly alarmed. He feared he and his family would be held hostage for the duration of hostilities and asked Charles Washburn to plead his case with the General. Washburn took the steam train to Cerro León and spoke to the General where, 'with more candor than discretion', the General expressed his view to the Yankee: 'the situation of Paraguay was such that only by a war could the attention and respect of the world be secured to her. Isolated as she was, and scarcely known beyond the American states, so would she remain till by her feats of arms she could compel other nations to treat her with more consideration.'[17] He had been expecting this war for many years. He had given thought not only to the fortifications of his own country but also to the difficulties Brazil would experience in getting sufficient troops upriver and overland to take them on. 'Having shown their strength and demonstrated to Brazil that they were not to be conquered except at ruinous cost and sacrifice, the imperial government would be glad to treat for peace on terms highly advantageous to Paraguay.'[18] He thought 'the old question of boundaries would then be settled and Paraguay would afterwards be recognised as a nation whose friendship was to be sought . . .'[19] The

Brazilian special envoy was allowed to leave, although the Brazilian consul was not. Requests came in from several other contracted foreign workers to be allowed to return home but no one was given permission to leave. The departure of the British, in particular, would have incapacitated the military. Washburn could do little for the other foreigners for he was engaged in preparations for his own departure. He had left behind a fiancée in New York.

News soon came that the Brazilian army was besieging the north Uruguayan city of Paysandú. 'The approach of a powerful Paraguayan army,' wrote the *Times* correspondent there, 'is expected at once.'[20] But before he marched south to relieve the siege of Paysandú, oust the Brazilian army and save the *blanco* cause, General López wanted to secure the rich northern front. A fleet to invade the Matto Grosso was gathering in Asunción bay.

On 14 December 1864, General López reviewed the troops of the northern expedition drawn up outside the new hospital.

Soldados!
My efforts to keep the peace have not borne fruit. The Empire of Brazil, not knowing our courage and enthusiasm, has pushed us into war and we are obliged by our honour and our dignity to accept its challenge, in defence of our most beloved rights.[21]

The bay was full of ships and the docks crowded with people waving the Paraguayan tricolour. Their navy was on its way to invade Brazil, reversing the humiliations of many years. Their destination was Corumbá, capital of the Matto Grosso. Eight steamers and four sailing ships were led by the *Tacuarí*, the fastest steamer on the Plate, blooded by British cannon in Buenos Aires and her own across the bow of the *Marquês*. Three thousand soldiers went smartly aboard, brilliant in new uniforms of white trousers, crimson jackets and red kepis with a black band and tassel, 'all Asunción was down at the riverside'[22]. Every envoy and government minister was there. Wives of the officers stood in a group apart with Elisa, there were *vivas* and cannon fired in the bay as each ship departed on the half hour. At midday, the last ship moved upriver at the tail end of the line. All week there were noisy demonstrations in the plazas against Brazil and for the General President and his forces.

By the first week of January, the Paraguayans had taken easy and brutal command of the riverside settlements and southern lands of the Matto Grosso. Garrisons were abandoned and settlers fled with families and slaves into the marshes, where they were hunted down by Paraguayans and the Gualo Indians. The Paraguayans left garrisons in the north and returned to Asunción as heroes. The *Ypora* flew a string from her shrouds to which were attached the ears of dead Brazilians, caught in the woods as they fled. Other ships brought 500 prisoners of war and more proof that the Brazilians had been amassing arms and ammunition upriver. A second returning column was on its way overland with 80,000 head of cattle from Brazilian *estancias* and the provincial Brazilian governor's 'patent of nobility', the certificate granting him his title, which had been snatched from his office wall. The officers gave it to Elisa Lynch, who framed it in gilt and hung it in an anteroom in Calle Fábrica de Balas. Silver ornaments were taken from the treasury and the silver chandeliers of Jesuit churches brought for a celebratory ball in the upper salon of San Francisco station. Colonel Barrios was promoted General. Soon women from the Matto Grosso were seen begging in the streets.

Elisa Lynch had particular reason to celebrate. Barrios had appointed a new Brazilian *intendente* to collaborate with his officers. The *intendente*, two steps removed from Elisa, had just put his name to documents which transferred into her name estates of enormous size in the new Paraguayan lands. At a stroke, she had acquired lands the size of Belgium, sufficient to keep her in the splendour of the fabulous Brazilian exiles of Paris, should the day come when she returned.

They heard of atrocities in Uruguay.

In December, 20,000 Brazilian soldiers destroyed Paysandú and besieged a garrison of 800 soldiers and the townspeople who sheltered with them. In Buenos Aires, hospitals were established for the wounded Brazilian troops far from home, the Brazilian fleet was accommodated in the waters of the Plate estuary better to prosecute the coming siege of Montevideo and *porteño* suppliers sent food, arms and livestock to the Brazilians troops. Flores, Mitre and Dom Pedro were not yet formally allied but already they were in smooth concert against the desperate *blancos* of Montevideo and their sole remaining champion, the President of Paraguay.

The Uruguayan Colonel Gomez of Paysandú surrendered on 2 January to General Barreto of the Brazilian army, assured he and his people would be treated honourably. His officers were executed, he saw women raped and children bayoneted and his throat was slit. Now the Brazilians were outside Montevideo, threatening to sack the city if it did not surrender within the week. No one believed their offer of honourable treatment and the government prepared for siege and blockade. On the other side of the river, the names of Gomez and Paysandú had become rallying calls among the gauchos of the Argentine provinces, who begged General Urquiza to mobilise and fight. López' envoys went back and forth to Urquiza's palace in Entre Rios, demanding to know when his army would be raised, where the two would meet, what their strategy would be. They returned each time with encouraging words.

To reach Uruguay, Paraguayan troops had to cross a neck of Argentine land, its scant population in sympathy with Urquiza and traditionally hostile to Buenos Aires. Obeying some vague and sporadic understanding of gentlemanly warfare, López asked permission of Buenos Aires. His troops waited on the banks of the Paraná until it came and Paraguayan spies in the northern Argentine provinces sounded the people's feeling towards a 'friendly invasion', should permission be denied and the ground have to be taken by force to allow the transit of troops to Uruguay. These provinces had little love for Buenos Aires. Popular opinion was in favour of supporting *blancos* against *colorados* and General Urquiza against General Mitre.

The siege of Montevideo lengthened; its people were sick and hungry; they asked when Generals López and Urquiza would arrive. The congress in Buenos Aires sent a curt and inevitable refusal to López' request. Still López did not send in his army but convoked his own congress to consider. Before it met, Montevideo had fallen to the Brazilians and Venancio Flores had been appointed provisional governor of Uruguay, backed by Buenos Aires and Rio. His *blanco* enemies were fleeing west across the River Uruguay and into the north Argentine provinces, where the gauchos who had wished to ride to their aid gave shelter and promised revenge against Brazil and the duplicitous president in Buenos Aires who had made Flores' victory possible.

Congress met amid a party atmosphere in Asunción. There were public balls each day in 'improvised saloons'[23]. Inside the senate, the deputies listened to the General, heard the sounds of exultation outside and declared war on 'the current Argentine government until it should guarantee and satisfy the honour and the dignity of the Paraguayan Nation and its Government[24]. Then they promoted the General to Mariscal

– Field Marshal. In the streets, triumphal arches were up by evening and churches, public buildings and all but the bravest of private houses remained illuminated until dawn. There were fireworks and the streets were full. Late in the evening, a military band headed a commission of notables who marched from the police station to the house on Calle Fábrica de Balas, headed by Benigno López, José Berges and Policarpo Garro, brother-in-law to Juana Pesoa, who stepped forward and offered congratulations in the name of the Paraguayan people.

> As the serenata arrived at the door of her house, [Madame] appeared . . . with a little basket hanging from her left arm containing bandages, thread, cotton etc and, after receiving the congratulations offered . . . she replied:
> People of Paraguay:
> I thank you for the congratulations you come to offer me for the appointment to Field Marshal of my señor, the President of the Republic, in the war you have just declared on those two large nations who, drunk on greatness, thought Paraguay would not confront them . . . No other explanation can be made of the provocation they have made to you, or of their blatant rupture of the agreements which existed between them and this country. I join the patriotic demonstrations you have made and from this moment I declare myself a Paraguayan citizen and, with this basket, I will march by your side to battle to nurse you . . .
> *Viva el excelentísimo Señor Mariscal Presidente de la República del Paraguay, Don Francisco Solano López!*
> *Viva!* responded the crowd amid the lively sound of the London carapé and the explosions of fireworks . . .[25]

Then Elisa stepped back to invite the commission and the crowds behind to enter her house and refresh themselves.

There were wines, liquors and champagne on offer and Elisa herself went from guest to guest to refill their glasses, her little basket still hanging from her arm. People who had never entered her house, and never thought they would, now wandered the halls and splendid rooms, touched the fabric of the sofas and gazed at her pictures. When her guests left, there were more *vivas*, to the Mariscal and the Mariscal's lady.

Deputy Centurión was deeply troubled that night.

I was pale, my heart oppressed by a great sadness, so great that I could not resist saying to my companion . . . 'my friend, this is bad! Paraguay might perhaps take on one nation, but to take on two, who will naturally make common cause, seems very bold to me. It is very imprudent.' He replied, his face as sad as my own, 'my friend, what can we do – we shall see what comes of it.'[26]

In Buenos Aires, a Paraguayan Legion was formed of exiles determined to fight the Mariscal and the first forced denunciations appeared in the *Semanario* from families whose relatives were associated with this act of treason.

I further say that if my son . . . persists in his misguided way, or does not publicly vindicate himself, he will receive the malediction of all his fellow-citizens and his afflicted mother who will against her will be obliged to curse him . . .[27]

Such declarations would become familiar.

Of the four countries now involved in the squabbles of the Uruguayan caudillos, Paraguay was the only one who had never, since independence from Europe, been at war, nor suffered internal revolt. She now faced a hostile alliance of three powers. Don Carlos had frustrated the plans of old enemies by a fixed refusal to elevate dissension to war, no matter the question, no matter the price, no matter the bribe. The General, now Mariscal, had fallen into their trap.

Chapter Nine

While the Mariscal met the alliance of Brazil and Argentina with a declaration of war, Brazil approached the alliance of the Mariscal and General Urquiza in a wholly different way.

The Brazilian General Osorio had been at Urquiza's side when they fought Dictator Rosas in 1852. Now he visited his old comrade in arms and brought fine horses. They chatted of old times, touched on the treaties bought by Brazilian envoys passing up and down the rivers in recent years and an offer was made: the Brazilian army required thousands of horses and was prepared to pay above the market price, immediately, to get them.

On 3 April, a Paraguayan envoy left for Buenos Aires with Congress' declaration of war. On 11 April, five steamers – including the *Marquês do Olinda* – left Asunción with troops abroad to occupy the Argentine city and province of Corrientes. They were to join the southern army, commanded by the most senior officer in the Paraguayan army after the Mariscal, General Wenceslao Robles, previously commandant of the camps at Cerro León and Humaitá, 'cunning and repulsive', with a reputation for cruelty and a tendency to drown his doubts in cognac. Two Argentine ships off Corrientes were attacked and taken that day and incorporated into the Paraguayan navy. Three thousand Paraguayan soldiers began crossing the Argentine border. Elisa's spies, men and women employed 'in a menial capacity around the camp'[1] went with them.

It was immediately clear from the reaction of the locals that the 'friendly invasion' was a mistake and Paraguayan spies had been misinformed. In Rosario, the Paraguayan consul was imprisoned, the Paraguayan flag burnt and a picture of the Mariscal used for target practice. On 17 April, Buenos Aires declared war on the government of Paraguay and Mitre appeared to give the speech the crowds outside congress wanted to hear: 'the barracks in 24 hours! Corrientes in two weeks! Asunción in three months!'[2] At the Council of Generals, the subterranean negotiations with Brazil emerged. General Mitre was appointed commander in chief of the allied army. Then General Osorio stood and proposed General Urquiza of Entre Rios as commander of 'the vanguard of the Allied Army'. There was one other country represented at the Council. Uruguay, announced General Venancio Flores, 'will, from today, lend all cooperation possible, considering her alliance with Brazil to be a sacred duty in the war faithlessly declared by the Paraguayan government, whose interference in the internal affairs of Uruguay is unjustifiable and insolent'[3].

A *Times* correspondent wrote from 'Paraná River' on 10 May.

The war fever in the districts on both sides of this river is assuming more troubled symptoms every day. At cafés, clubs and billiard-rooms, in shops, at street doors and in public offices, war talk is the general topic of conversation, with many, perhaps, as regular as their morning prayers, for palaver of this kind seems stereotyped out here as a sort of national institution.

'Battalions', 'bombardments' and 'revolutions' are so dovetailed with 'libertad' and 'la Constitución' and 'reaction in the provinces' that you feel yourself in a maze when involuntarily obliged to listen to political discussions. And still the changes are rung on events and probabilities, of which no one can give an explanation or foresee the end.

'Up to the moment,' he added,'nothing has caused such a universal feeling of satisfaction as the adhesion of General Urquiza to the Argentine National Government.'[4]

By the end of the month, the Southern Army was strung out over a hundred miles of enemy territory; a forward contingent under General Robles at the southern city of Empedrades, near Urquiza's border; and a garrison of 1,500 men to the north, in Corrientes, where Elisa's cattle-dealing partner Sinforoso Cáceres had just been appointed principal member of the government of occupation. It was a cold winter. Everywhere they went, they found hostility where they had thought to find support. Urgent requests came from Robles for better clothes, shoes and shelter, because the men were suffering greatly in the marshes of northern Argentina.

In Asunción and Cerro León, the Mariscal reviewed his troops. Fifteen thousand men marched past him in one day alone, glorious in scarlet jackets. In the bay of Asunción, the North American Mr Kruger demonstrated a torpedo, blowing a raft of palm trees into the air from the river with such vigour that he 'nearly blew himself up with it'[5]. Confident reports circulated that General President Melgarejo of Bolivia was about to send his army to join Paraguay.

On 1 May, representatives of Uruguay, Brazil and Argentina met privately in President Mitre's house in Buenos Aires to sign the treaty of the Triple Alliance. Article One stated that 'the Republic of Uruguay, His Majesty the Emperor of Brazil and the Argentine Republic contract an offensive and defensive alliance in the War provoked by the Government of Paraguay'[6]. Other articles shared commands and duties. It was stated that the war was not against the people, but the government of the enemy state and guaranteed respect for Paraguay's 'independence, sovereignty and territorial integrity'[7]. The heart of the agreement lay in its last, secret articles and these contradicted what had gone before. Paraguay was to be reduced to one-third her current size. Brazil was to get the lands she had been moving towards since San Ildefonso. Argentina was to acquire the whole of the Paraguayan Chaco. The rivers were to be held forcibly open for foreign shipping to penetrate to the new Argentine and Brazilian ports. The rump which remained between them would sink beneath her war debts and the clerical error which was Paraguay would finally be erased.

The Third Army had, at length, marched into Uruguay and was heading slowly south to engage the army of Flores and his Brazilian allies. Its commanding officers had both paid a call on Elisa before they left Asunción and doubtless when they crossed the River Uruguay in early May, some of her spies crossed with them. Theirs was a crack army of 10,000, well-trained and well equipped. Most had encamped across the river while a small force galloped on to reconnoitre, entering abandoned towns, meeting occasional enemy patrols, absorbing stray *blanco* fighters and the horsemen from Entre Rios who had disregarded Urquiza.

In Humaitá, the Mariscal was engaged on another operation.

He had left Asunción for the frosty Quadrilateral, in the extreme southwest of the country, leaving government in the hands of the aged Vice-President Sanchez. The Mariscal had wished to command the southern expeditions, but had been dissuaded by Bishop Palacios and Elisa Lynch, who pointed out that the war rested on his leadership alone. This was couched in fawning terms, at least by the Bishop, but it was true. Venancio was dull-witted and had recently contracted syphilis, for which reason Captain Fernandez had been appointed acting Minister of War. Benigno was officially in exile in the interior (although often seen about Trinidad with his mother) and to hand him the power he had coveted in 1862 would have been folly. So the Mariscal stayed in Asunción and the life of the leader was safe but his armies were hamstrung, for their commanders were not permitted to make even trivial decisions without consultation with the capital. The Mariscal was determined to run the war as he ran his government, centred absolutely on himself. When he left for the southern border on 8 June, the government in Asunción was as weak in autonomous power as his officers across the borders.

Panchito, now eleven, went with his father to Humaitá. The Mariscal had formally entrusted this adored son with the task of writing fair copies of dispatches. It was an administrative job but one which the boy performed with pride and it allowed him to be present at the meetings of his father's *état-major*. Elisa remained in the capital with the younger children. The war was expected to be over by Christmas. There was no need for her to go to the front.

The Allied fleet was on its way to cut off the river at Tres Bocas and strangle landlocked Paraguay. It was vital this blockade was swiftly broken and that no other, further downriver, was allowed to form. However, the Mariscal did not have enough ships to smash his way down the rivers. He had only one purpose-built man-of-war, the *Tacuarí*; his other seven steamers (which included the *Marquês do Olinda* and the two Argentine ships captured off Corrientes) were all merchantmen converted to war use by mounting a small number of cannon. Their guns were fewer than those of the purpose-built Brazilian ships, they lacked iron cladding and their boilers were above the waterline, exposed to enemy fire. The Mariscal had contracted and paid for two more warships, which would change the balance of force in the river, but they were still in a Bordeaux shipyard. The rest of the fleet was composed of *chatas*, low, manpowered barges generally used for towing and piloting, fitted with a single cannon on the bow when they were sent into active service. The Brazilian ships below the border must be put *hors de combat* or captured and this operation was to be executed immediately. The *Semanario* editorial which would announce victory and the ball which would celebrate it were planned before López left Asunción. A small group waited by the telegraph for confirmation of triumph on 12 June. Instead, they received the first garbled and frightening reports of failure.

The Mariscal had convoked senior naval officers on the afternoon he arrived in the Quadrilateral. The plan was this: the enemy fleet was anchored in the River Paraná at its broadest stretch, close to the mouth of the River Riachuelo. There was room by the side of the sleeping enemy ships for the Paraguayan fleet, engines cut, to approach in the small hours and divide. One part would drift silently downriver, then turn, and the Brazilians would wake to find Paraguayan boarding ladders over both sides. The superiority of ships and cannon would be outweighed by surprise and Paraguayan ferocity in hand-to-hand combat. His officers told the Mariscal that Riachuelo was seven hours' steaming away and the best time to attack was between three and four in the morning but when the meeting broke up the ideal hour of departure had passed. Although the fleet would arrive at Riachuelo when it was already light, the Mariscal was determined to press ahead and no officer would gainsay him. They left at midnight. Later, they discovered they had forgotten the boarding ladders. In the early hours, the propeller broke on the *Ypora* and the entire fleet waited while technicians fumbled below the waterline to mend it. It was nine in the morning when they reached Riachuelo and in broad daylight the Brazilians shouted 'Enemy fleet at the bow!', fired their boilers, loaded their cannon and shot them down. The battle lasted eight hours and the cannon was heard far downriver. The Paraguayan fleet stood no chance. Two of their precious ships were sunk and two badly damaged. Three hundred men died and others were taken prisoner. Commodore Mesa died from his wounds in Humaitá, unvisited by a furious Mariscal bent on finding a scapegoat for the disaster.

The men of the Quadrilateral swam downstream each day to salvage what they could of the ships damaged at Riachuelo. It was deepest winter and the water was icy. They were still gathering debris when the Mariscal received the news of Urquiza's defection and ordered Robles to retreat northwards. Robles gathered together his men, sick and cold and weary, inadequately clothed, unsure of what the guns of Riachuelo had meant, unsure whether General Urquiza was friend or enemy. He marched halfway back to the border and stopped.

In Asunción, the *Semanario* published news of a great Paraguayan victory at Riachuelo. Every city downriver knew that Paraguay had lost one third of her fleet.

In Entre Rios, General Urquiza wrote a letter and gave it to the go-between waiting to carry his final answer to General Osorio.

'If the army is about to enter into operations,' he wrote, 'immediate purchase is necessary. Your Excellency should in any case guarantee the contract immediately, although you should leave the horses until the last moment as they can rapidly wear themselves out in this season.'[8] The price was fixed at thirteen patacones per head, thirty per cent over market value. Thirty thousand horses were to be supplied.

It was Elisa's informers in Robles' camp, those employed there 'in a menial capacity', who first reported that 'something mysterious was passing between the general in command and the allies'.[9] They sent her stories of secret correspondence, of letters left in hiding places and offers of gold. Her messages whistled back down the wire to the Mariscal, '[beseeching] him at once to have Robles superceded'[10]. Colonel Resquin was promoted General and sent south to relieve Robles of his command and bring him to Humaitá for interrogation. The man who directed his trial was Silvestre Aveiro. The two men knew each other well. Three years previously, they had sat on the same side of the bench and judged Padre Maíz.

The story which came from their interrogations was a strange one. The principal charge was that Robles had 'received letters from the allied army which he kept for over a month without telling the Mariscal of them, although he sent him daily reports'[11]. The second was that he had attempted to communicate with the enemy at Riachuelo. There were other charges, of tyrannical behaviour and military incompetence.

As Robles sat smoking before his judges, the river was alive below the Quadrilateral, for every canoe, lighter and steamer on it was being employed to bring back the Correntine army. They brought guns, spoil and 3,000 head of stolen cattle with them and a grand piano from some merchant's house or *estancia*, as a gift for Elisa, who was expected any day to join them.

In Buenos Aires, they were jubilant at the news of the Paraguayan retreat. 'We will go to Paraguay,' promised *La Tribuna*, 'we will enter the tiger's own lair and our forces will tread enemy soil . . . once the Paraguayans are attacked on their own ground with their entire country laid bare it is very possible, indeed very probable, that these armed masses will abandon the battle grounds without a fight, certain as they will be that they can no longer be persecuted by the despot . . .'[12]

The only relief in those days of defeat came from Entre Rios, where Urquiza had called 8,000 horsemen to arms and told them they were to march on Paraguay. They refused.

'Never, General,' wrote Ricardo López Jordan, caudillo. 'That country is our friend. Call us to fight *porteños* or Brazilians. We are ready. They are our enemies.'[13] Urquiza tried to form a division of infantry, for all the horses had been sold, but this, too, disintegrated when the march to the front began.

William Whytehead was exhausted. His health had been failing for some years. He had been badly afflicted with 'tropical sickness' – probably amoebic dysentery – the summer he returned from England and in February 1864 he broke his hip badly in a fall at the docks. It had never quite mended; nor had his fever and his diarrhoea ever been completely cured.

He was also aware that his standing with Madame Lynch and President López had undergone an obscure change. Madame had visited him frequently at the *quinta* and had been solicitous in sending gifts and bottles of wine during his bouts of sickness. Privately, their friendship had remained solid but publicly, several noted that Whytehead was present at fewer of Elisa's dinners and his position there was no longer quite that of principal foreigner. By early 1863, the official invitations from Madame ceased almost entirely. His name began to appear in reports from the *piragües*.

Whytehead had been betrayed by his refusal to compromise his friendships with Washburn, Consul Cocholet of France and other foreigners whom the President regarded as potential or actual troublemakers. Ways were found subtly to humiliate him. Official dispatches did not give him his correct title or were sent over his head to embarrassed subordinates. His sickness worsened in the summer of 1864 but work at the shipyard did not allow rest: every ship in the fleet had to be brought in, examined and converted from merchant to military use. On 10 July 1865, he sent a note to the Mariscal, pleading for a rest 'because of an attack of nervousness brought on by accusations against his personal behaviour from subordinates'[14]. No answer came. On 12 July, he put cyanide in tobacco, put the tobacco into his pipe, smoked it and died. His body was found the following day.

It was a huge shock. No diarist left a bad word of Whytehead: he was gentle, mannerly, courteous, entertaining. The Mariscal, aware that he and Elisa were held at least partly to blame, ordered the garrisons to provide horses for the British community so that everyone who wished could attend the burial service at La Recoleta cemetery.

He was replaced by a sad friend and colleague, Mr Nesbitt, chief steam engineer of the *Tacuari*.

A feather-footed messenger from Madame bore gifts to commanders Duarte and Estigarribia in Uruguay.

To la Señora Doña Elisa Alicia Lynch from Comandante Pedro Duarte
Campamento en marcha, Uruguayana, August 15 1865
. . . Please believe me when I say that, although you are always in my thoughts, this proof of esteem which you have deigned to give me in such eventful times, persuades me to double my fervent oath to *el Supremo Hacedor*, He of Great Acts, not only that your own most precious life be preserved but also that of your most important family . . .

I will be most grateful if, in your goodness, you will permit me to beg you to give, in my name, many kisses and embraces to each of your noble sons and I hope you will always number me among your most devoted admirers . . .[15]

Estigarribia sent a similar letter of gratitude and a plea to 'remember him most affectionately to all the children'[16]. Neither reached Madame, for both were seized by the Allies and printed in *La Tribuna* that September. By then, Duarte, Estigarribia and all their men were dead or prisoners of war.

The mission of the Third Army was to march across Uruguay to the Brazilian border, relieving such garrisons as they could until Robles' and Urquiza's army joined them to march on Montevideo. By July, Urquiza had sold himself to the Brazilians and Robles was under arrest, his army scrambling back across the river to Paraguay. By August, there were Brazilians above and below them, General Mitre was on his way with a force from Buenos Aires and Venancio Flores was coming with savage, experienced troops. They vacillated, split into two columns and progressed slowly south either side of a river. On 17 August, Duarte's column was trapped and slaughtered by Flores' troops. Fifteen hundred Paraguayans and five hundred Allied soldiers died. A thousand Paraguayan prisoners were drafted into the Allied army or sold to the Brazilians as slaves. Then the Allies moved on to surround Estigarribia's army at the town of Uruguayana. On 2 September, he surrendered, asking only that his 5,554 men were given to the Brazilians, as the Uruguayans would have cut their throats. His terms were not honoured. Many prisoners were slaughtered: beheaded or slashed across the throat.

News of the surrender at Uruguayana reached Humaitá on 18 September and fell 'like a thunderbolt on Solano López . . . for three days he was so savage that even his son on whom he doted was afraid to go near him'[17]. On the 21st, he was seen for the first time, black-faced and red-eyed at a *besamanos*★. Bishop Palacios addressed a trembling, idolatrous stream of words to his master which the Mariscal scarcely heard. He stood to address the officers.

'*Cuidado!*' he said. 'Beware! Hitherto I have pardoned offences; I have found pleasure in being merciful. Henceforth, no pardon will be given.'[18]

Thirty-six thousand were dead or surrendered and the war had hardly begun.

In Asunción, public meetings were held at which Estigarribia was denounced and his wife begged to change her name.

In Buenos Aires, calls were made for the army to be reduced; already the war had gone on too long, the troops were expensive to support and trade was suffering. 'López has no option but to flee!'[19] *La Tribuna* assured its readers. A quick strike must be made and then everything must return to normal.

★ Presidential or royal audience.

Chapter Ten

When the Mariscal and Panchito went south, Madame had remained in the capital to complete the acquisition of two further city properties, both from the family of Hilario Marcó, the Mariscal's cousin and army officer: a *terrenito*, small plot of land, on the riverbank for 225 pesos and a larger one nearby for 4,400 pesos. The feverish construction across Asunción had not come to an end because of the war. Work had begun on an oratory for the Mariscal at the corner of Mercado Guazú, modelled on Les Invalides and Madame was continuing her redevelopment project around the riverside palace.

Other foreigners in Asunción were less sanguine than Elisa. A letter was on its way to the French legation in Buenos Aires, thence to Paris, calling urgently for a French warship to be stationed off Asunción. Consul Cocholet had no faith in López' ability to lead his troops to victory and when his inevitable defeat came, he wrote, there would be civil unrest, and the conscripted poor would turn on their masters. His fears were shared by 'rich native families resident in the interior [who] are returning to the capital, fearing a general disbanding of the semi-savage troops following a defeat and the excesses of all sorts which they will not restrain themselves from once liberated from the yoke of military discipline'[1]. Chief targets for the disbanded soldiery, he thought, would be foreigners 'of all nationalities [who] will run great dangers from soldiers of whom three-quarters are savages, whom the reins of discipline will no longer retain and the memory of pillaging in the Brazilian cities will animate to new excesses'[2].

Elisa Lynch was one of very few foreigners who accepted the genuine devotion which the Mariscal commanded among his people. The vast majority could never understand it, nor accept that it was not due solely to fear. It was not a threat from the *populacho* that López feared, but a stab in the back from the 'rich native families' and the 'foreigners of all nationalities' who thought as Cocholet did. In December, Elisa left the children with Isidora Díaz and Rosita Carreras and joined the Mariscal. It was a courageous decision for, despite the propaganda of the *Semanario*, she knew that the first campaigns of the war had been disastrous. An offensive campaign to liberate a neighbour had become a defensive one to save Paraguay. Fully one half of the troops trained and amassed with care and at huge expense were dead or prisoners of war. The Paraguayan fleet was reduced to two working vessels. The Allies had a stranglehold on the river and there was no prospect of relief.

The Quadrilateral was an area of about sixty-two square miles, 250 miles south of the capital and directly opposite the border with Corrientes. The River Paraguay flowed to the west; the River Paraná flowed to the south. Between the rivers was a peninsula of marsh, which froze in the winter and liquefied in summer, when mosquitoes bred in the red pools. The Allied army had set up a massive, visible camp on the opposite bank of the Paraná and the Brazilian fleet was at anchor off Corrientes. In the Quadrilateral, the Paraguayans woke every morning expecting the bombardment which would precede invasion.

Eight batteries barred the entrance to the River Paraguay: the *Londres*, the *Tacuarí*, the *Coimbra*, the *Octava*, the *Pesada*, the *Itapirú*, the *Humaitá* and the *Madame Lynch*. Seven chains had been twisted together and lay across the river, supported by three barges. These, and the guns, would keep the Brazilian ships indefinitely at bay, but a land army which managed to creep through the marshes and attack from the east would find only a single ditch between them and the Paraguayans. Colonel George Thompson's first war-time task had been a 'trigonometrical survey' of the peninsula and his sappers were now erecting all the defences they could on the landward side of the Quadrilateral.

The old fortress of Itapirú defended the Paraná coast and the great sandbank below it was considered the Allies' most probable landing place. The Mariscal, Elisa, Bishop Palacios and the bulk of the troops left a small garrison in Humaitá and established headquarters that month three miles inland of Itapirú sandbank. It was called Paso de Patria.

Even here in camp, Elisa had her own carriage – possibly brought by ship from Asunción, possibly looted in Corrientes and brought across the river. Madame Lynch, steering her pair of horses, seated in a high-wheeled carriage and dressed for the Bois de Boulogne, was one of the camp sights. She was a skilful horsewoman and when the tracks about camp were too rough for wheels, she accompanied the Mariscal in habit and neat Parisian side-saddle.

Camp life was more exciting than Asunción. Already many thousand adobe huts, roofed with river-reeds, had been built to accommodate the men. There were 30,000 soldiers here after 'vigorous recruiting'[3] to replace the southern armies, and many thousand others: a women's village where 1,000 workers were housed; children, muleteers, peddlers, prosti-

tutes, cooks, saddlers, errand-boys, money-lenders, entertainers, drinks-vendors, water-carriers, washerwomen. The
population of Paso de Patria was one and a half times that of
Asunción.

The camp was laid around a central plaza, where a large,
solid hut served as headquarters and accommodation for the
Mariscal and ten telegraph lines converged from the capital
and the outlying camps. A flower garden had been planted
outside. There were pots of roses and carnations on his
verandah, and two telescopes brought by Whytehead from
England were mounted on a table for the inner circle to enjoy
a panoramic view of the river and the camp beyond.

The bishop and Elisa Lynch were given a house to either
side of headquarters and Elisa assumed again her role of
hostess. She brought a touch of order and gaiety to those
occasions which can degenerate into boorishness when no
woman is present. A social circle formed around her and her
dinner parties as it had in the capital, with adjustments to the
guest list. The bishop was omnipresent, whispering in the
Mariscal's ear. Dr Stewart was frequently there, sometimes
with his new wife Venancia and the baby, Guillermito. Colonel
Thompson – who tuned her Corrientes piano – came with
George Masterman, in camp to take charge of the drugs
brought from Corrientes; and Colonel Morgernstern. Senior
officers also attended. William Whytehead was much missed
but dinners continued without him, and card parties and
musical entertainment from Madame's piano, as they had
done in Calle Fábrica de Balas, with the spice of uniform and
the thrill of a camp at war. She did not lack the company of
women, for wives of officers came and went and those whose
husbands received permission stayed for long periods in camp.
Juliana Insfrán de Martínez, now an army bride, lived in Elisa's
house throughout the Quadrilateral campaigns. Isidora Díaz
was often there as both friend of Madame and sister of José

Díaz, who had moved from chief of police to major of cavalry and was the Mariscal's shadow and favourite officer, fierce, gallant with the ladies, courageous and 'terrible in his punishments'.

Christmas was merry, despite the brooding presence of the enemy over the river; so were New Year celebrations. Elisa was López' constant companion, visiting the sick and wounded, attending balls and receptions, reviewing the troops at his side, looking beautiful, pinning medals to the chests of heroes. A magic lantern show had been among the last cargoes to reach Paraguay before the blockade began and Colonel Thompson and George Masterman had set it up. The Mariscal and Bishop Palacios had spent some hours studying the scenes of battle on the slides; doubtless it was erected also for the entertainment and instruction of the rank and file, sitting in obedient, barefoot rows beneath the orange trees and peering at the magic images each hot night.

There were other entertainments for the troops who waited each day for an attack which did not come. The mainmast of a Brazilian ship sunk at Riachuelo had been hauled upriver and erected in the plaza. It was the centrepiece of the dances held each Sunday: one for officers, in which Elisa participated with enthusiasm, dancing the 'London carapé, the Bolivian quadrille and the mamà cumandà . . .' and when she danced, Centurión wrote, 'the vivacity and enthusiasm reached its highest pitch'[4]. Music floated defiantly across the river. The melancholy waltz called 'La Palomita', 'Little Dove', was as familiar to the Allies as it was to the dancing Paraguayans 'who knew it by heart, all, young or old, men or girls, could whistle it; it accompanied their unknown dreams and helped them forget the many hardships of their life'[5]. No one who spent the Christmas of 1865 in Paso de Patria and survived ever forgot the tune of 'La Palomita'.

★

Beneath the public jollity, the Mariscal brooded on the loss of his armies, the treachery of his officers and the cowardice of his men. He began to see assassins in camp. He saw them in the men who had escaped the Brazilians at Uruguayana and were swimming back across the borders to join him; and among the Correntine cooks, carpet-baggers and camp followers who had returned with his army of occupation. Even among his favourites and his aides-de-camp he suspected treason and a hidden knife. The Mariscal breathed suspicion in the air; he heard words behind words and read thoughts on faces. The ring of sentries around his house with its pretty flower garden was doubled, then tripled. Any who came to see the Mariscal sat under a roof which jutted from one end of his house, under the silent surveillance of his sentries. Colonel Thompson was there one night and a curious sergeant began to put questions to him about England: ' "Did Queen Victoria always wear her crown when she went out to walk?" "Will you wear the Paraguayan uniform when you go to England?" '[6] At dawn, an aide-de-camp came and told Thompson to write down the entire conversation. When he took his report to the Mariscal at seven in the morning, the sergeant had already been shot, convicted of planning to assassinate his leader.

Orders went to the capital that those on whom the Mariscal's suspicion fell were to be brought south. Benigno and Venancio López were summoned and those foreigners who persisted in their request to be allowed to leave the country. Engineer Volpy had tried to resign, been refused, and saw his position shift: he was still an officer, still a guest at Elisa's dinners but it was understood he was not to leave Humaitá. Paddle-steamers docked through the summer months and apprehensive residents of Asunción, vaguely suspected of disaffection, disembarked beneath the batteries. Men who had been guests at Elisa's table now slept in straw-roofed huts to one side of the beaten earth plaza, stared at by soldiers. They were half guests, half detainees in a bizarre camp life of jollity and profound unease, warily greeting Madame and the Mariscal on the occasions they rode in from Paso de Patria.

Hector Decoud, godson to the Mariscal, was a little boy when war began. He wrote later of the moment that the policemen came knocking on the door in the night. He, his mother and three of his eight siblings were there, for Colonel Decoud and the four elder boys had been in Buenos Aires when war was declared and the Colonel was a member of the Legion Paraguaya, in league with the enemy. Mother and children were sent aboard the overnight steamer to Humaitá, where the children were held in the bow of the ship while Silvestre Aveiro interrogated their mother as to what she knew of enemy plans. She knew nothing, she said, and would have been shot as a traitor had not the Mariscal commuted her sentence to ten years' imprisonment in the Chaco, telling her she would be freed as soon as she denounced her husband and sons as traitors. Eight soldiers took her by canoe to a spot on the Chaco bank opposite the London battery, where, quite alone except for the guard allowed to make what use of her they would, she built herself a hut with 'a straw roof and walls of hide, a dress she wore served as both bed and shelter and she ate whatever meagre food was left by the soldiers who guarded her'[7]. Her children were taken to huts in Humaitá, where the girl, a *traidora* – female traitor – was another easy target for the guard.

On 8 January, the Mariscal rode along the track which linked Paso de Patria to Humaitá. The officers of the disastrous Corrientes expedition were taken from their tents, roped in ox-carts and drawn pitching to the execution ground. They were shot in the back. General Robles requested and smoked a cigar, ground it into the soil, refused a blindfold and received twelve bullets in the face. When the Mariscal left soldiers came and dragged away the bodies.

Some days later, Elisa Lynch's carriage was seen bumping along the same uneven red road. The officers of the fort lined up to receive her. Rain drummed on the roof of the dark hut, steaming hot and close. One by one they excused themselves and returned, relieved, to their duties. When Juan Crisóstomo Centurión attempted to leave, she called him back.

'Stay a moment,' she said, 'I have something to tell you.'

They were left alone.

'I regret,' she said, 'to have to tell you that His Excellency the Mariscal is very annoyed, extremely annoyed, with you. I cannot imagine what might have happened.'

These were words which every officer dreaded, particularly those who had gone south to Corrientes or Uruguayana. He stammered and protested: he was unable to imagine any offence he had given, he could think of no mistake he might have made, his devotion to the Mariscal could not be doubted. She cut him short and advised him to write immediately to the Mariscal. It was the oblique expression of the Mariscal's order. He was casting around for people to blame; each officer tried to ensure it did not come his way, some by honourable methods, others not. As soon as Madame's carriage had bumped away, Centurión set himself to write a long and agonised account of his actions in Corrientes. The letter went unanswered. The Mariscal had believed him, or his suspicions had been aroused by someone else and Centurión, for the time being, was forgotten.

The thunderous, continual rains of high summer came and the plaza round headquarters liquefied and trickled into the men's tents. The river flooded its banks and the troops lived ankle-deep in warm mud. The Correntine cattle died from eating the *miò-miò*, a poisonous grass to which Paraguayan animals were immune, and disintegrating carcasses poisoned the water which flowed sluggishly into foul lagoons.

In Asunción, State Treasurer Saturnino Bedoya, husband of Rafaela López, was ordered by the Mariscal to prepare chests 'with great discretion, for 2,500 ounces of gold and 10,000 patacones of gold coin, to go to Europe and buy arms and, in case, they fell into the hands of the enemy, the lid of each was to be marked "Madame Lynch" '[8]. The French gunboat *Decidée* came past the Allied camp that summer and anchored off Humaitá, ostensibly to take off neutrals who wished to leave. Her commanders were entertained royally at headquarters by Elisa and the Mariscal. When the ship left Paraguayan waters for France, she took with her Julie, the maid who had accompanied Madame from Paris ten years before, and a quantity of heavy chests marked 'Lynch'. They carried 'treasure'. Thompson stated it bluntly.[9] It was common knowledge at headquarters that money was being sent out of the country as an insurance policy.

January ended and still the Allied commanders hesitated. The Brazilian admiral would not pass the chains and guns of Humaitá unless Argentine infantry had already attacked from the land. General Mitre would not send his infantry onto Paraguayan soil until the Brazilian fleet bombarded. February passed and the men in the Paso de Patria watch-towers saw the camp across the river grow to monstrous proportions – twice the size of Paso de Patria; three times the size of Asunción.

Training of the militias was stepped up in the villages along the Paraná border. Local men were detailed to patrol the river coast. They were taught to look after horses, grow crops for cavalry regiments and cook food for large numbers. Every day, they received lectures on developments at the front, 'the justice of the Paraguayan cause, and above all on our liberty, because of which we were all aware that we would be taking up arms in defence of all the good things we enjoyed in our country'[10].

A letter to the Mariscal came from Bishop Palacios, briefly absent from headquarters on a campaign to 'excite the spirit of self-abnegation and heroism' across the country. 'We are continuing our pastoral labours with all possible care and force,' he assured his master, 'omitting no measure of diligence, using the power and influence of the Holy religion . . . with the end of directing it in the path of justice, good order and patriotism . . . by means of the confessional, in which daily we are engaged in confessing hundreds of soldiers, disposing and fortifying them for the struggle, and making them to understand, with the greatest clearness, that those who give their lives for their country will be recompensed and eternally rewarded by the Eternal Creator.'[11] Militia chiefs and judges of the peace reported participation in national fiestas, and expressions of feeling in their villages.

As the armies watched each other across the river through the wet heat of February, 62,000 Allied soldiers cursed their commanders as incompetents and cowards. By night, parties went out from the Paraguayan bank, slithering groups on trophy hunts, accompanied to the river's edge by a military band and Elisa Lynch, who gave them cigars and *caña*. They kissed her hand and disappeared. The raw Argentine levies across the river listened to the sounds of fiesta and sweated with fear of the grinning men who came up the shadowy riverbank each night to take back ears and scalps for the Mariscal and la Señora Madama. One day, Elisa came out of her house at dawn to find nine soldiers' heads piled on the verandah. The Mariscal sent them to the Chief of Staff to put them on public display.

February slid into the inferno of March and the troops

could hardly breathe. There was fever in the Allied camp, where the men sought relief from the heat by bathing in stagnant lagoons.

12 March: 'today,' wrote a Uruguayan officer in the camp across the river, 'the thermometer rose to 40 degrees centigrade in the shade, you could hear your blood boil in your ears and the sickness which comes when you can no longer breathe'[12].

In Paso de Patria, the first camp diseases had come among the men. Two hundred and fifty a day were dying of measles and the diarrhoea which followed it, for Dr Stewart's inoculation programme had begun too late. There was not always time to bury the bodies and they mounted in piles on the outskirts of camp.

Each evening that month, Elisa and the Mariscal sat on the verandah outside headquarters and watched a show. The crew of the little steamer *Gualeguay* had stumbled upon an activity which López, happening to see it from his verandah, had found immensely diverting and ordered to be repeated. As he and his circle sat with a digestif, the *Gualeguay*, for López' 'personal entertainment . . . went out . . . to the point of the island off Itapirú and defied the allied fleet, firing her 12-pounders, which were answered by the whole fleet, with every kind of projectile, from a 68-pounder to a 150-pounder. These used to fall around her like hail, throwing up immense waterspouts into the air. She used to retire a little before sunset. She did this every day for three weeks, without being hit, except by one ball, which passed through her funnel.'[13]

On 25 March, a new order was issued:

by order of His Excellency the Mariscal President of the Republic and Commander in Chief of its Armies, the following punishments are in force:

172

For all those who fall asleep on guard:

1 The officer to be arrested, and reported to His Excellency
2 The sergeant to receive 50 lashes standing
3 The corporals to receive 40 lashes
4 Privates to receive 50 lashes each

In case of desertion of a soldier when detached from his company:

1 The rank and file next to him on each side to receive 25 lashes
2 The officer in charge of the company in which a desertion takes place, to be arrested and reported to the Supreme Government
3 The sergeant to receive 50 lashes and do duty in his company for one month as common soldier and one month as corporal; at the expiration of these 2 months to be reinstated
4 The corporals to receive 40 lashes in circle and do duty in their companies as common soldiers for 2 months, after which to be reinstated[14]

The men in the trenches, the sentry posts, the earthworks and batteries and rings around headquarters spied on each other's movements and listened to each other's whispered conversations and no one trusted his neighbour.

Among those who escaped their Brazilian captors at Uruguayana and swam back across the rivers to rejoin the Mariscal was a sadist called Germán Serrano. He showed the Mariscal's guard an interrogation technique he had seen practised by the Uruguayans, who had themselves borrowed it from the forces of Simón Bolívar and knew it as the *cepo boliviano*, the Bolivian hold. Later, it was described by one of the men on whom it was inflicted in the Paraguayan camps.

> The torture is as follows and this is how I suffered it: I sat on the ground with my knees up, my legs were first tied tightly together, and then my hands behind me, the palms outwards. A musket was then fastened under my knees; six more of them, tied together in a bundle, were then put on my shoulders and they were looped together with hide ropes at one end; they then made a running loop on the other side, from the lower musket to the other; and two soldiers hauling on it, forced my face down to my knees and secured it so.
>
> The effect was as follows: first the feet went to sleep, then a tingling commenced in the toes, gradually extending to the knees and the same in the hands and arms, and increased until the agony was unbearable. My tongue swelled up and I thought my jaws would have been displaced; I lost all feeling in that side of my face for a fortnight afterwards.[15]

Its name was changed to the *cepo uruguayana*.

A letter from France was delayed because it had come overland through Bolivia.

When the Allies closed off the rivers, the balance due on the Mariscal's ironclads under construction in Bordeaux had yet to be paid. Smooth-talking Brazilians presented themselves with an offer. An 'arbitration' was staged at which the Paraguayan government was represented by one Aquilles Tamberlich, bag-carrier at the Paris legation. He failed, dismally but honestly; or he was bought by Brazilian gold.

The company [ie the shipyard] acquires the right to dispose of the ship under construction, undertaking to build for [Paraguay] another for the sum of 1,800,000 francs as indemnity. [The arbiter Tamberlich] chose this settlement, with my assent, in preference to absolute rescission from the contract, in which case no less than 236,000 to 300,000 francs would have been adjudicated to the company, that is, half or two-fifths of their account – 500,000 francs – for prejudice and loss of interest.[16]

Thus were the ships disposed of to the Brazilians on the other side of the arbitration table. It was a reminder that modern wars were not won on battlefields, but in the boardrooms of banks and at embassy receptions. Paraguay had no credit agreements with the banks of Europe. Paraguayan diplomats were few: there were only two in Europe. Candido Bareiro had written to Lord John Russell, Prime Minister of Britain, asking him to protest to Argentina. A Foreign Affairs committee examined his request and told the Prime Minister it would be 'ludicrous'[17] to intervene.

The Mariscal had thought he could win the war with the cash-crops of his *yerbales* and the ignorant courage of soldiers.

In April, the first thunderstorms came and temperatures began to fall. Along the Allied shore, rafts and barges lay against the bank, ready to carry the troops across. Tons of provisions had been disembarked and stored. The river rose higher each day; soon it would be high enough to allow the boats from Corrientes across the canoes filled with stones which the Mariscal had sunk in the channels. Allied commanders took their first cautious step under cover of heavy rain and lightning. By dawn on 5 April, 8,000 Brazilians were perched on the sandbank below Itapirú fort. They clung there for twelve days. Eight hundred men under José Díaz went out in canoes on the Mariscal's order to dislodge the enemy. 'It was madness,' said Colonel Thompson, 'to send his men there, with no object, to certain death'[18]. They retreated at daybreak leaving 500 dead or prisoner of war. Then orders came from Allied command for the final push and wave after wave of Brazilians came over the side of their landing craft and 8,000 men dug into the beach. The following day, 10,000 Argentines joined them. Then, for five days, no supplies came across the river. As they captured stray Paraguayan oxen to relieve their hunger, the Allied soldiers on the beach heard the rumble of carts going from Paso de Patria towards Humaitá fort. The artillery was being taken to safety.

The 113 ships of the Allied fleet lined up off Itapirú, in a position to fire over the trees and straight into Paso de Patria. At any moment, the bombardment might start, and then the Allied advance from the beachhead. The men looked to the officers and the officers looked to the Mariscal for orders: should they retreat further inland out of range, should they attack, should they dig in? The Mariscal gave no orders.

During the night, other officers ordered riflemen down into the trench which encircled the little hill on which Paso de Patria stood. After them went soldiers with chairs, tables, chests, boxes, trunks, anything which could be hurled at the enemy as it appeared over the lip of the trench. Still the Mariscal brooded silently behind his verandahs and his sentries while the troops worked, not knowing whether they would be called on at any moment to advance, retreat or hold firm.

At daybreak, they were woken by enemy guns. Tumbling from her bed, dressing in whatever was to hand, Elisa emerged to see a camp in commotion, the air dense with smoke and shrapnel. Grapeshot flew over the treetops and the first dead lay on the ground. Officers were bursting from tents with collars flapping, buckling on swords as they ran to López' house for orders. It was empty. The Mariscal had gone. They asked Elisa where he was but she had come to ask them the same thing. There was no time to seek him out; they turned and faced the attack.

It took Elisa all morning to find him. Smoke obscured the ground; the topography familiar from daily rides around camp borders and through tent villages changed with each shell. Where there had been solid land, there were pools welling up; where groups of men had sat to boil their maté, there were empty spaces. Stretcher-bearers passed her between the front and the hospital on the Humaitá road. She guessed that López was somewhere out of shell range where he could observe the action in safety. He must be on a rise in the ground to the north or west of Paso de Patria and this was the area she went to search, on horseback, as the fighting continued below her.

She found him at midday, on a small hill three miles inland. He was observing the fighting through a telescope and his aides sat their horses in a loose group around him. Late in the afternoon two balls came suddenly close and the Mariscal was sure he had been seen. They left immediately and went further inland, where they spent the night. There was dinner for the Mariscal but no one else, for no stores had yet been brought up from Paso de Patria.

Below, the last Paraguayan troops fought, then torched the camp when the enemy could not be held back. Lines of women with baskets on their heads came across the marsh passes amid the smoke. The troops destroyed the storehouses, the baggage carts, the hospitals, pharmacies, stables, cattle yards, officers' quarters, troops' tents, latrines, chapels – everything but a tannery, a telegraph office and the building which had housed the arsenal. The crops sown for spring were burnt and the soil left scorched. The curiosity of the Allied troops to see the camp of their elusive enemy was given its first sad satisfaction in this wasteland. 'We toured the field of combat,' an officer wrote home; 'it is sown with enemy corpses, there are more than 300 of them, largely children of 15 or 16 years old – it breaks my heart to see them . . .'[19] The Allied soldiers used the beams of smouldering houses to grill their meat that night.

When the last Paraguayans left Paso de Patria, the smoke was so thick behind them that they could not see the enemy but they knew they were there because the church bells rang all night across the marshes, in taunting victory.

The Allies had secured the coast of the River Paraná. Now they must find some way to pass Humaitá, the 'Sebastopol of South America' on the coast of the River Paraguay.

By May, 62,000 Allied soldiers were camped in Paso de Patria, 30,000 Paraguayans were camped four miles north and between the two lay the impassable Tuyutí *esteros*. Each tide seeped into the marshlands which housed the armies, squelching and sinking in the mud. The Mariscal waited for the Allies to push further into the Quadrilateral but they did not move from their toehold on the north bank of the Paraná. The Allied command had relapsed into indecision and sloth: now the men were north of the Paraná, it would take weeks to ferry across the stores, horses, cattle and weaponry to keep 62,000 fighting men in the field. An army, Napoleon said, marches on its stomach and the Allied army, separated by the river from its stores, was marching nowhere. Soon, the nights were cold. More Allied troops came off the boats from Corrientes and squeezed into the camp which clung, vulnerable, to the extreme southern edge of the Quadrilateral. They were short of shelter, food and wood. Scores of men fell sick each day of dysentery and fever and the horses ate the *miò-miò* and died. There were mass graves and the smell of flesh. Bodies rolled in the shallows and corpses emerged grotesquely when the marsh gas heaved.

'Here,' wrote a Uruguayan diarist, 'we breathe air which has been poisoned for a long time. What will be said of this vast cemetery where we are camped? Death visits us at every hour here; our minds dwell on death because the graves of the Paraguayans are dug among the tents; you could say this is a place where only death is breathed, cold, stoic death; the death of martyrdom and resignation.'[20]

Not all were martyrs, or resigned, for where there were troops to supply and entertain, there was big money to be made and the Allied camp at Paso de Patria had become a bazaar. There were shops among the tents, and liquor stalls and brothels and newspaper kiosks. War tourists came from the city and bought postcards of prisoners. The Paraguayan camp across the marshes had few of these for the blockade had begun its slow asphyxiation of the country and yerba, tobacco and cotton for export sat useless in store in Asunción. The troops relied on their meagre army ration and food parcels sent by relatives and what was brought back by men and women who went silently each night through the passes only the Paraguayans knew and returned with food, beer, clothes and trinkets from the stores in the Allied camp and, sometimes, information for the Mariscal. Other times they did not return at all but became *pasados*, deserting to the enemy.

The men and women who sold food and drink, or postcards and photographs of prisoners to the war-tourists from Buenos Aires and Europe, or ran entertainment tents, or charged to write letters home for the illiterate, were only the front line of a massive commercial tide which had stormed downriver, sweeping up the little merchants of the northern provinces and the big ones in the estuary, galloping along the coast into the eager hands of the Bank of Mauá in Brazil and on, a tidal wave of greed and opportunity, across the Atlantic to the banks of Europe as soldiers gasped in the heat of a tiny damp circle ringed by the American rivers.

In March, the secret articles of the Treaty of the Triple Alliance had been leaked by a horrified British diplomat and read aloud in the House of Commons in London. When the outraged editorials of the British and French press reached Buenos Aires, there was criticism of Mitre by the many who felt dishonoured. All *porteño* papers, except Mitre's own, were brutal. But Argentine suppliers had gained contracts for food for 48,000 Brazilian troops. The Empire of Brazil had contracted war-loans of £10,218,920[21] with the Rothschild bank in London and more with other banks in Paris. Merchants from Buenos Aires, Corrientes, Santa Fe, Montevideo, Rio de Janeiro and even the European capitals had arrived at the front to set up business. Currency from a dozen countries circulated. The Banco Mauá, the largest of America, had even opened a branch at Paso de Patria. It would take more than the embarrassment of exposure to halt a war which generated such riches.

The Mariscal called José Díaz to his temporary headquarters on 1 May and promoted him to colonel. He was to attack the Uruguayan vanguard at Paso de Patria with 7,000 soldiers. At midday on 2 May, they erupted into Flores' unsuspecting camp and set the entire Uruguayan force on the run. Flores' tent was sacked and their success would have been great had not Colonel Díaz, in his excitement, ordered his men to advance on the Brazilian camp, for there General Osorio was ready for them. What was left of Díaz' forces crawled back to the Mariscal that night. A thousand men were left dead on the ground between the two armies. The survivors were acclaimed as heroes. The cannon they had seized were put on display at headquarters and Díaz was decorated. It was a vindication of Paraguayan bravery.

In May, a new Paraguayan headquarters was established at Paso Pucú, two and a half miles across the Tuyutí marshes from the Allied camp. Between the Paraguayans on a rise to the north and the Allies on a rise to the south lay the treacherous *estero*, threaded with secret paths the Allies would enmire themselves finding. Their navy made a tentative move north but was held back when the Mariscal ordered demijohns to be floated in the river to signal torpedo positions. There were no torpedoes there, but the Brazilian Admiral Tamandaré believed him, and stopped. Again 'La Palomita' floated across each cold Sunday night and the sound of the gomba drum. Naked men with knives in their teeth came through the marsh in the inky dark and returned with trophies and boasts of killing.

The men at the southern end of the Allied front heard strange sounds the night of 23 May. The water birds were uneasy. They screeched and called to each other and would not be still. They heard cartwheels along the tracks which divided them from the enemy and voices close by speaking Guaraní. The Mariscal gave his last orders to senior officers and finished with fiery words: it must be victory or death, he said. Resquin, Barrios and Díaz left his tent to ride along the lines, encouraging the men. Charge firmly, they said, and the enemy, being cowardly, would run. This would be the last battle – the Mariscal had said so himself; they would win, or die in the attempt. If they did not die, they would be made slaves by the Brazilians. Rum mixed with gunpowder was passed among the men. Just before dawn, the Mariscal and his companions rode out of camp to a hill three miles away from which they would observe the engagement.

Dawn came but no one moved. They had mistaken the passes; the junior officers were ill prepared. At midday they attacked. 'It was a whirlwind of fire; through the thick cloud of smoke which hung over the front, in flashes we saw, flying through the air, the limbs and clothing of the cavalry and the saddles and legs of their horses.'[22] Sixty thousand men thrashed at the feet of their commanders, trampled by horses in their agony, face down in the red mud and lilies. Between 6,000 and 8,000 soldiers died that day in Tuyutí marsh. It was a horror. The Mariscal ordered the bells be rung throughout that night to signal victory.

About 16,000 were wounded and the stretcher-bearers were unable to carry all the mashed and mangled flesh to hospital. The medics could not cope. Men lay in piles where the stretcher-bearers left them, under temporary verandahs outside temporary hospitals which had few drugs or surgeons. Wounds could not be disinfected and amputations were performed without chloroform. Orders were telegraphed to the capital and the great salon of San Francisco railway station was turned into a hospital to receive the wounded. They bled in lurching bullock-carts on the road to Humaitá and aboard the steamers to Asunción. Some died on the way; some held on to limbs attached by a strip of skin. Gangrene killed many before they reached the capital.

At midday on 25 May, great clouds of smoke appeared above the enemy lines but no gunfire. The smoke came from pyres, where dead men of all nationalities had been stacked for their last destruction. They burnt until late that night. Some of the corpses sat upright and twisted and then there was a pile of ash and a ghastly smell. The last dead remained scattered across no man's land, preserved by frost.

It took eight days to bring in all the wounded. Men crawled across the marshes and into the ditches, scrambling over corpses too numerous to bury, to find those left alive after a night, two nights, a week of open wounds, rats and frost. At night, both sides heard thousands of women searching the fields, calling names in Guaraní, Castilian and Portuguese. The armies waited for rain to wash the deliquescence from the *esteros*.

June came, intensely cold. The Mariscal had 5,000 able men left. The Allied soldiers waited for the order to advance and finish the war. It did not come. The interminable quarrels between the provinces and Buenos Aires had re-emerged and troops were diverted from the front to crush provincial rebellion. Stalemate ensued and orders went across Paraguay that children from the age of twelve must be sent to the front.

Chapter Eleven

Elisa Lynch left for Asunción, to visit her family and Minister Fernandez.

The city was vastly changed. There were few men in the streets. The markets were empty. The ladies who had used to walk in bright colours, with flowers in their arms and hair, now went in black to the hospitals at the docks and San Francisco station. The sick lay on floors, begging for the knife, as gangrene was worse than amputation. Bodies from the battles of May rolled in the river, tossed there by the steamers which arrived with half their cargo dead. The streets between the docks and the railway station were crowded with carts full of sick men. 'Almost or quite naked, with their wounds untended, dirty and famished and so emaciated that when dead they dried up without decomposition, they were carried from the pier to the hospitals; and then they had to lie, perhaps for a week, or till they died, on the ground; but one never heard a word of complaint: they bore all with a silent heroism.'[1] Half-qualified surgeons desperate for sleep worked among piles of limbs. The apothecary George Masterman had presented himself to Dr Stewart; within ten minutes, he was carrying out his first amputation. 'As well

The young Elisa Lynch (South American Pictures)

Above left: Carlos Antonio López, father of Francisco Solano López and president of Paraguay 1844–62 (Mary Evans Picture Library)

Above right: Doña Juana Pabla Carrillo de López, mother of Francisco Solano López (South American Pictures)

Francisco Solano López, Elisa Lynch's companion and president of Paraguay 1862–70 (South American Pictures)

People of Paraguay curing *yerba maté*, Paraguayan tea (South American Pictures)

Passengers meeting a train on a jungle track (Mary Evans Picture Library)

A view of the Paraguayan Chaco (South American Pictures)

Above: 'The crossing of the San Joaquín River, Paraguay' by Argentine war artist Candido López (Museo Historico Nacional, Buenos Aires, Argentina/The Bridgeman Art Library)

Left: 'Paraguayan prisoners and the wounded after the Battle of Yatay' Candido López (The Art Archive/Museo Nacional de Bellas Artes Buenos Aires/Dagli Orti)

Right: 'Argentine military camp near Curuzú on the Paraná River' Candido López (The Art Archive/Museo Nacional de Bellas Artes Buenos Aires/Dagli Orti)

Below: 'After the Battle of Curupaity' Candido López (Museo Nacional de Bellas Artes, Buenos Aires)

Dr William Stewart, army surgeon and godfather to Enrique Lynch López (South American Pictures)

A member of the Paraguayan cavalry (South American Pictures)

The ruins of Humaitá church in the Quadrilateral (South American Pictures)

Panteón de los Héroes, Asunción
(Tony Morrison/South American Pictures)

Government Palace, Asunción, built but never inhabited by Francisco
Solano López (South American Pictures)

Francisco Solano López and his eldest son by Elisa Lynch, Panchito (South American Pictures)

The old Elisa Lynch (South American Pictures)

as the hospitals in Humaitá and the camp,' Consul Cocholet wrote to Paris, 'they have had to create temporary hospitals in Pilar, Villa Oliva and other places . . . in Asunción, although only 2,500 sick came here, the railway station, the tobacco warehouse, the barracks and private houses were taken over, as there was not enough room in the hospital. To remedy the lack of nurses and surgeons' assistants, women were conscripted; the Ladies were put in charge and women of the people looked after the men. Each family had to give, according to its rank in society, one or more people to permanent service in the hospitals.'[2] There was no one in the city who was not in mourning for a husband, a son or a brother and Elisa was a link to the front which even those who had snubbed and despised her might use in their desperation for news.

She returned to camp with a sheaf of documents to be authorised by the Mariscal, for she had been on a shopping spree. Her later description of this was disingenuous. 'At the end of 1866,' she explained, 'Benigno [López] put up for public sale his real estate, which caused shock and the rumour that the war was about to end badly for Paraguay. To counteract this, I offered to buy any real estate put on the market and began by buying certain properties which belonged to the state . . . later, I bought as a favour to people who wished to dispose of their land . . .'[3]

In the ten weeks of her absence, the Mariscal had gathered together 20,000 men and boys at the new Paraguayan camp in Paso Pucú to replace those dead, decomposing or burnt to ash on the vast pyres of May. Most came voluntarily. Men left their farms to their womenfolk to support the Mariscal against *los macacos*. A few did not: 200 Payagua Indians and 6,000 slaves were conscripted. Young boys were brought by their mothers. Whole families now lived at the front and tatty orphans who ran errands and begged for food, dressed in cut-down uniforms, dead men's kepis falling over their brows, uncannily handy at loading ammunition and squirming towards the enemy sentries.

Watchtowers were erected in both camps to peer across the marshes. They were fifty feet high, constructed of tree trunks at four corners with platforms lashed between them. One incorporated ladders surrounded by hides and matting, 'an unusual precaution intended to conceal [the] petticoated ankles'[4] of Madame. The Mariscal rarely left headquarters.

He wished to launch the next attack from a trench dug on the battlefield of 24 May, which lay between Paraguayan and Allied lines. George Thompson was sent to survey the land and reported a trench could be dug in a gully called the Sauce. Work began that night. Every spade and shovel in the army was sent down; battalions experienced in earthworks for railways and fortifications were detailed to Thompson. They worked in silence, among trees which showed the passage of bullets, spent cannon ball and mummified corpses, 'the skin having dried on to the bone and the bodies looking tawny and thin'.[5] The enemy was just beyond. In the dark, the snipers who lay among the diggers to protect them were indistinguishable from the dead.

On 16 July, the Mariscal attacked. The trench changed hands three times. By 18 July, 2,500 Paraguayans and 4,500 Allied soldiers were dead. In Buenos Aires and Rio, there was despair: the Paraguayans could not win this war against three nations but their defence was unbreakable. Again stretcher-bearers carried the dying from the Paraguayan lines, the hospital carts went to Humaitá and the steamers loaded the wounded for Asunción. One of them also bore correspondence from Elisa Lynch to Minister Fernandez.

Paso Pucú, 21 July 1866, Madama Lynch to Francisco
Fernandez
Muy apreciado Don Pancho,
I very much appreciate the trouble you have taken over
both the house and the plot of land. I am sending you
today the permission of purchase which *el Señor* has granted
me so that you may conclude the necessary paperwork. I
would like the house to be let, whatever the rent, as much
money is lost while it stands empty. A temporary rental
agreement could be made in case a better tenant is found –
however, you understand all these things so much better
than I do so I leave it to your discretion to arrange as you
think best . . .

Don Sinforoso Cáceres has just come in and he says he
is very interested in my new house but he thinks the
staircase is dangerous. Let me know if this is the case and,
if it is not too much trouble, see Doña Dolores about it.[6]

There are problems implicit in interpreting a few tatty
documents which once belonged to a rich archive and trying
to reconstruct from them the nature and scale of the business
they represent. The frequency with which diarists and declar-
ants made comments on Elisa's business operations, together
with the extraordinary number of properties she acquired
during the war years [twenty-seven] and these scant but dated
documents give a picture of an efficient business overseen by
Elisa and administered by Minister Fernandez. As authorisation was given for her various war-time transactions, letters
were sent up on steamers to one Captain José Maria Areco in
Asunción, who delivered them to Fernandez or Madame's
other agent, Doña Dolores Sion de Pereyra, receiving sometimes 100, sometimes 200 pesos for his work, always on the
order of 'Madama' and charged to the account administered
on her behalf by the Minister for War.

July 30, Paso Pucú
To José Maria Areco from Elisa Lynch:
On the *Ybura*, and entrusted to Captain Thomson, you will find a round box. Give this to Doña Tomasa and then distribute the documents inside it to the various addressees . . . you will also receive, today or tomorrow, 3,000 pesos which you will give to Don Pancho [Don Francisco Fernandez], whom you may ask for 100 pesos.[7]

What was in the round box for Doña Tomasa remains a mystery; the documents Areco was to distribute were the permits signed by López. Cash followed. On 6 August, Fernandez signed the back of Areco's instructions: 'I received the 3,000 pesos and have given 100 pesos from them to José Maria Areco . . .'

Rafael Zavala, who had borrowed heavily from Elisa in 1863, had not been able to repay the loan and eight per cent interest at the end of the two years agreed. The sale of his house on Calle Uruguay was in the hands of Minister Fernandez. Elisa's request of repossession was authorised on 20 July.[8]

In the midst of these business transactions, there was a personal note.

August 22
To Captain Fernandez from Elisa Lynch
Please tell Areco that I am very annoyed he has not sent Leopoldo's baby carriage and that he should send it on the next transport. Leopoldo is better but still not out of danger.[9]

A telegram addressed to Areco himself, also mentioned the children:

Madame orders that you go to Ibirai to see Leopoldo and the other children and tell Isidora [Díaz] that a steamer is leaving tonight and she must write to Madame . . . Tonight, send a detailed report by telegraph on Leopoldo's health . . . and news of the other children.[10]

24 July was scarcely celebrated in Paso Pucú that year. The following month, the Mariscal took to his bed. He was suffering a severe bout of dysentery and possibly of cholera, for that disease had come to the Brazilian camp, blamed on an infected slave from Rio, and crawled across the marshes to where the malnourished and feverish Paraguayans fell easy victims. One of them, in Villa del Pilar, was Adelina Pesoa López, who died that winter. The hospitals, already over-stretched by the wounded of the winter's battles, had no staff nor drugs to spare for the sick of this new scourge. In July, Allied numbers had fallen by a third from disease but in Brazil there were inexhaustible reserves of slave and conscript cannon fodder. In Paso Pucú, surrounded by the sick, the young and the wounded, even the Mariscal was forced to see that the supply of peons he had used to fling at his enemy like so many sandbags was dwindling, and so were the crops that dead and fighting men could not grow.

The first of September began with a roar from the south and the Mariscal rose from his bed: the Allies had begun the bombardment of the island of Curuzú in the River Paraguay, halfway between the confluence of the rivers and Curupayty, the southernmost fort of the Quadrilateral. It continued all that day and into the night until General Díaz, commander of Curupayty, hopelessly outnumbered, ordered evacuation and the firing of the arsenal. Allied soldiers moved onto Curuzú and Curupayty was exposed. If Curupayty fell, Humaitá was in danger; if Humaitá fell, control of the river passed to the

Allied fleet and the war was lost. At headquarters, George Thompson was given orders to start immediate work on a trench between Curuzú and Curupayty to hold the Allied army back. Díaz was upbraided and the regiment which had failed to hold Curuzú was decimated. The Mariscal would not tolerate failure in anyone but himself.

Defences had now to be built between Curuzú and Curupayty to hold off attacks from infantry, cavalry and the fleet. Curupayty fort stood on the highest point of the bank, about thirty feet above the river, with cannon above and a line of torpedoes below. The river was narrow in front and the Chaco coast within rifle range. Attack by the incompetent Brazilian navy was the least pressing problem; Thompson and General Díaz turned their attention to the landward side from where the cavalry from Paso de Patria would appear. They set their men digging a trench from the river to a vast, natural lagoon 650 feet inland, first felling trees, then digging a network of broad sunken walkways among the palms, where hidden riflemen would shoot the oncoming enemy. They worked under the expectation of attack.

That day, or the next, a stray shot from the Allied fleet flew over the trees and killed three people outside the Mariscal's house. The Mariscal left, mounted his horse and rode 2,000 yards from headquarters. From a safe spot, he sent for Thompson, who left the trenches at the riverside and rode to find him. Orders were given that men must be diverted from the trenches to build an earthwork next to his house in Paso Pucú to shield it from the guns of the fleet off Curupayty. For several days, sweating men were brought from the trench at Curuzú to build an earthen shield, fifteen feet high, ninety feet long and twelve feet wide at the top.

Twenty thousand Allied troops were now packed into the tiny space of Curuzú. Small boats carrying messages from one commander to another sped past. At any minute, enemy cavalry could appear on the defenceless landward flank and the men digging trenches would have to drop their spades and engage in hand-to-hand fighting. They worked in furious relays.

Two days after work began on the trenches, the Mariscal decided to add another element to his defences.

A member of his *état-major* later said that the idea for a parley came from Elisa Lynch. Certainly there were few others in the inner circle whose position was so secure that they could offer such an idea without being accused of cowardice or treason. The Mariscal sent a message to General Mitre, asking for a 'personal interview between the lines, on the day and at the time Your Excellency wishes'. It was arranged for 9 a.m. on 12 September at a spot called Yataity Corá.

Before dawn that day, a rifle battalion crept silently into place beside the road, where the Allied commanders and their escorts were expected. After breakfast, the Mariscal, Elisa Lynch and Bishop Palacios climbed into a four-wheeled carriage. Twenty-four scarlet-shirted dragoons trotted behind. In the rear were thirty officers and the two López brothers. They reached a pass in the marshes, where the human debris of the winter's battles lay and a hut stood by the path, where Elisa and the bishop were to remain. The Mariscal mounted his bay horse and the commission moved off towards enemy lines, their scarlet backs visible against the grey-green scrub for many yards before the path twisted and they disappeared from view.

On both sides, work ceased that day and there was hope. No bombs fell and no snipers shot from trenches or the high palms. There was music and dancing and, while Madame and the bishop waited in their hut, Allied officers approached the Paraguayan lines and called across. Paraguayan soldiers stood and called back, exchanging news of prisoners and cousins and old friends separated by war and politics, the gossip of camp and anecdotes of battle, *vivas* and best wishes for the coming peace. At three in the afternoon, the line of scarlet and the dust of hooves came back around the bend in the path and Madame left the hut and scrutinised the approaching Mariscal. His first words were to her.

'Nous ne sommes pas arrivés à un accord. La guerre continuera' – 'We did not reach an agreement. The war will continue.'

Venancio Flores had walked out of the meeting after telling the Mariscal that 'responsibility for the war and the bloodshed' was his alone. The Brazilian commander had refused to attend, limiting his participation to a letter handed to Mitre in López' presence, that his orders from the Emperor were to fight 'that man' not to 'enter into social relations with him'. Hamstrung by the treaty which allowed none of the parties to make a unilateral peace, Mitre could do nothing. The two men smoked and chatted for many hours, exchanged souvenirs and rediscovered the pleasure in each other's company they had found seven years ago, after Cepeda, but the war would continue.

They were sombre as they rode back to Paso Pucú. The Mariscal convened his *état-major*.

Gentlemen, [he said] my effort to end this war was rejected. *El generalisimo* Bartolomé Mitre demanded, as required by the iniquitous Treaty of the Triple Alliance, that our country surrender unconditionally. As Paraguay's primary defender, I did not accept. Henceforth, the war will be one of victory or extermination.[11]

In the enemy camp, the Allied commanders discussed the attack on Curupayty which would end the war. It was set for 17 September, at dawn.

Thompson's men were the only ones who had not stopped work that day. They were in mud to their knees, water to their waists, still digging the trenches of Curuzú.

The morning of 17 September was cool and cloudy. At Curuzú, there was still a dangerous neck of dry land between trench and lagoon through which Brazilian horsemen might come, if guided by *pasados*. Men threw up damp earth from the trench which crawled towards the lagoon, cutting off any route the horses could take without sinking to their withers in bog. Dawn passed and the clouds bunched thickly. Still no ships appeared. No one knew it in the Paraguayan camp but at midday General Mitre sent a message to the Brazilian admiral demanding to know why he had not attacked at dawn. The admiral sent a message back: 'It may be about to rain.' At midday, it did, and continued for four days. Beneath the storm, the Paraguayan trenches lengthened. Cannon were pulled into position on walls of packed sand behind them. Powder was brought from the Humaitá arsenal and stored in bunkers dug into trench walls. Still the Allies did not move. On 21 September, General Díaz came to Paso Pucú and told the Mariscal that the defences were ready.

The sun was radiant in the early morning of 22 September. It glinted on the first ships of the Brazilian fleet moving upriver towards Curupayty and the Argentine guns on the Chaco bank opposite. At eight o'clock the bombardment began and nothing could be heard beneath the bombs until midday, when there was a moment's sudden silence, broken by the 19,000 foot soldiers who marched to the sound of bands across open ground towards the Paraguayan positions, their uniforms new and fine. The Paraguayan cannon fired from behind the trench walls. It was a massacre. Nine thousand

Allied soldiers died, mown down before they even reached the trenches, left hanging on the hawthorn bushes where Paraguayan bullets had killed them. The Paraguayans lost twenty-three men.

Elisa Lynch presided over a great supper, hastily compiled of the Mariscal's favourite dishes, among them orange *budín*. Champagne was served and the Mariscal raised his glass to General Díaz: 'Your name,' he said, 'will live for ever in the minds of your countrymen.' Soldiers worked the marshes behind Curupayty that night and the next, stripping the corpses. They asked the wounded if they could walk. If they could not, they were lanced where they lay. The men brought in guns, uniforms, watches, coin, letters, rosaries, miniature portraits and unexploded shells. Two Paraguayans taken prisoner at Uruguayana and pressed into the Allied army were ordered hanged by Díaz. 'One of them was a long time dying,' Thompson recalled.[12] Word came from headquarters that all coin taken from the pockets of the dead was to be brought to Madame Lynch, who would exchange it for paper money at an official rate.

The lagoons were clogged with naked corpses, disintegrating in the rain.

Among the soldiers taken prisoner was one John Neale, an Irishman from County Wicklow, mercenary in the Brazilian army. The soldiers took him to Curupayty, where General Díaz asked his nationality. 'English,' he said, and was sent to Paso Pucú. On the fourth day of his captivity, Madame Lynch drove out in her carriage:

> and seeing me take off my hat to salute her she drew up near me as if to speak to me.
>
> 'Good evening your ladyship,' said I, 'I am proud to see your ladyship for I often heard tell of you before. I hope you are well.'

'I am quite well thank you,' she replied, 'and what part of the world do you come from?'

'I am a rambling Irishman, my lady' – and then I told her my latest adventures.

'Well I understand the President is going to send all the Englishmen and prisoners to Asunción,' she said, 'where you will be set at liberty to make a living as you choose. Meantime if you send the sergeant of the guard to my residence, I will give him whatever provisions you may require.'

'I thank your Ladyship. I have enough to eat and am well treated.'

She then bade me good evening and the next day sent me a fine poncho, 2 shirts and a box of cigars worth altogether about £10 sterling.[13]

John Neale spent three weeks in Paso Pucú. He was embarked on a steamer to Asunción in October, with one hundred European prisoners of war. All except the 'English firemen', who had been crew aboard an Argentine gunboat, were freed to make their living as they could. Neale's poncho was stolen by the seamen.

The battle of Curupayty was 'a disaster', wrote an Argentine officer in the letter which bore the news of his friend's death, and one 'which revealed the incapacity of the Commander-in-Chief', General Mitre, who 'should have been tried by military court and shot'[14]. Mitre retired from the front that month. Command of the Allied forces was given to the Brazilian Field Marshal the Duke of Caxias, sixty-three years old, a veteran of Uruguayana and older battles, an outlander and confidant of the Emperor. Admiral Tamandaré was replaced by a bolder man, Vice-Admiral Ignacio. Venancio Flores left in disgust for Montevideo. In Argentina, Brazil and Uruguay people opened the newspapers fearfully that month to read the names of the endless dead. Thirty-four thousand men had died in battle that year; more had died of disease than battle. In the Argentine army, men deserted in twos and threes, then tens and twenties until whole companies walked away from the front and back to their villages, disgusted with a command which had sent them defenceless into the mouths of Paraguayan cannon, disgusted with this war against their republican brothers, fought in league with the slave-owning Brazilians, a war few now remembered wanting. Within weeks, insurrections had begun in the northern provinces of Argentina, led by those who had refused to fight under Urquiza. The government in Buenos Aires ordered more men conscripted but they slipped away; groups of outlaws formed in the hills. By the end of the year, most of the Argentine army had been withdrawn from the Paraguayan front to put down rebellion in their own country.

Chapter Twelve

On 11 September, a ship had docked at Humaitá and a long-haired forty-four-year-old man with the grey skin of a cell-dweller was taken under escort to Paso Pucú. He was Padre Maíz, just released from the Central Police Station of Asunción. His guards left him in a thicket of hawthorn, put irons on his wrists and pointed out the sentry who would shoot him if he moved. He was not alone. Many of *los politicos* had been there for over a year: the Brazilian consul Amaro Barbosa; the governor of the Matto Grosso; officers from the Corrientes and Uruguayana campaigns; suspected spies, foreigners and groups of cold, sick men. During the great battle of 22 September, the low huts of *los politicos* were exposed throughout to enemy fire, for they were the enemy within and the Mariscal was determined that the battle which defeated his army should be the battle in which they died. They all expected to die; some survived, and among these was Padre Maíz. When the firing stopped at the end of that day, the priest was consumed by an almost mystical transformation.

Just after the battle, a chaplain came. He had been one of Maíz' pupils at the seminary, had fallen under the Mariscal's suspicion and been imprisoned but was now an army chaplain. He had come to warn Maíz of Bishop Palacios, for Palacios was having him watched and had said that if, sleeping, Maíz showed no signs of nightmare, it was proof that he had not repented his sins against the nation. Maíz simulated sleep each night while priests bent over his face to watch his expression, his breathing, his movements and any sign that devilry was being cast out. They watched him for ten days, then a man came from headquarters and handed him a document. It was a copy of the Treaty of the Triple Alliance.

I read and re-read that monstrous document. I had recently realised the character of this war and [that] it was, indeed, a case of victory or death . . . Poor Poland of the Americas! Such was the impression that embittered my soul as I read the iniquitous document by which the Allies, like those who crucified Christ, partitioned in advance the sacred soil of *la patria*. And I reflected: if the war could have been avoided and had not been, now we had not to avoid it, but to confront it, confront the enemy until victory or death . . .

I, who knew [the Mariscal's] spirit, his decisiveness and his energy, his courage and his abnegation, his ardent patriotism, his pride and his military honour, capable of leading him into martyrdom before he would yield, far less surrender, to the invaders, I was able to forget the sufferings I had endured in the grim prison to which he had sent me and, with my Paraguayan heart, I was enthused and firmly resolved to follow [him] as my true leader and supreme commander of the war in defending la patria . . . *Lopismo* appeared to me as the symbol of pure and true nationalism.[1]

Padre Maíz was reborn.

The Mariscal went walking among the detention huts and

the hawthorn and the two men spoke at length. The priest was relieved of his irons.

Charles Washburn attributed Maíz' return to favour to a new coldness in the Mariscal towards those whom he thought had encouraged him into a war which, despite victory at Curupayty, had gone so grossly wrong. 'Madame Lynch,' he said, 'Colonel Wisner [ie Colonel Morgernstern] and others who had been most ardent in advising him to begin it, were very much out of favor.'[2] Padre Maíz' tense and uneasy relationship with Elisa entered a new phase, for he was now on the edge of the inner circle which accompanied the Mariscal everywhere, shared his dinner table and transmitted his wishes to the outside world.

In the *Semanario*, the first letters appeared above his name, confessing to conspiracy with Benigno in 1862.

Unhappy wretch that I was! How could I have avoided it? . . . those charged with my education and training . . . caused me to drink at the fountain the fatal principle or fundamental root of all my aberrations, misfortunes and miseries, the lack of respect to the Supreme Authority, disaffection towards my country and its government . . .
Who could bring me forth from such a desolate state? . . . None but the very God of Heaven – none but FRANCISCO SOLANO LÓPEZ, who occupies His place on earth . . .[3]

He vied in adulation with the bishop.

In November, a US gunboat brought in Charles Washburn to resume the post of US consul with his new, pregnant wife, and anchored off Humaitá. They had been held up for six months in Corrientes by Allies reluctant to admit this gesture of support from the United States. The Mariscal was too sick to receive him, and Washburn continued upriver to Asunción, where he rented the house of the Saguier brothers and re-established the US legation there, distributing luxuries not seen for many months in Paraguay among his friends. He had come authorised by the US president to mediate peace, should the Mariscal permit. The great republic in the north, now emerged from its own battles, was a natural friend to a sister republic at war with a slave-owning emperor. One of those whom he was surprised to see roaming freely in Asunción was Benigno López. Pardons had been granted after the great battle of Curupayty and Benigno had been released from his sentence of exile to the interior and given permission to move about the country. Among the hawthorn, other *politicos* watched for a messenger but the relief from the Mariscal's paranoia was brief. Perhaps it was Padre Maíz, restored to the post of father confessor, or Benigno, restored to that of brother-confidant, who began whispering to the Mariscal that there were those who did not love him as they should.

It was an alarming sign of the growth of his suspicion that he now looked askance even at *los ingleses* in whom he had previously placed his greatest trust. These men were not politicians or diplomats but salaried professionals and López appreciated this straightforward contractual relationship. Somewhere below his need for adulation was the knowledge that this precluded the critical advice which might have saved his armies from disaster. In Asunción, George Masterman and Dr Fox had been arrested and imprisoned, they did not know on what charge.

Foremost among the couple's British friends was Dr William Stewart, godfather to Enrique. It was during the Mariscal's sickness before the battle of Curupayty that he first took against the doctor. Then, it might have been due to the delirium of disease but it continued, later, when his mind cleared.

Near the end of 1866, Madame Lynch sent for Dr Stewart and he went to her hut. She said to him: 'Dr Stewart, I am afraid López is going to do something for which I will never forgive him.' This was at the time López was showing his displeasure to Dr Stewart and the doctor knew well enough that Madame Lynch's words meant he was going to hang, shoot or torture him. A little more conversation ensued, when Madame Lynch said: 'I want to transmit money to Europe . . . I want you to give me a bill for £4,000.' Dr Stewart replied he had not any such sum. She replied that was nonsense, he had married a wealthy lady in Paraguay and must have plenty of money. She insisted he should provide her with the money and at last he consented to give her a bill on his brother in Galashiels on condition that she should take her chance of his declining to accept it if he had not the money. Dr Stewart knew that if he had refused to do so his life would be in danger, and he was only too pleased to get away from her by making the promise . . .[4]

Neither Madame nor the Mariscal was aware that Dr Stewart had not been entirely truthful in his account of himself when he came soliciting a job in 1857. He had allowed it to be understood that his younger brother was director of a bank in Scotland. He was in fact a functionary with little power. Now was not the time to confess.

The first couple's murmured conversations in French after the aides-de-camp went to their huts and only the barefoot Guaraní-speaking sentries were left in earshot will never be known. It was the Mariscal's duty always to present a resolute and hopeful face before his army. There was no member of his family before whom he removed the mask. Venancio and Benigno were no good to him. Even before the officers he might have considered brothers – General Barrios, Inocencia's husband, and General Díaz, his shadow – he maintained the warrior front. There remained only Elisa, despite the coldness towards her Washburn suspected. The battle of Curupayty was interpreted to the troops as the beginning of the end of the war but Elisa was placing her bets both ways. She applied pressure to Dr Stewart to get money in Britain; and she began arrangements for the acquisition of more property in Asunción. She could not leave while war continued. All foreigners in the country were detained indefinitely and Elisa's departure would be a clear signal that she, privy to secrets, believed the war was lost. Futhermore, there were her sons, of whom Panchito was as bewitched by the prospect of glory as his father. It was unlikely he would leave with her.

The soldiers remained resolute. They believed in their cause and their leader.

'God be thanked, the Mariscal was gravely ill,' wrote one soldier home on 30 November, 'but he is now completely recovered and has been getting up again for the past two or three days; yesterday he left his house. *Los negros* [the Brazilians] are completely silent. You would not even know of their existence if we did not stir them up sometimes by dropping bombs on them . . . the alliance is breaking up and the world is falling in on top of it . . .'[5]

Neither Elisa nor the Mariscal knew that on 7 November, Field Marshal Caxias had received unequivocal orders from Rio: he was not to accept any terms for peace other than unconditional surrender and the permanent exile of Mariscal López.

Christmas passed, and New Year. Temperatures rose.

One morning in January 1867, José Díaz and some friends went fishing in canoes. It was a favourite pastime, although the Mariscal had forbidden it, for they were in range of the

Brazilian ships. That morning, the shell of a Whitworth cannon exploded thirty yards away, shattering the canoes and Díaz' leg. He would have drowned had not his Indian sergeant dragged him out and pulled him up the bank. In his tent he was given *caña* and wrote to the Mariscal. Dr Skinner was dispatched but gangrene had already started. The leg was amputated with only the anaesthetic of rum and a cigar. When he could speak again, the General asked for his leg to be embalmed and given its own little coffin.

When the telegraph came to Paso Pucú that Díaz had survived the operation but lost a dangerous amount of blood, Elisa drove her coach to Humaitá hospital and brought him back to headquarters to keep a personal eye on his convalescence. He was put into General Barrios' hut near the Mariscal's house and the Mariscal came immediately to see him.

'What the— were you doing with the *camba*?' he asked with forced jocularity.

'I was testing their marksmanship,' replied Díaz, 'and I discovered it is good.'

He lasted another three weeks. The Mariscal spent days at his side and the army waited for news. On 7 February, Díaz called the Mariscal and Elisa, asked the Mariscal's pardon for disobeying orders and recommended the young officer Bernardino Caballero to him. He died that day.

His funeral was a day of mourning throughout the Quadrilateral, for Díaz had been revered, talismanic. The procession around the gun carriage was hushed. Men cried when his body was loaded onto a steamer for Asunción, where he was taken to La Recoleta cemetery and his sister Isidora was chief mourner. Ladies laid their jewels on his tomb.

In Curupayty, Colonel Paulino Alén took charge of a garrison in mourning.

★

In 1870, Charles Washburn wrote a book about his experiences in Paraguay to defend himself against grave accusations. He had been called before a congressional hearing to answer charges of conspiracy against the head of state to whose government he was accredited.

The conspiracy started in 1867.

Washburn and his wife had spent six months as reluctant guests in the Allied camp below the rivers in 1866, now more properly called a Brazilian camp for the Argentine presence had decreased to negligibility. He knew of the Brazilians' intransigence and their insistence on the Mariscal's exile and replacement by another leader. In Asunción at the end of that year, he learnt that there were those in sympathy with the Brazilian plan, for the first, dangerous whispers of revolt were circulating. They cohered around Benigno López, old rival to the Mariscal, periodically free, periodically detained, the obvious candidate to replace him.

Nevertheless, no definite plan to overthrow López had been formed and Washburn pressed ahead with his attempts to bring peace by negotiation. In March, he took a steamer south to Humaitá to mediate a treaty. His mission was well known in the capital and he left it in a state of joyful anticipation such as had taken hold of the Quadrilateral the day of the parley at Yataity Corá. The Asuncenos believed that peace at last was coming and the men and boys would soon be home. It happened – by accident, perhaps, but probably by design – that Benigno was on the same steamer south. Despite Elisa's mistrust, he had been restored to the status of beloved brother and uncle. Many hours passed between Asunción and Humaitá. They were spent in conversation.

'We speculated,' wrote Washburn carefully, 'as to what would probably be [the Allies'] next move and, if successful, what would be their succeeding step.'[6] He already knew what this step would be; it would be the removal of the Mariscal and the appointment of a new government, probably led by his shipboard companion. At Paso Pucú, the two men were entertained at Elisa's table, where there was still burgundy for dinner and port afterwards and their hostess dressed in silk. On 9 March, Washburn was escorted to the Allied lines by thirty Paraguayan officers and Panchito Lynch, who was so rude to the officers on the other side that Washburn thought he should have had his face slapped. 'Madame Lynch,' he said, 'afterwards professed to be greatly mortified at the rudeness of her son and the evidence of ill-breeding he had exhibited on an occasion that demanded the strictest courtesty and propriety.'[7] No one in his escort, not even the Englishman Colonel George Thompson, was allowed to cross the lines. Washburn returned two days later with Caxias' offer.

It was a favourite maxim of the Brazilian commander that a mule bearing gold could storm the best defended fortress. The offer he now made, through Washburn, was exile over *un puente de oro*, a bridge of gold such as Dictator Rosas had crossed to Southampton in 1852. No other terms would be considered.

One of the more preposterous accusations later made against Elisa Lynch was that it was she who dissuaded the Mariscal from accepting this offer, for the prospect of Parisian exile funded by New World gold had surely influenced her decision to come to Paraguay over a decade ago. But the Mariscal refused. Washburn put argument after argument to him: common sense: 'it were better to look the truth in the face and act with reason, rather than attempt the romantic'; honour: 'his name was already known in all parts of the world . . . and he would be received abroad with welcome and greatly honored wherever he might go'; humanity: 'it would be more to his fame and credit, to save his life and the lives of thousands of others, rather than uselessly and recklessly thrown them away'[8]. None was accepted.

No, he said, there was no future for him, he should
leave no one in whom he had an interest, save only the
children I saw around him [Madame Lynch's] there was
nobody else in the world that he cared anything for . . . it
were better to fall at the pinnacle of honor than to live
longer a fugitive, his country given up as spoil to the
enemy.[9]

When Washburn returned, defeated, to Asunción, a little
Brazilian spy went behind him, a *pasado* who had worked so
well that López trusted him more than his own *piragües*.
A telegraph to José Berges followed: 'Keep watch on the
American and what he says in company.' The Mariscal was
aware that his refusal to accept terms had opened another
front, within Paraguay, and that the Yankee had not told him
every detail of his conversation with Caxias any more [he
hoped] than he had told Caxias every detail of his talks with
the Mariscal. The Brazilian proposal that direct communications be opened with Benigno, or some other appropriate
Paraguayan, was probably made at this meeting, if not during
Washburn's six months in Corrientes the previous year,
although Washburn would never admit such gross misuse of
diplomatic privilege.

He received and visited many friends on his return to the
capital. Consul Cocholet of France, Consul Vasconcellos of
Portugal, Minister José Berges, the López ladies, the Treasurer
Saturnino Bedoya, husband of Rafaela López, the foreign
merchants prevented from leaving the country, Antonio de la
Carreras and his henchman Larreta all came, for the US
legation was now the salon of choice in Asunción. There was
little left in the pantries of the Club Nacional and few private
homes had reserves of food and wine to offer guests. They
were disbelieving, and angry. He told them that the British
and Italian legations in Buenos Aires would shortly be sending

up gunboats to take off their citizens and that he intended to ask Washington to recall him. He could see no point in staying.

Elisa Lynch had heard of the Paraguayan legend around Saint Thomas, who doubted the resurrection and spent his later life in obscurity. His ancient presence was claimed by the Syrian Christians of Malabar, who said he came among them with baptism and was killed by a heathen spear. His bones are disputed: the people of Mylapore insist they lie in India but the faithful of Odessa contradict them. They say the remains of San Tomás were brought by holy men in 304 and buried there. In Paraguay, however, they believed that he did not go to India but to the Americas, and lived in a grotto near lake Ipacaraí, whose corridors ran back into the dark rock and held treasure from the times of Dr Francia.

On the feast of Saint Thomas in 1867, a small party with a crowd behind them entered this grotto to beg the saint's protection for Paraguay. It was an inspiration of Elisa. She 'invited the whole country around to attend . . . at the cave and offer up prayers to heaven for the defeat of the Allies; such was the attendance that not half of the people could get into the cave.'[10]

They gathered just outside, peering into the gloom where the Mariscal, Panchito, Elisa Lynch and Inocencia López de Barrios knelt and prayed together. When the ceremonies were over, Elisa 'gave money to the poor people'[11] and the party returned to the Quadrilateral, where preparations for San Francisco Solano Day were underway.

They received there the gloomy news from Mexico that the forces of Benito Juárez had closed in on the Emperor Maximilian. On the night of 10 June, he slept in a room in the Capucin convent in the town of Queretaro. At dawn, men came to his door and took him, dressed in plain black, to the square at the top of the Hill of Bells. Seven men faced him with rifles. The Emperor gave each an ounce of gold and asked them to aim well at his heart and make his death a clean one. They said that he pinned a piece of scarlet cloth to his white shirt as a target and asked the men not to shoot at his face, as he wanted his mother to see him once more in his coffin. They took aim.

'I forgive everybody,' the lonely Emperor said. 'I pray that everybody may also forgive me, and that my blood which is about to be shed will bring peace to Mexico. *Viva Mexico! Viva la independencia!*'

They shot him through the heart.

Birthday gifts had been prepared in Asunción, and commissions to take them to the Quadrilateral for the Mariscal's birthday, but presentation was not possible. Cholera had struck both camps. From the Paso Pucú watchtowers, they watched the Allied men on graveyard duty burying 250 men a day. The fumigation of headquarters was so thorough and so frequent that it was almost impossible to remain there. The Mariscal was unwell and raged at his doctors that they were trying to poison him. No one was allowed to speak the word cholera in camp. There was another reason Paso Pucú was not safe for a commission bearing gifts that July. Despite their heavy losses, the Allies, under the new energy of Field Marshal Caxias, were moving swiftly up the landward side of the Quadrilateral and this time they seemed unstoppable. The Emperor had recently 'engaged to send out 2,000 men per month to keep up the army to its present strength'[12]. President Mitre had returned to the front 'with a part of the forces lately employed in quelling the insurrection in the Argentine provinces . . . fully supplied with every requisite for a campaign . . . 8,000 are cavalry and well mounted, since fresh horses are daily arriving in large numbers . . .'[13] Few reinforcements would come from a country whose men were dead and scarce supplies from harvests left to rot in the fields. Soon the fresh and veteran troops would have thrown a ring around the depleted Paraguayan army. The *esteros* flooded again; the whole country about Curuzú was under water and the Brazilian fleet was preparing to make another attempt to pass Curupayty. When land and river forces met, the Mariscal's army would be trapped.

The Allied vanguard was heading towards the river-port of Villa del Pilar. Every day, Paraguayans went out on their skeletal horses to harass the mule trains which took supplies from the Allied base at Tuyutí to the forward camps. In June, they were astonished to see hot air balloons rise from the Brazilian lines to survey their trenches. Artillery was drawn up to shoot them down and the troops ordered to burn whatever they must to hide their lines in smoke.

A British gunboat from Buenos Aires arrived in mid-August, bearing Mr Gould of the British legation. His task was to persuade the Mariscal to release British citizens detained against their will but he was also authorised to mediate peace should the Mariscal accept. Washburn's failure was recent and few supposed the Mariscal to have become less intransigent since. Nevertheless, Gould began complicated talks with the Mariscal's secretary, Luis Caminos, who took proposals to his master and after several days of what everyone considered to be hopeless negotiations, there was astonishment in the inner circle. The Mariscal had agreed to a golden exile. Gould left for Caxias' camp to settle the terms of the *puente de oro* and General Barrios sent a coded telegraph to his wife in the capital that there would be peace. Inocencia gave the news to Benigno; it went round the circle of diplomats and foreigners who met in their *quintas*, the Club Nacional and the US legation. There was elation. Then a second, bitter missive from Barrios came. When Gould returned from Caxias' camp, the Mariscal had changed his mind. He would not accept exile; nor would he allow any male British citizens to leave on the British gunboat. 'The fact of the matter is,' wrote Dr Fox, 'he does not wish anybody, Englishman or Frenchman, or Native, who knows anything of this country and Government, to escape from the general slaughter.'[14] The mediation had been a farce.

Mr Gould compiled a shocking report on the condition of Paraguay for the Foreign Office in London. His information had been limited, for, he said, he was 'closely watched and tacitly circumscribed to the small open space around these headquarters'[15]. He had been allowed no private conversation with the British.

The Paraguayan forces amount altogether to about 20,000 men of which 10 or 12,000 at most are good troops. The rest are mere boys from 12 to 14 years of age, old men and cripples, besides from 2 to 3,000 sick and wounded. The men are worn out with exposure, fatigue and privations. They are actually dropping down from inanition. They have been reduced for the last six months to meat alone . . . They may once in a way get a little Indian corn but that, mandioc and especially salt are so very scare, they are, I fully believe, only served out to the sick. In the whole camp there is absolutely nothing for sale. There must be, judging from what I saw, a great scarcity of drugs and medicines, if not a total want of them for the sick, whose number is rapidly increasing . . . Cholera and smallpox . . . are spreading. The horses have nearly all died off and the few hundreds that yet remain are so weak and emaciated, they can scarcely carry their riders . . . The draught oxen are in a dreadful state and cannot last much longer. The cattle in the Camp, some 15 or 20,000 head, are dying very fast for want of pasturage . . . Many soldiers are in a state bordering nudity, having only a piece of tanned leather round their loins, a ragged shirt, and a poncho made of vegetable fibre.[16]

Across the marshes, the Allied camp of Tuyutí was a city, with shops and banks, saloons, gaming halls, theatres and accommodation for the tourists, cattle corrals, stables, depots of cannon, powder and provisions.

Only one house in the Paraguayan camp still unfailingly ate and drank well. Each night, the Mariscal sat to a table over which Elisa presided. Bishop Palacios was always there, and Panchito. Padre Maíz, Colonel Thompson, Colonel Morgernstern, the generals of the army and foreign visitors were guests. On the verandah, there were still smartly dressed troops from the Mariscal's personal guard. Inside, the Mariscal was served with one wine, Elisa Lynch and the guests drank another and several courses were brought. Then there were games of cards, port and cognac, some brief entertainment from Madame at her grand piano or the magic lantern show. Then the guests went to their tents, Madame and the children went to their rooms at one end of the verandah, the bishop retired to his at the other and the Mariscal slept between them. Sentries watched through the night and the spies crept about the camp and listened.

It was the spying and the constant, terrible suspicion which most struck Mr Gould, the 'most abominable system of espionage, such as the world has perhaps never before witnessed, children being taught to betray their parents, and adults punished whenever they fail to spy on each other'[17]. Abominable it was, but effective; and necessary, for there was treachery in Paraguay that winter.

Caxias was pushing his forces ever harder around the landward rim of the Quadrilateral and this time he was not pushing blindly into enemy territory, as the Allied army had been forced to do since they groped uncertainly onto the Itapirú sandbank over a year before. The Brazilians' immediate advance to Tuyu-cué, the next camp in the ring they were throwing around López' army, was based on information received.

'The semicircular movement which he made to go from Tuyutí to Tuyu-cué, that, you can be sure, was not the work or inspiration of any military genius. He did it because Benigno told him to, because the country would be left open to the [River] Tebicuarí and forces could be sent to Asunción, whose support was indispensable for the outbreak of revolution . . .'[18]

Now there was blockade from land as well as from water and continued Allied bombardment. Shot from the Whitworth cannon, the *fiù-fiù*, whistled over Paso Pucú and a new earthwork was built, eighteen feet high, to protect headquarters from the guns of Tuyutí. 'Still considering he was not safe,' George Thompson wrote, the Mariscal 'had a *casemate* – a bunker – made, in which he would dine and live when any firing was going on – one shot in any quarter being sufficient to make him get out of bed and go there. This casemate was formed of immense logs of iron wood, nine feet long, stuck in the ground side by side, in two rows nine feet apart, and covered over with larger logs of the same timber. The whole was covered over with nine feet of earth.'[19]

The Paraguayans in the outlying trenches responded to Allied cannon by beating pots and pans and blowing a crude horn known as the *turututú* for the infernal noise it made and by hurling stones and arrows at Allied sentries from the watchtowers. Detachments were sent to halt the Allied advance and men desperately needed were killed in futile sorties: 500 one day, 100 the next, 200 in the night. The hospitals in Humaitá and Asunción overflowed again.

The combats in which men uselessly died through

September did not stop the Brazilians from reaching Villa del Pilar and cutting the telegraph wires to the capital. The encirclement of the Mariscal's forces by land was complete. After dinner in the bunker, they called trumps above incessant noise. Atop the earthwork, a sentry held up flags, each with a capital letter indicating where the next cannon ball was predicted to fall. Another, below, dashed in and out with the news.

On the river where the water flowed fast and high, still the Allies hesitated before the torpedoes of Curupayty but their bombardment was constant. A shell entered the hospital in Humaitá and broke Dr Fox's leg. Curuzú was flooded and its garrison in peril. 'It is believed,' wrote a reporter, 'that the whole place which cost millions to organise and arrange will also have to be abandoned; these floods are now causing great loss and damage to the allied army, when in reality they should be turned to good account by the Brazilian admiral, to ascend the river, shell Humaitá and pass up to Asunción.'[20]

In mid-August, the first step was taken. Admiral Ignacio ordered sandbags to be piled inside and outside the turrets and gunports of his ships to deflect the force of cannon ball from Curupayty. It would protect the men inside 'both from the splinters and from the fine heated dust, to which the projectiles are often reduced on striking the iron plates and which, in spite of every other precaution, even when the ports are closed, finds its way in and disables the men at the guns'[21]. Then the ships left Curuzú, shut their ports, and steamed before Curupayty, and 'keeping close under the cliffs on which the guns are mounted, avoided in a great measure their fire, as they could not be sufficiently depressed . . . Only one of the ironclads was disabled by a shot striking the condenser, and was exposed to a very heavy fire, until another vessel came to its assistance and, lashed to its side, towed it up past the batteries.'[22] This time there was no wait, no long delay before the next operation. They anchored a mile below Humaitá and started shelling. The Curupayty garrison was brought to Paso Pucú with the artillery. All villages for one hundred miles north of the Quadrilateral were evacuated and their crops burnt. Homeless families were sent to the villages of the cordillera east of the capital, or begged in Asunción and the Quadrilateral camps. A wasteland opened up across a tract of central Paraguay; a belt of scorched earth to prevent the Allies from surging north.

On the Chaco bank opposite, an escape road was being swiftly built as far as Monte Lindo, opposite the estuary of the River Tebicuarí. Lieutenant Colonel Nuñez was given the task of getting the precious horse and cattle herds to Tebicuarí. They had to be swum across the Paraguay just north of Humaitá, herded along the new Chaco road, and swum back across at Monte Lindo, where the river was 560 yards wide and the current very rapid. There were various ways of getting the animals across the rivers. One was a *manga*, or funnel, constructed with fences. Cattle were forced into the wide end on the bank and emerged twenty yards away, where a canoe with cows lashed to its side was waiting. The animals which came snorting through the *manga* were supposed to follow the tethered cattle across to the other bank; 'many were drowned, however, by this method. Another was to fasten four animals on each side of a canoe by their horns and then paddle across; they also tied the animals' legs and horns together and carried four across in a canoe. But the best plan, and the one most used, was a large pontoon towed by a steamer.'[23]

Dispatches also went up the new Chaco road and crossed by canoe to San Fernando, a government *estancia* on the Tebicuarí and the nearest telegraph station not in enemy hands. The women in the Quadrilateral camps were told they could return to the capital if they wished. Some had been there for three years as unpaid labourers. Many walked the 250 miles to Asunción.

There remained one small gap through which the Mariscal could communicate with the capital: the stretch of river between the enemy fleet below Humaitá and Caxias' forces at Villa del Pilar. It was only a matter of time before the Allies closed the gap. In October, the bombardment from the river ceased briefly when an Italian gunboat deposited Lorenzo Chapperon at Paso Pucú. He was the first representative in Paraguay of Victor Emanuel of Italy. Consul and Madame Cocholet were also at Paso Pucú, awaiting the French gunboat on its way to take them off and bring in their replacement. They had been ungracious envoys, reluctant to appear at receptions and balls, contemptuous of Paraguayan society, constant complainers, absolute in their refusal to meet Elisa Lynch. When Consul Comte de Cuverville arrived, their grievances poured out: the slights and the snubs, the food, the weather, the outrageous attempts of Madame to be friendly, her wealth and entertainments and large family, her pro- liferation of houses and her scandalous past. Cuverville listened, absorbed and made no judgement. His first dispatch was hopeful.

Paso Pucú, 9 October 1867
I was received by Mariscal López and had the honour of talking at length yesterday evening. He received me with a courtesy, I would even say cordiality, which I consider exceptional and augurs well for my mission. I am sure he would continue war if necessary but he regards peace as desirable and would cease the war if a powerful friend organised this for him. I have no doubt that both sides would like the French to mediate peace. Mr Gould's mission, despite its failure, has at least laid the foundations.[24]

At the end of October, Cuverville and Chapperon took a steamer to Asunción, a sad and desolate city. There were cripples and amputees and beggars and women in black in the streets. Police in the city had started requisitioning eggs brought by the few market women who still came in. Few shops traded. Everything was scarce. At the riverbank, the peons working on the Mariscal's palace had been conscripted and their place taken by child slaves, 'little fellows made prematurely old by the labour to which they were condemned . . . constantly watched, that they should never idle away a moment.'[25]

'The fact cannot be hidden,' wrote Cuverville from the French consulate, 'that the Paraguayan government is currently experiencing its worst moment yet.'[26] He had been in the capital only days when he was contacted by the disaffected and spoken to about the need to remove the Mariscal from power. Newly arrived from Paso Pucú, recently in transit through the Brazilian camp where men, food, horses, arms and medicine abounded, Cuverville did not think the conspirators would be called on to act. He, like Gould, thought the war must end within weeks. Then news came from the Quadrilateral.

At 4.30 in the morning of 3 November, 9,000 Paraguayans stormed the Allied camp at Tuyutí. This time their timing and their tactics were perfect. Panic spread along the line of enemy camps as far as Paso de Patria, where opportunistic boatmen charged fleeing officers £10 for passage to Corrientes and left those who could not pay on the shore. No one had thought the starving and depleted Paraguayans capable of such an attack. At nine, they left Tuyutí in smoking ruins and returned to Paso Pucú, bent double beneath booty, dressed in comical layers of looted clothes with packs of stolen food strapped to their backs and chests, cases of liquor in their arms, rough sledges piled with provisions and roped to their shoulders, bumping across the tussocks, staggering into camp with muscles stretched to the extreme. There were letters to General Mitre from his wife, new officers' uniforms from a sacked tailor's, 'parasols, dresses, crinolines, shirts [Crimean shirts especially], cloth . . . brought in in large quantities, every man carrying as much as he could. A tripod telescope was brought from one of the watchtowers and gold watches, sovereigns and dollars were abundant' and 'the only artichokes I ever saw in Paraguay'[27] were brought to Colonel Thompson. The men also brought 453 prisoners of war and left 3,000 dead on the field. The money chests were opened in the Paso Pucú bunker. Elisa Lynch relieved the men of their coin and returned its official value in notes.

The Quadrilateral was *en fête*; the peace party in Asunción was in despair. The previous year, the country had been almost brought down by military combat, then victory at Curupayty paralysed the war. A year later, they had hoped twice for peace and an even more astonishing victory chased the enemy from Tuyutí. It was a disaster. It prolonged privations. It meant conscription of ever younger and older soldiers to replace those killed. It meant the men were not coming home. Even Vice-President Sanchez and Minister Fernandez failed properly to organise public celebrations this time.

At the end of November, Madame took the steamer to Asunción. Doña Dolores had recently acted for her in the acquisition of a row of houses between Calle 25 Decembre and Calle Oliva, in what was to be the shopping district; and plots on Calle Palma and Calle Estrella, where the merchants' warehouses were falling empty. The purchases needed to be settled.

No doubt on arrival she was greeted with enthusiasm by the *populacho*, still staunchly behind the Mariscal despite the conscription of children, the requisition of livestock, the encouraged donations of milk, eggs and cheese. Her reception was different in the Club Nacional where she found faces falling blank and nervous silence when she entered rooms. The merchants whose warehouses were closed and useless greeted her carefully but without warmth. When she made her hospital visits, Dr Rhind and Dr Surgeon Fox of Southampton looked at her sourly for they had endured three months in the Mariscal's gaol for reasons they did not know. The apothecary George Masterman was sourer still, for he had spent eleven months in gaol on the whim of some suspicious officer and been released only by the pressure of Charles Washburn, looking, he wrote to his sister Fanny, 'the most extraordinary figure you can imagine, my hair hanging in heavy curls on my shoulders, a beard like a Jew and the complexion of a bilious ghost . . .'[28] He had immediately taken up his work in the hospital. 'I have performed 30 capital amputations,' he wrote just before Elisa's visit, 'included one of Shoulder and 13 of thigh (4 recovered) and having had charge of 800 wounded for weeks altogether, I have learnt no end of practical surgery . . .'[29] The hospitals were full. 'In each narrow bed lies a wounded man, some on bags of sacking stuffed with moss, others on the bare thongs, which emboss themselves deeply in their flesh, if they have any. Most of them are nearly naked, save for the bandages over their wounds and shattered limbs . . . there are no blankets . . . the air is so close and fetid, for the poor, shivering wretches *will* close the shutters of the unglazed windows at night, that a stranger can hardly breathe it, and yet it is full of visitors, almost all women.'[30]

But one man in town was delighted to see Elisa again. 'The change of consul,' wrote Dorotea Duprat de Lasserre, a French merchant, 'was a disaster for the French community. By night a certain person charmed him with the various wines for which, unfortunately, Monsieur had a great liking, and . . .

without his realising it, got everything he knew out of him.'[31] Consul Cuverville was smitten. The tartness of his dispatches fades into a most unprofessional soppiness on the subject of Madame Lynch.

'I am much angered,' he wrote home, 'by Mme Cocholet's opinion [of Elisa Lynch], but having lived for ten years in Paris, I believe I may consider myself as accustomed as she to distinguishing a lady of real society from one of a different sort, and I can assure you that Mme Lynch not only belongs to the best society, but she is generally loved here, her charity is proverbial and her greatest detractors are those to whom she does most good.'[32] Even though she would not see forty again (he thought wrongly), her company was *agréable* and her conversation *charmante*.

What Consul Cuverville knew, and Elisa Lynch got out of him during their tête-à-têtes, was that a group in the capital was already planning the administration which would follow the Mariscal's defeat and removal. Benigno López was at its heart, Ministers Berges and Fernandez were aware of it, Washburn was actively concerned in it and so was Treasurer Saturnino Bedoya, Rafaela López' husband. On the fringes of this group of planners and plotters were the wealthy foreigners who hovered around the US legation and the Club Nacional, angry at their detention, sickened by the Mariscal's refusal to put peace before personal honour: Simón Fidanza, Genovese shipowner; his compatriot Antonio Rebaudi, Madame's favourite merchant; Nin Reyes, Uruguayan trader; Antonio de la Carreras and Rodríguez Larreta; the British medics and engineers whose requests to leave the country had been rejected. Both Cuverville and the chancellor of the French consulate, M Libertat, had been recently approached and questioned 'on the intentions of the Emperor Napoleon's government, should the allies enter Asunción . . .'[33] In a dispatch home that month, he was specific. 'Here,' he wrote, 'in the event that President López were obliged to resign, it is believed there are three candidates for the post, José Berges . . . Don Saturnino Bedoya . . . and Don Benigno López.'[34]

For Cuverville, a new arrival and unknown quantity, to have been given such information, there must have been extraordinary confidence in the circles to which he referred, for no one doubted that these discussions were treason and that the Mariscal's punishment would be terrible. But the Mariscal was far from the capital, surrounded by water and land, his forces weary and they knew that the victory of 3 November could only detain the Allies temporarily.

When Elisa Lynch visited Minister Fernandez to settle her property purchases, she viewed her right-hand man with new eyes, but said nothing.

Another task in the capital required Elisa's delicate intervention.

Many would later say that she was creator, instigator and prime mover of the Ladies' Commissions, with the sole aim of acquiring the national jewel collection, but she was not. Rather, she subverted the ladies' own expression of patriotism for gain.

The first Grand Assembly of Paraguayan Women was an outdoor rally on Plaza 14 Mayo, Asunción, on 24 February 1867. At eight in the evening, the plaza was milling with ladies dressed in red, white and blue. There were *vivas* to Paraguay, to National Independence, to the invincible armies of the Republic and to the Glory of the Madre Patria. Then an old lady stood. The daughters of Asunción, she said, had resolved to: 1) offer all their jewels to the war effort; 2) appoint a committee to execute this resolution; 3) ask the Mariscal's permission to use the national colours instead of jewels for their personal adornment; and 4) order the creation of an elegant album to be signed and delivered to the Mariscal in homage.

'Hail, patriotic woman!' wrote the *Semanario*. 'The national press . . . congratulates you and salutes you . . . the women of Paraguay have made themselves famous . . .'[35]

Collections began throughout the country in March.

Viva la republica del Paraguay!
Ibicui, 11 March 1867
Jewels belonging to the undersigned Rosa Isobel Rodríguez who hereby states to the Commission responsible for the collection of these objects in this locality for the offering to be made to the Supreme Head of the Republic towards the heroic defence of the country: 1 gold necklace and a pair of gold earrings, each weighing 6½ grammes.[36]

There were over 2,000 such entries in the *Libro del Registro*.

Viva la republica del Paraguay!
Ibicui, 11 March 1867
Jewels belonging to the undersigned Juana Pabla Santandez . . . 1 gold rosary weighing 6½ grammes and one pair of gold and topaz earrings, each weighing 3½ grammes.[37]

An unknown number of earrings, rosaries, bracelets, necklaces and rings was packed into chests by commissions in the villages and brought to the capital by patriotic ladies. In Paso Pucú, they realised the astonishing potential wealth on the necks, wrists and fingers of the villages. Soon, the ladies of the foreign community had begun their own collection to make an *ofrenda* to the Mariscal, this time under Elisa's 'personal direction'[38], and those of the Paraguayan ladies were officially encouraged. Gently, the project was taken from the hands of volunteers and given to state machinery. The lady commissioners who had received the first jewels were gradually replaced by 'judges of the peace [who] called upon everyone, even those who had not volunteered to give it, to deliver at once the whole of their jewellery'[39]. More earrings and rosaries trickled into the depots in the capital.

Some donations were extensive:

> Dolores Vasquez de Acosta with her daughters Barcilia, Cecilia, Rosa, Candida, Balbina and Valenciana Acosta: two rosaries, one weighing 2oz 11 adarmes, the other 17 adarmes; a gold chain, 2oz; a coral rosary with 11oz gold, 4 adarmes; two coral and gold necklaces, one coral and filigree necklace, three pairs of gold earrings, two with topaz and one with a fake stone.[40]

Others were simpler:

> Higinia Sara de Aguirre: one pair of earrings adorned with six fine stones weighing 9 adarmes.[41]

There were other patriotic demonstrations. Twenty girls in Aregua 'got lances and white dresses with tricolour bands and a sort of Scotch cap, designed by Mrs Lynch, and they used to go about Asunción singing patriotic hymns.'[42] Pretty requests were made and publicised in the *Semanario* of young ladies who begged to be allowed to take up arms. 'The hints and ideas for all these things emanated,' said Thompson, uncharacteristically coy, from headquarters, 'López "lady-friend" . . . being the medium'[43], but the ladies acted upon these hints out of a desire to ease the sufferings of husbands, sons and fathers at the front and a belief that this was a just war.

'With every day which passes,' wrote one soldier son and brother in February, 'the cause for which we fight is more sacred and more beautiful and as, with each day that passes, we are more united in our efforts and our action, our eventual victory cannot be doubted . . . it is thought the war is nearly over . . .'[44]

By 1867, there was not a family which did not have a man fighting or buried. They knew that no shops traded in Paso Pucú or Humaitá. Their men were poorly dressed and hungry. They had lice and suffered cramps because there was no salt and they were cold in winter. They relied for new uniforms and luxuries, such as salt and soap, on the loot which remained from robbing the dead of Curupayty and Tuyutí. Everyone, 'from the minister and the general to the rank and file'[45] was a trafficker and a barterer. A black market flourished. Women in the camps, although they performed semi-official tasks like laundry and cooking, received no rations at all and were dependent on what their men gave them, or, when these were killed, what they could get for their services. Certain commodities had run out entirely. There was no paper. The karaguata palm was used to make a rough and fibrous substitute. There was no ink. A crude black juice was produced by drying and grinding a species of black bean with water. Officers' commissions were written on parchment made from sheepskin. Soap was made by boiling together fat meat and wood ash. There was no salt, except for the Mariscal and the hospitals. The men urinated into cauldrons left to evaporate in the sun, and the salt in their urine was mixed with iron pyrite and turned into gunpowder. The women had revived the art of weaving, which had almost died out in Paraguay because of the cheapness of imported cotton. They made serviceable broadcloth shirts but the trousers cut from cured hides for officers were so stiff when it rained that the men could not bend their legs.

This was the suffering the ladies wished to ease. They had sent food parcels, cigars and soap. They had torn up their petticoats to make bandages. They had sent their horses and their cattle to the army corrals. They had rifled their bureaux, bookshelves and family albums when the chiefs of militia came to collect 'useless paper', for the army had run out[46]. They had taken up their carpets to be made into ponchos for shivering troops. Now they gave their jewels.

Their intentions were good but the currency of their wealth was useless for, with the rivers shut, their jewels bought nothing. On the anniversary of the battle of 24 May, the ladies announced they would make a present to the Mariscal of an album bound in gold and a jewel-encrusted sword. It was arranged by Doña Dolores de Sion, Elisa's agent. A meeting of foreigners was organised in the Club Nacional to decide on that year's homage to the leader and organise subscriptions to pay for it. Illness and the march of the Allies had prevented the presentation planned for the Mariscal's birthday, but on 22 December 1867, just after Elisa returned to the Quadrilateral from Asunción, a deputation followed her down the new Chaco road. It was composed of Saturnino Bedoya, Don José Berges and Padre Solano Espinoza, an army chaplain and fervent admirer of the Mariscal. They brought with them the fruit of the sacrifice of ladies throughout the country, translated into a Book of Gold and a Golden Sword. The national wealth had been diverted into a gift for one man. The sacrifice of family treasures would aid *la patria* only in so far as *la patria* was identified with the person of the Mariscal.

On Christmas Day, *caña* was given to the troops and the bishop stood to offer a speech of abject homage. The gifts were presented, the sword passed from hand to hand for admiration and then strapped on. Elisa dispensed champagne to her guests. When the commission prepared to leave Paso Pucú for the long journey back, Saturnino Bedoya was detained. No charges were made. He was not put in irons or questioned.

Chapter Thirteen

It was only a matter of time before the Allied navy passed Humaitá and encircled the army. Each day, the tide rose higher. The rains were of a force and duration unequalled in local memory and Paraguayans and Allies waited for the moment to come when the ships could slip over the sunken chains and break out of this tight circle at the bottom of the country. On 19 February 1868, they did so. In these bleak hours, even the Mariscal realised his capital was lost. Immediately, Thompson wrote, 'he sent Mrs Lynch to Asunción to take out into the country all valuables in his house and in her own. This was done at midnight, in order that it should not be known.'[1] Saturnino Bedoya was with Bishop Palacios and a group of officers when the ironclads fought their way past the batteries. 'I wonder what they are doing in Asunción?' he quipped nervously. 'Who knows – they might think *los negros* have taken us prisoner and set up a new government and we will have to go up and teach them a lesson . . .'[2] When Bishop Palacios reported this indiscreet joke, the Mariscal sent him back to ask Bedoya what he had meant. All then noted Bedoya's 'paleness; he was tongue-tied; he was terribly scared'[3]. General Barrios and the bishop were ordered to conduct a formal interrogation. This was reported in the coded telegraph Barrios sent to his wife before the enemy cut the wires, to tell her the Brazilians were coming and Bedoya had been foolish.

Elisa Lynch arrived in a city given to panic. The Mariscal had telegraphed Vice-President Sanchez that Asunción was to be evacuated to Luque, twelve miles inland at the start of the cordillera, and lines were already forming along the road to the cordillera, 'the roads full of men, old people, children, women with babies in their arms, hungry soldiers, long queues of carts laden with baggage . . .'³ The midsummer rain was incessant. The roads were steaming clay.

No one knew how long the city had before the Brazilians came to harvest victory. Elisa could do nothing to safeguard the vast palace on the dock; the properties which were to have been mansions and arcades; the house on Calle Fábrica de Balas and the *quinta*. These must be left to their fate. Her priorities were to place in safety those documents which proved her claim to properties whose ownership might be contested under a non-López government; and to ensure that portable wealth – jewels, pictures taken from frames, the debris of the refugee existence – were stashed away for easy removal.

They were packing at la Presidenta's *quinta* in Trinidad, too, and Benigno was talking of his brother's inevitable and imminent defeat to his mother, sisters and their relative and confessor, Padre Acosta. Rafaela López de Bedoya took Acosta to her house nearby and spoke urgently.

She told me that her brother Benigno and other people had agreed to bring down the Mariscal's government and end the war; that López must die or fall; that they had reached an understanding with the enemy, who had promised to send the ironclads a little upriver from Asunción so all those who wished could take refuge aboard them; that they

. . . were going to do so, that that night they were going to take some trunks to General Barrios' house on the riverbank so they could go aboard at any moment . . . and they expected that I, as a relative, would go with them, safe in the knowledge we would all soon return . . .[5]

At the docks, the machinery of the arsenal was dismantled, thrown into wagons and taken to the railway station, repacked and reloaded, transported down the line to Aregua and discharged onto the banks of Lake Ipacaraí. As the trains went back for more, soldiers set out in laden canoes for the far shore, where others with ox wagons waited to drag the machinery into the cordillera.

Now the Mariscal was unreachable. Telegraphs could no longer be sent or received. On 21 February, Vice-President Sanchez convened a council of notables to decide what action should be taken when the Brazilians came. He was seventy-three, sick and frightened. The meeting was called in his name but was led by Benigno, who justified his presence by claiming to be proxy for Venancio, Minister of War, ruined by syphilis. Only one man proposed active resistance. He was Padre Solano Espinoza, who had been with the Christmas commission to the Quadrilateral. The council took no decision that day and agreed to reconvene the next, without Benigno, who was to travel to the town of Paraguarí to talk to the chiefs of militia of the interior.

Benigno's clandestine presidential campaign was underway. It had started during his first conversations with Washburn and the opening of communications with Caxias, however these were effected. The chiefs of militia could not have been convened so swiftly in the upper saloon of the railway station in Paraguarí had they not been forewarned to come when the defeat of the Mariscal was no longer just a dangerous dream but an imminent, perhaps consummated, fact.

His host in Paraguarí was a friend and relative of Saturnino Bedoya, Don Gregorio Molinas. Benigno's last words to Don Gregorio were later recalled by the Molinas daughters:

Quédate tranquilo, stay calm. Many foreign commanders are with us and have signed a great agreement with us. What does this mean, Gregorio? It means we are on the right road.[6]

The capital continued to empty beneath the storms. The archives, cathedral statues, powder depot and treasury were taken away. Consul Chapperon put seals on the Italian legation and joined the exodus to Luque; Consul Cuverville would shortly join him but Charles Washburn had refused to leave. On the night the notables met, the first refugees arrived at the legation, intending to give themselves to the Brazilians, who would treat them as neutrals. Two itinerant Yankees were there; George Masterman and many British families from the docks; Carreras and Larreta of Uruguay.

On 22 February, as Washburn's staff were engaged in issuing receipts for the goods of the fleeing wealthy, sure the US legation was the only house in Asunción not about to be sacked, Elisa Lynch sent to ask Washburn to call at her house. He found her in 'great tribulation'[7].

The war had polarised positions in Paraguay. Although before 1864 Washburn had been a frequent and appreciative guest at Elisa's house, he had inevitably taken his place on one side and Elisa had equally inevitably taken her place on the other. 'She questioned me,' he wrote, 'of what the Brazilians would do now they had passed Humaitá. I told her they would probably keep López and his army shut up where he was and advance on Humaitá with such force as to take it, and then, by cutting off his supplies at all points, he would be obliged to capitulate or else to attack them in their entrenchments which, with his unequal forces, could not be done successfully. The cause was lost, and she could see it as well as I.'[8] His assessment was a logical one. It seemed impossible that the Mariscal could escape the ring thrown round him. The reduction of his troops by starvation and disease was an open secret.

'She asked me,' Washburn continued, 'if I would receive her most valuable items into my house, I replied that I had done that for many other people, and had offered to do it for all; that if she thought her property would be more safe there than elsewhere, she could send it, and I could answer that while there it would never be taken by the Allies unless they forcibly violated the US legation. She was very despondent and said that she did not know what would become of her, and seemed to be aware that she neither deserved nor could expect any mercy if she fell into the hands of the enemy. She intimated that she might, at the last moment, apply to me for shelter ... The ambitious plans which had induced her to invest such large sums of money in furniture and adornments not to be found elsewhere except in palaces seemed to have miscarried ... the illusions of the López dynasty, with her first-born as the heir apparent to her paramour, and her other sons as royal princes, had all vanished and she only thought then of saving her life and the lives of her children, and escaping with her ill-gotten gains to Europe.'[9]

That night she left for Patiño-Cué and a stream of families making for the hills called and sought information from her. Among them was Hector Decoud, whom she had last seen playing in the huts of Humaitá while his mother expiated her husband's treason in the Chaco. He wanted to know where and how his mother was, for two and a half years had elapsed since he had been sent back to Asunción. She was well, Madame told the boy, because his godfather, the Mariscal, made sure that she was always looked after. If he wanted, he could send her some gift and she would make sure his mother received it. He returned three days later with a wooden box containing clothes and twenty gold coins.

Asunción was deserted, but for a plague of cats. Washburn, Cuverville and Masterman stood on the flat roof of the US legation and watched the Brazilian ships approach. Padre Espinoza was among the gunners but Comandante Gomez of the garrison had given them dummy shot. In the breathless heat, the three foreigners saw the inexplicable that afternoon: the Brazilians fired a few desultory shots at the city, turned, and steamed out of the bay. One of the towers on the Mariscal's new palace was damaged. A soldier carrying trunks from Madame's house to the US legation was injured. Two dogs were killed. Then the city was left in silence and at least two of the men on the legation roof were stunned and suddenly scared.

Later, when writers began fitting explanation to event, the failure to take Asunción on 22 February 1868 became one of the great mysteries of the war. Had the sailors been scared some skeletal, silent horde lay in ambush? Had there been a fatal but banal failure to pass orders down the line? Had Caxias decided victory in the Quadrilateral was so secure that the conspirators in the capital did not require the protection of his fleet? Or – the favourite explanation of those who saw genocide behind the Treaty of the Triple Alliance – did Caxias and his masters not wish the war to end in February 1868, but to continue until every last Paraguayan was dead and the ancient province had reverted to the *terra nullius* the first Portuguese saw in 1537, licensed for occupation by a Christian monarch?

The conspirators were alone and unprotected when the Mariscal re-established telegraphic contact with Asunción on 24 February and the first telegraphs were alarming. The Republic of Paraguay was declared to be in a state of siege. Military law was imposed throughout the country. Minister

Berges and two of the other notables were ordered immediately to Paso Pucú for explanations. Someone had sent a telegraph and told him of their council, and its strange passivity in the face of threat.

When the three nervous notables took the Chaco road south, Elisa Lynch went with them to deliver them to the Mariscal.

Paso Pucú was now a camp besieged and a plan of extraordinary daring had been devised: the army of the Quadrilateral was to be transferred, silently and secretly, to the Chaco bank. The artillery was brought in from outlying defences and stored in Humaitá fort. Horses and cattle were rounded up. In Paso Pucú, Madame packed her possessions: clothes, china, books, carpets, furniture, her grand piano from Corrientes and her carriage were all to be taken by steamer, raft or canoe across the river.

Late on the evening of 2 March, the Mariscal, Elisa, their children, Bishop Palacios and other officers left in stealth and took the road to Humaitá. When they left, the bunker in which they had lived was completely destroyed.

Already stores, livestock, troops and weaponry were being ferried to Timbó, a position recently defended and garrisoned six miles upriver on the Chaco bank, at the head of a deep lagoon. It was shelled each morning by the Brazilian ironclads who now had the run of the river. Two men were to be left in charge of a garrison in Humaitá to hold off the enemy while new positions were consolidated upriver. Senior officer was Paulino Alén; second-in-command was Francisco Martínez, husband of Elisa's friend, Juliana Insfrán.

In the same canoe as the Mariscal were the Bishop, Madame Lynch, his sons and his aides, these last rowing. The canoe behind them carried the men who worked at headquarters

. . . Afterwards came the troops. There were about 100 canoes, prepared in advance, so heavily loaded that they were no more than 2 inches above water . . . Our landing was difficult and tiring because of the strong current. The canoes entered the lagoon at Timbó on the rising tide.[10]

Light began to break when they were halfway across and a crocodile broke the surface alongside Elisa's canoe. Then they saw the first of the Brazilian ironclads coming to bombard Timbó.

We still had 400 yards between us and the lagoon of Timbó and the ironclad could easily have wrecked . . . us. But it did not move . . . and firing started only when the last canoe in the great caravan arrived in the lagoon. The war could have ended then and there with the fall of López.[11]

It was another piece of unexplained cowardice, incompetence or sinister strategy. 'The bombardment lasted all that day, and the day following.'[12] They lay in mud or shade and waited for it to stop.

'After dark that evening, we set off for Monte Lindo . . . [about forty miles upriver] . . . the road leading through the woods and most of it through deep mud. Solano López went most of the way on horseback, having his own horses, and his carriages and carts with provisions were also drawn by good animals.'[13] Everyone else went on foot.

It was heavy going, through virgin country. The guard-houses and the new road along the river's edge were the only European hold on Indian land. It was part mud, part sand, part water – the same treacherous mixture of land and liquid as the *esteros* of the Quadrilateral. Every few yards a stream emptied itself into the River Paraguay. Some were shallow enough to splash through at a canter; others, a little wider, allowed a rider to swim a horse across without dismounting, only pausing to brush off the leeches. Carriages and carts racketed through fords, their axles in peril. But some of the inlets were wide and edged by marsh penetrating too many miles into the interior to ride around. They were passable only by bridge. Beams had already been laid across the water by the roadbuilders but they had not had time to lay sod, which would raise the bridge and provide a surface suitable for hooves. Brushwood had been laid in tangles of long, stretchy twigs ripped from the undergrowth. It was dangerous; it trapped the horses' hooves and threw their balance. Many tripped and fell into the river below. George Thompson could not understand the jollity of the troops. They smiled and laughed and worked and thought the tumbles hilarious. The Mariscal went among them cracking jokes in Guaraní, and they loved him as much as they always had.

At about midnight, the gleam of lanterns off the river began to throw back a red richer than the mud and they knew they were close to the River Bermojo. The track wound down through woods and they spent the night on its banks. The López family commandeered a guardhouse. Their companions 'wrapped ourselves upon our ponchos'[14] and slept beneath the stars. Behind them came the first of the 8,000 people who crossed to the Chaco that week, struggling silent and semi-naked through the mud with cattle, horses, food, clothes, documents, liquor, poultry and possessions in bundles. Saturnino Bedoya, Minister Berges, his fellow notables and *los politicos* were among them, some with iron bars between their ankles.

Breakfast was a grim affair for most; 'nothing but maté except for some, who were given soup by the medics'[15]. The López family had their private stores. Early in the morning they set off. By now, they were well out of sight of the enemy's patrolling grounds. Only a vessel reconnoitring far upriver would spot the winding, mud-caked line on the far bank.

They crossed the red Bermojo in canoes, three horses roped to either side. The oarsmen propelled their cargoes across, and back, and across again. A carriage was sucked into the mud. The horses could not manage the pace. Up to their withers in the mud, pulling uphill, some died. Colonel Thompson was 'forced to prick his sword to move [my horse]. Then it died, and I went on by foot to the next posthouse'[16] where he found López, Elisa and the ubiquitous bishop taking a siesta beneath trees.

The cooks had been sent ahead and had dinner ready. After dinner, they remounted and rode on to the wide stream of Paso Palenque. The bridge was unfinished. López ordered a hut built for his family. Everyone else slept on the grass. 'The troops had to work all night to finish the bridge . . . and they were in and out of the water all night, in the greatest good humour. As soon as the bridge could bear the carriage, López got into it and was dragged across by men on foot, the horses swimming.'[17]

It was 5 March. Many evacuees had caught up with the Mariscal during the night, slept where they dropped and marched on with him in the morning. They went six miles north to Paso Puente, where four cannon lay waiting to be dragged across the river. On the far side, the straggling column rode or walked through eighteen miles of bamboo forest, crossed another river, had dinner as the light faded and continued through the dusk. Now the track was widening and solid ground was more frequent than marsh. López 'began to gallop and those who could, kept with him',[18] and, as darkness came, the first riders reached the woods opposite the Tebicuarí estuary and made camp.

Night after night, silent boats went out from Humaitá with animals roped to either side, disguised as *camalotes* by giant lilies wrapped around them, and went back for more, and more, so long as darkness held. Alén and Martínez wondered how many more nights would pass before the Allies realised their prize was slipping away. A trail of Paraguayans six miles long walked in single file, swam and slithered north up the muddy Chaco bank, across the rivers, the mudflats and the temporary bridges which collapsed beneath the weight of so many feet. When the Brazilian ships steamed past, they froze among the bushes or stood neck-high in the mud. Finally, they arrived in the clearings around Monte Lindo, filthy, hungry but happy. Over three weeks, the Mariscal's army regrouped upriver and the Allies had not noticed a thing. If Martínez, Alén and the last few troops could get away, the extraordinary evacuation would be complete.

On 23 March, the Allies woke to realisation. Two Allied ships were stationed between the Chaco bank and Humaitá, trapping two Paraguayan ships in the lagoon. The commander of the first, seeing capture was imminent, sent his crew over the side to swim for the Chaco shore and fired his ship. The other was the *Tacuarí*, and she made for a creek and away. When her paddles thrashed the air, the crew scuttled her, threw her artillery into the mud and fired her hull.

In Paso Pucú, an Argentine division wandered and looted the Mariscal's headquarters. In Elisa's house, they found several unopened packing cases with the label of a Parisian warehouse stamped on the side. They contained large quantities of furniture which had come in just ahead of the blockade and never been used. Someone looked beneath her gilded bronze bed and found a pair of black satin shoes. An Argentine general sent them to his wife in Buenos Aires.

'I received the booty of Mme Lynch,' she wrote to her husband. 'After three years' blockade, Mme Lynch leaves her elegant latest fashion shoes lying about . . . it is a pity that woman is not López' wife. Her heroism would be worthy of every eulogy, for following the destiny of her husband.'[19]

In Humaitá, completely cut off from the Mariscal's army, Alen, Martínez and 4,000 people were surrounded.

In Luque, now capital of the Republic, those who had compromised themselves were scared. They had thought the Mariscal trapped and starving in the south. 'How great,' wrote Centurión, 'must their surprise have been when the Mariscal came through the Chaco and presented himself . . .'[20]

At camp in Monte Lindo, Thompson and other foreign officers wondered quietly if the Mariscal was about to make a bolt for Bolivia and why the Brazilians had not cut off the Chaco road when they took control of the river. Eight thousand people slept in huts and hammocks, played their harps and danced, drank maté and waited. The *politicos* lay in their irons as they had in Humaitá and Paso Pucú. Bedoya and Berges wandered in semi-confinement and rehearsed craven stories of inability and fear. Madame talked in French to the Mariscal of events in the capital and the Mariscal wrote a letter to Vice-President Sanchez.

An extraordinary event has been brought to my notice: that the vice-presidential government called a council as three ironclads approached Asunción, to decide whether or not to attack them. Such . . . was the cause of my calling Minister Berges and his companions . . . Such alarming facts induced me to interrogate Bedoya and it has emerged that he, in agreement with Benigno, was to cause an uprising which was to become a revolutionary government which, in cooperation with the enemy, for shame! would surrender the country. And that Vice-President Sanchez was involved in all this . . .' [as the] vile instrument [of Benigno].[21]

Orders went to Luque that those who had attended the council of notables were to present themselves at Monte Lindo: Comandante Gomez, Minister Fernandez and others came fearfully across the river.

The Mariscal was shooting in the dark. Neither he nor Elisa had real proof that the confused events in the capital were not the product of incompetence and confusion among the notables, manipulated by the ambition of Benigno and Bedoya. The interrogations which now began in Monte Lindo seemed to confirm this. Bishop Palacios presided, with Secretary Aveiro at his side 'with the object of asking them for explanations about what had happened when the ironclads arrived at Asunción, and about the hesitation over firing on those boats . . .'[22] Coherent stories emerged from the men called before the Mariscal's unsmiling secretaries: alone and leaderless, they had convoked the meeting without the Mariscal's permission because he could not be contacted; they had allowed themselves to be led by Benigno. Then Benigno himself was ordered to Monte Lindo. The first words between the brothers were cold.

'Well,' said the Mariscal. 'And what were you all up to in the capital?'

'Sir, as we had no news of you, or of the army since Humaitá was besieged by the enemy, we thought the moment had come to consider and to resolve how to save ourselves and our interests.'

'You see, Caballero,' said the Mariscal to his favourite officer, 'they are more Brazilian than the Brazilians.'[23] He did not know what to believe and who to blame. He had refused his ministers the power to act without consultation and they had not been able to consult him. He had left a syphilitic and incompetent brother at the Ministry of War. He had left his capital guarded by a garrison too small to offer effective resistance to an invading enemy.

Benigno ate that night *en famille*. Bedoya was treated less gently.

During the interrogation that afternoon 'Berges and Bedoya became somewhat heated. The latter . . . was chivvied by Berges and the others and, irritated, Bedoya rolled up his sleeves and said in a menacing tone to Berges and the others that if what they had proposed had taken place, things would be different . . .'[24] When Bedoya left the session, he walked crossly through camp and in front of López' tent, neglecting to raise his hat as he did so. 'López ordered one of his adjutants to take his belt to his brother in law until he learnt respect for his superiors and this happened, to the considerable surprise of those present . . .'[25] Later, Bedoya was asked what his comment had meant. He referred, he said, to 'a simple family conversation, in which Berges had joined, about who would succeed the Mariscal' should he be captured or killed by the Allies, 'and that all had said it must be Don Benigno'[26]. The interrogations stopped there, for the time being. No proof of malice, or true conspiracy, had emerged.

The River Tebicuarí was to be fortified to hold back the Allies, advancing overland from the Quadrilateral towards Asunción. George Thompson was given eighty men and 120 boys to erect defences to close off the estuary, 500 yards wide. He chose to defend Fortín, a promontory accessible from the land only over one narrow neck of dense *estero*. From here, a garrison could observe enemy shipping to the north and south and had the entire width of the estuary within firing range. For three days, his naked sappers went down to the red river's edge and built their defences. When troops marched through the bog to take up their position, the way was safe for the Mariscal to cross.

The canoes slid silently out from the banks of Monte Lindo. The precious cannon were taken across; the beasts were swum.

Elisa's boxes and crates, her wardrobe, carriage and piano went over, followed by Elisa, the bishop, the boys and the notables while observers in the reeds above and below watched for the Brazilian ironclads which steamed occasionally by. Past the new defences at Fortín, the land was flat and wet for four miles, formed of the same bogs and floating pastures of the south. As they approached the ford on the high road from Villa del Pilar, the land rose slightly and a few houses stood about an earth plaza of thirty square yards, where the soil was solid enough to support them in the shade of an orange grove. This was San Fernando.

The army camped squalidly in the mud and drained the land. Huts were built. Arsenal workers were brought from Asunción and set up workshops to repair guns and cannon; there were hospitals and a little octagonal church near the central plaza where the Mariscal spent much time, for he had 'taken a fit of church-going'[27].

The interrogations of the notables had ceased; their stories, after all, had been plausible. In Luque, there was relief when one after another returned, reinstated in his post and doubly cautious. Four men continued in semi-detention in San Fernando. They were the three named as presidential candidates in Cuverville's dispatch and Vice-President Sanchez, now seventy-four and trembling with fever.

They waited in Luque too, a city crowded into a village. It was the fourth winter of the war; families wrapped in blankets lay on the verandahs and war widows begged to feed their children. Some asked permission to return to Asunción and take food from their houses; a few obtained it. Those who had been sure the war was over in February could not understand what had happened. The Allies could have taken Asunción; they could have attacked López on the Chaco bank; they could have replaced him. Now the Mariscal was running the country from San Fernando and Benigno, Bedoya, Berges and Vice-President Sanchez were in his grasp. The peace party was headless but there were few officers, officials or merchants in Luque who had not had some dealing with these men and proximity was complicity in the eyes of the Mariscal. Everyone was jumpy; the slightest of pressure was felt.

From the temporary French consulate in Luque, Cuverville reported that Washburn was now 'most embarrassed by his current situation; he too thought Paraguay completely lost and did not doubt the Allies would occupy Asunción . . .'[28] Realisation had come for Washburn as soon as the Allies sent their few pathetic shots into Asunción on 19 February. The vague understandings between Benigno and Caxias had been given greater weight by the Paraguayans than by the Brazilians. Washburn also realised grimly that he had over-exposed himself. The Mariscal had ceased or suspended interrogations but if these were resurrected, the name of the US envoy would rapidly surface. The wrath of the Mariscal might be withstood by the deft threat of a US gunboat but his own government would be horrified.

Nevertheless, those who had used Washburn's diplomatic bag or other shady routes to Caxias had begun to breathe more easily as the notables returned to their posts. Major Fernandez was once again at the Ministry, representing Venancio; Major Gomez was back in charge of the garrison, the functions of Vice-President Sanchez had been entrusted to three of his fellow notables. At the end of April, Minister Berges returned to his *quinta* on the outskirts of Asunción, publicly reinstated in the Mariscal's confidence, visited by Charles Washburn, who quietly took away a sheaf of documents to be hidden in the US legation. Still those who had any inkling of what might have been uncovered at Monte Lindo sweated. No one knew what the others knew; no one was completely sure what the Mariscal knew.

At the end of April, news came that the US *Wasp* was in

Allied waters off the Quadrilateral. Washburn's urgent requests to be relieved had been answered and the gunboat had come to take him and his family off. His guests in the legation, now nearly forty in number, begged him not to go for this was the only shelter in Paraguay from the arbitrary wrath of the Mariscal. They knew that as soon as the consul left and his house was divested of its immunity, they would be seized and taken to San Fernando to join the *politicos*, exposed to the elements and the fire of the enemy; or forced to fight in the trenches at the front; or shot. The French and Italian consuls could not be trusted. Chapperon was little known and little liked and he shared a house in Luque with Cuverville, known to be Madame's creature. Masterman, Vasconcellos, Carreras and the other frightened foreigners waited to hear when the *Wasp* would be let through by the Allies.

Around the Mariscal, brooding and suspicious behind the triple cordon of sentinels who ringed his new house, the life of San Fernando regained the rhythm of Paso Pucú. Every fifteen minutes, a sentry came to check the sentinels and these sentries were in their turn observed by López' personal bodyguard. He received daily reports from his spies in the US legation and pored over details of menus and the number of people who sat at Mrs Washburn's table each night. He received desperate dispatches from Paulino Alén, still holding Humaitá, hungry and sick and in dire need of relief.

The troops sat and smoked. They read the *Cabichuí*, a newspaper edited by Centurión, full of stories of heroes, coarse jokes about Mitre and Dom Pedro and woodcut cartoons of naïve perfection. They cleaned their weapons and made their reverences to the Mariscal and his lady, should they ever come by, were flogged and beaten and punished by their father-officers for transgressions, danced and played their drums and waited. There was nothing the Mariscal could do now to take the initiative. They must wait: wait and see where and how the enemy would attack; parry, and wait again. Sometimes they heard bombardments from the estuary, when the Brazilians steamed past and lobbed a few shots at Thompson. They squatted and drank maté until they were dazed and motionless and stared across the marshes to where they could not see the enemy. They were tired.

Life for the First Family, too, fell into a familiar pattern. Madame and the boys lived in a house near the Mariscal's. The boys ran in and out of both, followed by Major Fernandez (unrelated to Minister Fernandez), an aide appointed escort to the Lynch-López sons. He accompanied them about the camp, to lessons and meals, taking them to see their father, bringing them home safe to their mother. There were all the familiar faces in the huts and houses around: the generals, Secretaries Caminos and Aveiro, the Mariscal's bodyguard, the British doctors, George Thompson when he was not in Fortín, engineers Volpy and Burrell, the men from the arsenal, Padre Maíz. At dinner, they chatted to the bishop, General Resquin, Uncle Barrios and occasionally Uncle Benigno and Uncle Bedoya. The Mariscal sat at one end, drinking his accustomed bottle; the others sat below, drinking an inferior one just as they had in Paso Pucú, Calle Fábrica de Balas, and the house on Mercado Guazú. There was conversation, below the lingering stink of treachery which the council of notables had stirred up and the Monte Lindo interrogations had not quite dispelled. The unseen enemy beyond the low horizons held everyone's life suspended. It was Benigno, the constant thorn, who took the first, secret action.

Before the war, he had been on terms of easy acquaintanceship with the boys' escort, Major Fernandez. In April, a cornet-player of the corps which guarded Benigno's hut was bribed by 'an offer of abundant recompense'[29] to pass messages to the Major. If these were written, the cornet-player may not have understood them. If they were verbal, he was a brave man, for Benigno proposed assassination. The only people who had access to the person of the Mariscal, outside the inner circle of Madame, the bishop, Padre Maíz, generals and private secretaries, was Major Fernandez. It was an appalling and a terrifying request. The major hesitated and feared. Finally, he approached an ironworker in the camp, commissioned a knife and waited.

Then Bedoya's guards came with the news that they had found him dead. Aveiro thought it was suicide. 'He refused to take any food and the cuts inflicted by the irons on his legs, he himself tried to aggravate, and thus . . . he died in prison, his leg gangrened.'[30] Others suspected poison, but not on the orders of the Mariscal, for there were those in camp who feared Bedoya's indiscretions.

In the first week of June, Elisa Lynch went to Luque. She moved into the house opposite the Ministry, on the street from the railway station, and was besieged by supplicants wanting news of their men at the front. The Mariscal's birthday was approaching and his gift from the ladies of Paraguay was to be finalised. This year it was to be a golden inkstand costing 5,310 pesos and a bejewelled Phrygian cap, the conical cap which symbolises the liberty of ancient Europe, designed by Alessandro Ravizza, at a cost of 400 ounces of gold. The *comisionada*, the lady commissioner, was Señora Mercedes de Roca, who had been a friend of Elisa's since she and her husband arrived in Asunción. One day a week, she came to Luque from her house near the lake, to discuss progress.

Dr Tristan Roca was a chemist and had been employed in the hospital corps when the couple first came from Bolivia in 1858. He had recently been made editor of an army newspaper, *El Centinela*. All Bolivians in Paraguay were cautious that year. The Bolivian president, General Melgarejo, had dangled the possibility of help before the Mariscal for years. He had just been bought by the Brazilians and declared his neutrality. From the *Centinela*, Dr Roca declared his disgust. All commerce with Bolivia, across the only border not blockaded, was banned. Officially, it stopped immediately; unofficially, contraband continued. Money was being sent out of Paraguay down secret routes and many of the foreign merchants in Luque knew it. Some even participated: Roca himself, despite his editorials, was accused of receiving goods from across the frontier. Even Simón Fidanza, the Genovese shipowner, arms-dealer and millionaire whose loyalty had been unquestioned, despite one early request to be allowed to leave Paraguay, was involved in clandestine dealings with the *altiplano*. Benigno's name was mentioned, and those of the Portuguese semi-diplomats, Leite Pereira and Vasconcellos. Even the Phrygian cap was tainted, for Fidanza was proposing to send into Bolivia more than the cap would cost; his twenty-five per cent 'commission' on 400 ounces of gold would not come back into Paraguay.

One night, over-trusting, slightly drunk or tired, Dr Roca talked of all this to Gumersindo Benítez, one of the notables just reinstated after the hearings of Monte Lindo, and Benítez' report was at San Fernando within hours. Suspicions were immediately ignited in the Mariscal's mind that the Monte Lindo interrogations had been a sham. On 15 June, police in Luque arrested Simón Fidanza. On 16 June, Leite Pereira and Vasconcellos fled to the US legation.

When Benigno López heard that Fidanza was being brought to San Fernando for interrogation, he realised that the illegal transfer of money abroad was unimportant compared to what else the man might confess under torture. He sent urgently for the cornet player. They were in conference when a guard came unexpectedly into the hut, the cornet-player was taken away to confess and Major Fernandez joined

Simón Fidanza in irons. On the orders of Bishop Palacios, he was tortured. In his pain, he implicated Benigno, Comandante Gomez of the Asunción garrison and a priest, Padre Moreno, in conspiracy against the life of the Mariscal. Padre Moreno was subjected to the same foul treatment and gave his tormentors the name of a woman, Ramona Eguisquiza de Decoud. It was on 8 July that she, interrogated without torture, according to Secretary Aveiro, confessed to the true, terrifying extent of the conspiracy. 'She told of having seen letters exchanged between certain foreigners and Comandante Gomez, [and] had seen the list of people who composed the Directory and various others of different nationalities who were affiliated to the conspiracy.'[31] One was Simón Fidanza. She gave her interrogators the names of over 100 foreigners and Paraguayans in Luque, San Fernando and Cerro León involved in the conspiracy. The Mariscal had been hood-winked by the united front presented at Monte Lindo. There was a grand conspiracy afoot. Orders were telegraphed to Luque. On 13 July, Dr Roca and over fifty others were arrested, ironed and sent aboard a steamer for San Fernando.

The terror of San Fernando had begun.

Chapter Fourteen

When Tristan Roca was sent south, his wife Mercedes fled to Madame's house where Elisa kept her 'with many other foreigners, sewing day and night, being most tender with her'[1]. She spent six days there. On 20 July, Elisa gave her a present for Tristan and she left to ask news of her husband from the Luque police. When she came back, Elisa's door was barred and Elisa had gone to Asunción.

Many in Luque must have suspected that it was Elisa who had discovered the conspiracy, in conversation with Cuverville, and reported it to the Mariscal. They would have been wrong and, separated from the Mariscal in San Fernando, knowing as she did his eternal suspicion, his tendency to believe the worst and his addiction to brain-fuddling drink, Elisa was in as much fear as anyone. She had already sent money out of the country down her own secret routes and the Mariscal knew it. She had been in Luque when the contraband traffic with Bolivia was discovered and had said nothing. She had in fact been impeccably loyal – her name never appeared in the denunciations made at San Fernando – but in those days of terror, while the Mariscal drank and raged, there was no reason he should trust Elisa

Lynch any more than the other friends, relatives and officers who were being exposed as traitors. She could not compromise herself in any way. Señora de Roca must fend for herself. She did so in the streets, for her landlady would not take her back, *traidora* as she now was, and she slept with her two infants on verandahs, and sold her clothes to feed them. The arrests continued. Dozens of men and a few women were taken away each day, by train to Asunción, in ox-carts through the streets, onto steamers in the bay. It was a wet and unpleasant night on 21 July, when they came for Alonso Taylor, master mason.

> After working hard at the soap works of Luque, [Taylor wrote] I returned to my house at 10 o'clock at night. Shortly afterwards, a cavalry soldier knocked and told me through the door that I was ordered into the capital by the Minister of War and Marine [Fernandez] but he could not tell me why. But I knew that it was useless to resist . . . [At the dock, he found] a crowd of men. I dismounted and was immediately, despite my remonstrances, put in irons and placed with 8 or 9 other prisoners until the morning.[2]

Elisa Lynch was in Asunción that night. She left her house on Calle Fábrica de Balas after dark and walked to the US legation, a small and lonely community in a deserted city.

> I knew instantly, [Washburn said] that her visit portended something important, either good or evil. I hoped for the best and in conversation with her expressed my surprise at what I had heard had taken place; so many people had been arrested, some of whom I supposed were the most loyal men in the country and many of them I had believed to be the most devoted friends of López. I could not understand what it all meant. [He was lying.] She said that

a great conspiracy had been discovered, but of the details of it she would not give me any information, she would not be allowed to do so, but there was no crime conceivable but that the conspirators had not contemplated committing. I said, if that were the case, it was as much in my interest as that of anybody else to have it discovered, for if they were contemplating any general massacre, as they had none of them ever confided anything to me about it, but had studiously kept it secret from me, evidently I should be one of their victims. She said, 'Oh no, that is not in their plans at all, I believe.' She said, the discovery of this plot had been a great blow to the President. Many of his best friends, those for whom he had done the most and on whom he most relied for support had been proven false and treacherous.

They flirted about each other, neither sure exactly what the other knew. No one, said Washburn, from the US legation could possibly have been involved.

'But they have confessed,' she said. I replied that under certain circumstances confession was no evidence. People under fear, or on promise of reward, might confess to facts of which they were not guilty. 'Oh no', she said, 'there has been no constraint put upon them. It has all been voluntary. The President could never use restraint, or force them to confess against their will. He is very kind-hearted.'[3]

The following day, Alonso Taylor and the other prisoners from Luque went aboard a steamer and waited.

Mrs Lynch and her eldest son Francisco [Panchito] came on board with some officers about 11 . . . As she left the steamer, Mrs Lynch looked, but she took no apparent notice of me, although she used to be very kind to me, and my daughter was often in her house. I had asked an officer who was on board and used to be very intimate with me, if he would let me speak to her, but he said that being a prisoner I could speak to no one, much less to her. He abused me, and seemed to delight in my misfortune.[4]

San Fernando, said Centurión, was hell.

Wherever one looked, one saw only prisoners, all respectable, well-known people, with whom one was linked by family ties, friendship or obligation. On all sides, one heard only the groans of suffering, moans of pain and desperation and the shouts of the many innocent people who slander had thrown into an infernal vortex from which no one emerged alive. Our state of mind is indescribable. Terror and suspicion reigned. We watched and observed, but we did not say a word, offer any thought of generosity or inquire about the fate of the condemned, or know what went on in the tribunals. Any manifestation of charity, compassion or humanity, such as a sensitive heart might feel, was considered an act of treason.[5]

Six tribunals were established, each under the jurisdiction of two *fiscales de sangre* – 'judges of blood'. They acted according to the old Spanish *leyes de partida*, the military law which the Mariscal had declared when the Allies passed the Quadrilateral, and the *leyes de partida* defined any who had known of treason, and not denounced it, as traitors. It was a witch-hunt. People named others in fear and pain, threatened with the lash, the *cepo uruguayana*, the stocks, the hammer which smashed fingers pinned to a block. No one knew who was under suspicion and who had already been incriminated. All foreigners were suspect. All those they knew were suspect, and those who knew the people the foreigners knew. The net was thrown wider, and wider again.

Elisa returned to San Fernando just before the Mariscal's birthday, in time to hear Bishop Palacios' suggestion. 'As the case [against the conspirators] was so far advanced, and as its subject matter was such that even nods and winks could be taken as full proof, the trials should be ended and all the accused should be hanged.'[6] General Barrios supported the suggestion. The bishop added, 'as the reason for his haste, that an attack was about to be made as the land forces were so near. To which the Mariscal replied that he did not want to proceed thus, that the trial would carry on until the last day in which events of the war would prevent its continuing.'[7] Neither Palacios nor Barrios knew that they were already marked men. When George Thompson came from Fortín to dine with López shortly afterwards, Palacios and Barrios were still guests at his table but General Bruguez, another old favourite, was not. 'One of López' little boys asked where he was and everyone smiled and told the child, "He's gone away".'[8]

It rained incessantly. The nights were icy. The prisoners slept in the open, in corrals marked out by hide stretched around stakes. 'The mode of securing us was simple but dreadfully painful. To one of the stakes a hide rope was made fast; prisoner No. 1 lay down on his back, and loops were knotted fast round both ankles; then No. 2 lay down two yards off, and was tied to the same rope. This was repeated until the row was full; then another was commenced the same way and so on. The ends of the ropes were secured to other stakes and they were stretched by the full strength of 2 or 3 men until they were taut as harp strings.'[9] It was called the cepo de lazo. 'My ankles were soon covered with sores,' Mr Taylor said, 'and almost dislocated by the strain on them.'[10] Female prisoners were flogged in the 'A-shaped huts' where they slept. The men in the corrals could hear their screams.

Hundreds of people lay in irons behind the trees on the far side of camp. They were tortured each day. Every member of the meeting convened by Benigno López above the station of Paraguarí was there. Tristan Roca was in irons; so were José Berges; Pedro Burgos, father of the Mariscal's mistress; Ramón Franco, in whose house Madame had spent her first night in Asunción; Sinforoso Cáceres, her business partner, who had received the money for the golden inkstand; countless others, now almost unrecognisable in their squalor, their faces bruised and skinned. Before their inquisitors, they named Venancio, Rafaela and Inocencia López, judges, ministers of government, deputies, priests, seminarists, the dean of Asunción cathedral, foreign diplomats and the hangers-on at their consulates; Herr von Treuenfeld, who had come to lay the telegraph line; Mr Stark, English merchant; Mr Watts, ship's engineer from Limehead; M Anglade, one of the French merchants from whom Madame used to buy her haber-dashery; Gustave Bayon de Libertat, chancellor of Cuverville's consulate, less astute than his superior; the Italians, Swiss, Germans, French, British, Uruguayans, Argentines, North Americans, Brazilians who had dutifully gone to the Club Nacional to subscribe to *ofrendas* and pay for the arches, illuminations and public balls which celebrated the army's 'victories'; even the name of Juana Paula Carrillo de López emerged from those in pain. All except la Presidenta were brought to San Fernando, went before the *fiscales de sangre*, were lashed with ropes made of hide or jungle creeper, tied by their feet to the rope-fence of the corral and tortured.

In Humaitá, they were starving.

General Caballero's men across the river in Timbó sought desperately to send relief. They killed bullocks, lashed their carcasses to a bamboo raft and covered them over with grass and flowers to resemble a *camalote*, but most were caught in the current and floated back to the Chaco shore further down. When the Mariscal sent a futile order to resist to the last, Colonel Alen put a shotgun to his head. The bullet took out one eye and his brain lost control of his limbs, but he did not die. When, at last, the Mariscal sent a telegraph to evacuate the last 9,000 and bring them to San Fernando, the messenger who swam through the ironclads with the order gave it to Lieutenant-Colonel Martínez.

The Mariscal's birthday, 24 July 1868, was marked by extraordinary events. Colonel Martínez ordered shouts and laughter and the sound of fiesta. The bands played throughout the night and under their cover, the first of the starving garrison slid into their lily-draped canoes and crossed to the lagoon, with Timbó at its head. With them in a stretcher went the broken mind and body of Paulino Alen. Martínez was to bring up the rear. Over 4,000 crossed before dawn, then two Brazilian ships spotted the suspicious *camalotes* and opened fire. The last 4,000 were caught in the lagoon. They scrambled onto a little island and were surrounded. Ten thousand bombs exploded over and above them that week. They had nothing to eat. There was frost each night. Boys swam from the island with knives between their teeth to board the besieging Brazilian vessels; each night, canoes put out to paddle silently among them and make Timbó, where the vanguard waited. Two thousand more people crossed to the Chaco bank that week amid the flashes and crocodiles and spray from explosions. Each evening, a telegraph went from Timbó to San Fernando to give the Mariscal the numbers arrived, the numbers still marooned.

On the eighth day, (they said) the Allies realised there were women and children on the island. The bombs stopped and men with white flags and proposals came. Martínez rejected them. For four more days, no one ate. Then a Brazilian priest landed with a crucifix in his hands, and persuaded Martínez to save the lives of those on the island. Martínez was swaying so badly from hunger and fatigue that he could hardly salute the Argentine general who came ashore, but he demanded his officers be allowed to keep their swords and no men be forced to enlist in the Allied army. When the last Paraguayans left the island, there was applause from the Brazilian ships. Of all the acts of courage of the wretchedly misled Paraguayans, the last evacuation of Humaitá was the most extraordinary.

Colonel Martínez was called for courteous interrogation. What, his captors asked, held the Paraguayan men at their posts? He replied it was fear of what the Mariscal would do to their womenfolk if they refused or deserted.

When news of Martínez' surrender arrived at San Fernando, the Mariscal sent a telegraph to Luque and soldiers went to Elisa Lynch's house, where Juliana Insfrán de Martínez was living and brought her back.

She went before the judges of the fourth commission. They gave her a chair and asked her what she knew about 'the revolution'. She knew nothing. Was she aware that General Vicente Barrios and others had declared she was involved? Their accusation was false, she knew nothing of any revolution. What had her husband told her last time she saw him in Humaitá about the plot to depose the Mariscal and hand the country over to the enemy? Her husband had said nothing about it, she told them; her husband was incapable of dishonour and treachery.

The Mariscal read the report of her first interrogation and ordered she be whipped until she give a satisfactory answer. The first flogging took place within hours; the second, third, fourth, fifth and others over the next weeks. When it became clear that even scraped of her skin she would not yield, the Mariscal ordered she be put into the *cepo uruguayana*. It was done in his presence. In the grossest pain, Juliana shouted her innocence. Unless she confessed, he said, she would be tortured to death. She was put in the *cepo uruguayana* six times.

Executions of the traitors in the corrals all around San Fernando began on 4 August. Forty-five people died that day and the firing of the execution squad was so prolonged that the sentries called in alarm that the Brazilians had come. 'Those who could not walk were taken in carts, the others marched down two by two in irons. Then a volley and a few straggling shots gave us food for meditation. If the victims had good clothes on, we saw the guards and the lower grade of officers come back wearing them.'[11]

There were executions every day from 4 August. When there were not enough bullets to spare for firing squads, those to be killed were tied to trees and lanced. The executioners waited for the names of their next victims. Their leader was Toro Pichai, 'one of the most barbarous and inhuman officers in the army'[12], a man made for the dirty side of war. He delighted in the torture fields of San Fernando and, under his leadership, the lancers of the Cabeza Florida regiment became expert practitioners of death. Their appetite for the infliction of pain consumed them. They became vampirical. Fearful parties were offered them after their executions, and the camp women were brought with armfuls of flowers which they placed in the killers' kepis. Sometimes children took their place in the execution squads and then the deaths were slow, for they did not have the strength to kill cleanly.

Lieutenant Maciel, *fiscal de sangre* and secretary to the Mariscal, divided his time between the tribunal and headquarters, where he wrote up correspondence for both his master and Madame. He was one of few who knew that while López tried his citizens for treason, he was writing letters to 'the consuls in Rosario, Montevideo, Buenos Aires and other places, asking them to send the various sums of money they had in their care to different parts of Europe'.[13]

Maciel remembered other administrative operations. 'To Madame Lynch,' he stated, 'I made out *Escritos de Transferencia* of houses which had been confiscated. Large stretches of land were made over to her at nominal prices. López was informed of these transfers, all of which were carried out with his approval.'[14]

The property of those convicted of treason was forfeit to the state and could be sold to private individuals at whatever price the state wished. This was not a principle peculiar to Paraguay: traitors have everywhere been dispossessed by the country they betray. What was peculiar was that the Mariscal was the state of Paraguay and the property which became forfeit to him in one little house in San Fernando was acquired on the other side of the plaza in another, where Elisa Lynch lived.

The roles assigned by Maciel to Elisa and López in these dealings are unequivocal. López, he said, 'was informed'. Elisa was the instigator. Although López' notion of the state as himself and of dissent as treachery was horrific, sincerity looms through the horror. He appears genuinely to have considered those executed at San Fernando as traitors. Elisa inspires a different horror: she looted from the dead, acquiring their estates with the same cold cupidity as the soldiers who tore rings from dead fingers after battle.

The arrests continued, and the torture and executions. No one was safe from the denunciations of those in the *cepo* and those tied to the pole to receive 100 lashes with a cowhide rope.

One day, when the bishop was lunching with [López] and seated at his side, a spy approached and spoke to him arrogantly: 'get out of that chair; it does not belong to you,

you do not deserve to sit there, you are vile, you are odious, you are a traitor to the country and *el Supremo*, the best monarch in the world . . .' Seeing himself thus insulted, the bishop went white and looked uncertainly at López, as if imploring his mercy. López, seeing his friend thus, exclaimed . . . 'is it really possible that this great friend of mine is in league with the vile traitors of the *patria* and the government?' The bishop sought to defend himself but could not because of the hail of blows which fell upon him, accompanied by insults and blasphemies as [the guard] shoved him from the dining-room . . .[15]

He went before the second tribunal, presided over by Padre Maíz, wept, and confessed he had not denounced the treasonable plans of General Barrios. The soldiers then brought General Barrios, who took off his sword and placed it on the Mariscal's table, then made for the hut where his wife waited her turn before the tribunals. From outside, an officer heard his shout: 'You wished to see me brought to this!' and entered to find Barrios with his throat slit by his own hand and Inocencia, bloodied, screaming for help. The incision was not deep enough.

Intelligence came that the Allies were moving north and camp broke before Bishop Palacios could be interrogated. The next line of defence would be just south of the capital, where Pikisyry creek emptied into the River Paraguay and the gentle hills of Lomas Valentinas overlooked the last lagoons and *esteros*. The army was set in weary motion. Colonel Thompson and his men began to dig the last great trenches of the war along Pikisyry creek. They erected the last river defences in the bay of Angostura. The condemned, and those under interrogation, went north in irons with the marching soldiers. Antonio de la Carreras, Benigno López and the Portuguese consul were locked in one swaying, stinking, cart.

Alonzo Taylor saw the covered bullock-carts in which Rafaela and Inocencia López were imprisoned go by, 'about 7 foot long, 4 foot wide and 5 high . . . the front and the windows had been blocked up and the door behind was secured with a padlock but an opening had been made in front, about 6 inches high, through which I suppose the food etc. would be handed in to them.'[16] The bishop struggled in the irons Padre Maíz had ordered, the same ones Maíz had worn when Palacios convicted him of conspiracy in 1862.

Behind them, in San Fernando, the tiny garrison left to guard the Mariscal's back was massacred. 'Vultures rose from the bloated carcases of cattle; and Paraguayan corpses, in leathern waist-wraps, floated face downwards, rising and falling after a ghostly fashion, with the scour and ripple of the stream.'[17]

On 10 September, the US *Wasp* was off Angostura, Charles Washburn and his family left Asunción and his house guests were at the mercy of the police who had been waiting outside the legation for three months. As soon as the US consul turned the corner of the street, they were arrested. In the police station, they were manacled and bars were attached to their ankles then, seated sideways on mules, they made the fourteen-hour journey in pain and fear to Villetta, a few miles from Pikysyry creek, where the first of the San Fernando detainees were encamped. Rope corrals had already been prepared.

'What a scene of misery!' wrote Masterman. 'Within a gently sloping hillside, which had been roughly cleared of brushwood, and about 100 feet square, lay forty prisoners in huts, or under blankets on the ground.'[18] He recognised Dr Antonio de la Carreras, whose 'fingers had been smashed into a shapeless mass'[19]; Venancio, Alonzo Taylor and others. None dared greet each other. Some prisoners of war were with them, 'in the last stage of misery, almost, some quite, naked, covered with wounds and the majority too feeble to walk and lastly, a group of felons, distinguished by a single iron ring on the right ankle; these seemed scarcely human, were without a rag of clothing and generally lay in a huddled heap on the ground . . . blows, kicks and the vilest abuse being showered on them by the soldiers.'[20]

That evening, he was taken before one of the *fiscales de sangre* and told to confess he and Mr Washburn had conspired to depose the Mariscal. He refused, and was put in the *cepo uruguayana* until he agreed to tell them what they wanted. Then he returned to the corrals on the hill.

> From one of the hovels near me crept out on all fours Don Benigno López . . . – he was well-dressed, but heavily ironed; and from another, a spectral old man I was long in recognising as the ex-Minister for Foreign Affairs, Don José Berges . . . Then two very old men, evidently in their second childhood; they were without a rag to cover them: one was in irons and could only crawl tremblingly on his hands and knees; the other looked round with a timid smile on his silly face, pleased with the bustle around him and evidently but faintly conscious of what was going on . . . what would their offence be? A wailing complaint for the loss of their few comforts, a passionate lament for the death of their sons or grandchildren; an idle word spoken in garrulous old age and construed into treason . . .[21]

From their vantage point on the hill the next morning, the newcomers saw a 'dense cloud of dust and a heaving tumultuous throng . . . men, women and children in three vast herds, hemmed in by soldiers on foot and on horseback, fully armed and with sticks in their hands, with which they thrashed those outside and those who fell from exhaustion.'[22] These were the last 600 prisoners from San Fernando.

Then Madame Lynch appeared, driving a coach and pair. As she passed the prisoners, 'she bowed with a gracious smile, we took our caps off to her, all well knowing that a word from her could send us to the scaffold, or worse, on the morrow'[23]. She must have recognised every face there.

They marched six miles to Lomas Valentinas, through grass thick as reeds, along tortuous paths, those in the rear passing the bodies of others who had lain down from exhaustion and been kicked to death by the guard. The rain came down in torrents. Just inland of Pikisyry creek, a camp was created as it had been on each stage of the retreat: huts, headquarters, urination cauldrons, powder dumps, a chapel, a house for the Mariscal, another for Madame. The first survivors of Humaitá began to arrive. The interrogations began again, and the torture. Masterman saw Benigno taken away and saw him return, 'his face frightfully distorted by the agony he had suffered'[24].

A letter came to the Mariscal from la Presidenta. She begged for news of the two daughters and two sons under arrest and still uncharged.

September 10, 1868, Pikisyry
My dear mother
I received your welcome letter of the 3rd inst. and I still live to acknowledge this upon the 6th anniversary of my father's death, through the mercy of God, who has vouchsafed to spare me, despite so many machinations of my own ones and of strangers . . .

I cannot express to you, Mamma, all the pain with which I read your letter . . . I should have expected, however hard it might have been, something more natural and frank. Poor Mamma! You perhaps do not know that I have already passed through every possible bitterness in this monstrous affair without daring to complain. But my martyrdom reached its crisis when I learned the facts. I fear on my part further to embitter this day by dwelling on a subject not less bitter than the worst which happened six years ago [when Benigno and others opposed his election to the presidency]. Useless were all my endeavours and vain were all my hopes; and again I explain – or rather others will explain for me – the cause. All arrayed themselves against me and none busied himself save with his victim. But God permitted light to shine through the darkness; my enemies were all confounded and I am still here. I am all in all to you and would to heaven! – would to heaven! that I could be so for all those who did not think to require my help.

Venancio, Benigno and Inocencia are in good health.

Were I allowed a word of advice, I would recommend you not to show excessive alarm concerning all that is happening. It would hardly be prudent, though a mother's tender heart request expression.

I receive your welcome letter rather as that of a mother to her son, than as of a supplicant to the magistrate; the latter case would only do harm.

Please be assured, Mamma, of all the love with which your blessing is begged by

Your most obedient son

Francisco Solano López[25]

The Mariscal was in constant pain. He had toothache and indigestion, aggravated by heavy drinking. He was anxious about his sons and spoke continually of his fears for them. Late one night, Elisa's household was awoken by the frantic barks of the dog, Loto, and the sound of overturned chairs in the room where the children slept. Elisa rushed from her own and saw a large and thrashing viper in the dog's jaws, damaged but alive. Behind her came a soldier of the Mariscal's guard, bayonet fixed, who killed the snake as the family watched. The next morning, Loto was gone. Soldiers joined the children to search for their pet on the outskirts of camp where the prisoners lay chained among their huts, but he was not found. Their parents explained he had gone to a quiet place to die.

One day, a party brought in a stretcher bearing something half-living, half-dead, 'in a leather sling suspended from a plank, an almost naked man, his head resting on his knees. I would have thought he was dead were it not for his pathetic cries when they tipped him out onto the ground.'[26] He was Colonel Alén, the traitor who had failed to hold Humaitá and attempted suicide rather than face the Mariscal.

In another hut, Juliana Insfrán de Martínez waited to know when and how she would die in expiation of her husband's crime. She was 'given' to an officer who took charge of her 'with great pleasure'.

The soldiers waited for the Allies to come as they had at San Fernando and Thompson's men built trenches along Pikisyry creek. To the south, the enemy would have to cross the last of the *esteros*, and the Paraguayans would trap them in the marsh and murder them as they had at Curupayty.

Three foreign warships were moving regularly between Angostura and the Allied base in the south for Britain, France and Italy had all sent missions to take off their distressed citizens and this time, López was letting a few of them leave. Madame and the Mariscal had determined not to keep the neutral captains away, but to charm them. The strategy had worked on the consuls, Chapperon and Cuverville. On 4 November, HMS *Beacon* moored in the river and Captain Parsons came ashore to be given a special tour of the camp, cleaned for the occasion, no prisoners in sight, no instruments of torture left about. Madame cooked plum pudding that night and at dinner they explained he could, of course, take any British away who wished, but none wished to go. Only one Briton was allowed to approach him, and then in López' hearing. Colonel Thompson, now sick of the war, was forbidden to enter camp. Dr Fox, his leg broken by a Brazilian shell, went aboard with several British women.

The captains of the French and Italian steamers, were frequent guests at dinner, along with the French and Italian consuls, who travelled regularly between Luque and Pikisyry. The Italian community had been second in size only to the British before the war. Now most were in irons. Their consul ate dinner every night with the Mariscal and held Madame's stirrup when she mounted for her daily rides about camp; 'if he did not carry the hem of her dress it was only because her skirt was short'[27]. When Italian prisoners were brought before the *fiscales de sangre*, the first question was always the same: 'Have you deposited money with the Italian consul?'

The reply was always yes, for all foreign citizens left their valuables at the consulates of France, Italy or the United States when Asunción was evacuated and Consul Chapperon had brought the copies of all receipts issued from the consulate in Luque.

'So,' the judges said, 'you do not trust the Supreme Government of the Republic. You are a traitor.'[28]

'The Italian vessel . . . took away fifty-two women and children and the Frenchman a smaller number.'[29] Both – and possibly the British ship as well – 'took away a number of heavy cases, each of which required from six to eight men to lift; they probably contained some of the ladies' jewellery,' wrote George Thompson, 'which had been collected in 1867, as well as a large number of doubloons'[30]. It was common knowledge that Elisa Lynch was lining a desperate nest outside Paraguay.

In December, a US steamer moored off Angostura and General MacMahon, the consul sent by Washington to replace Charles Washburn, stepped ashore to be greeted, wined, dined and charmed. His time in camp was brief, for spies brought reports that Caxias' troops were not approaching across the marshes, as expected. They were marching up the Chaco road and crossing the River Paraguay to the north, from where they would attack the Mariscal's army in the back. On 6 December, the first Allies advanced southwards towards Pikisyry. They reached the bridge of Ytororo, three miles above Lomas Valentinas, and thinned out to cross the little river. On the other side, General Caballero and 5,000 Paraguayans waited in silence. Three thousand Brazilians and 1,200 Paraguayans died in the ambush. The Brazilians retreated but that day, the rest of the Allied force crossed the River Paraguay and there were 27,000 fresh soldiers against 7,000 weary Paraguayans. On 11 December, the Allies reached Avahi, a mile south of Ytororo. Six thousand five hundred died in that battle. In Lomas Valentinas, they told each other with relief that the last battle was coming. The prisoners waited for the Brazilians to come and save them.

The children came shouting to Elisa for Loto had reappeared, thin, with patches in his fur, but alive, for a species of grass called *mboi ka'a* grew in that area which was the antidote to a viper's bite. A party was given.

On 16 December, Juliana Insfrán de Martínez was taken away by soldiers and shot.

On 18 December, a tribunal met and pronounced a death sentence against Benigno, Venancio, Rafaela and Inocencia López. Their execution was postponed. On 20 December, it met again. The Mariscal 'passed a note to the council begging the capital sentence for these three be commuted to exile in the interior of the Republic'. The council agreed. The two sisters would be sent to join the other *traidoras* at a detention camp in the interior and Venancio would continue with the army.

On 21 December, the first Allied cannon were heard at dawn. The Mariscal's carts were already prepared for retreat. The remaining conspirators were brought into his presence and their sentences read out. Those to be shot were taken away immediately; Rafaela and Inocencia were returned to their locked and stinking carriage to watch the condemned marched away by a squad of child soldiers commanded by their cousin, Hilario Marcó. General Barrios was among them.

The Allies were advancing as the children were drawn up in line. Shot was exploding around the condemned and their executioners when Marcó gave the order to fire. Some of the children were crying. The Mariscal was present; Elisa was not. Among those killed that morning were men she had known since Paris. Bishop Palacios and Juliana de Martínez died with them, and Paulino Alen, who went half-blind and demented to his death. Those who did not die after the first round of bullets were killed by the children's bayonets. The bodies lay where they fell and the firing squad went immediately to face the enemy without.

López exposed himself to enemy fire for the first time during the seven-day battle of Lomas Valentinas. More than one person thought he was courting death. A bullet took off the tip of his tie, but death did not come.

The fighting continued throughout the following day and night. On the morning of 23 December, the Mariscal requested the presence of General MacMahon and gave him a letter.

Distinguished Sir
as the representative of a friendly nation, and in precaution against anything which may occur, I permit myself to confide to your care the enclosed deed of gift,

by which I transfer to Mrs Elisa Lynch, all my private property, of whatsoever nature.

I beg you will have the goodness to keep that document in your possession until you can deliver it safely to the said lady, or return it to me on any unforeseen contingency which may prevent me from seeing you again on this subject.

I shall also permit myself to beg you at once to do all in your power to carry into effect the dispositions made in the said document, thanking you in anticipation for all you may do with that view, towards obliging your very attentive servant.

Francisco S. López

[Enclosure]: I, the undersigned, Marshal President of the Republic of Paraguay, by this present document, declare formally and solemnly that, thankful for the services of Mrs Elisa A Lynch, I make in her favour a pure and perfect gift of all my goods, rights and personal actions.[31]

General MacMahon took the deed of gift, a few of the European wives and the Lynch-López children, except Panchito, and drove by carriage to the hill village of Piribebuy thirty miles away, where the *traidoras* lived.

Seven thousand died on the field that day. On the 24th, the Mariscal was invited to surrender and refused. It was Panchito who galloped to the enemy camp with a white flag and an escort to hand the refusal to Caxias. As he galloped back towards his father's headquarters at the end of the parley, watched by his mother, the Brazilians fired maliciously low over his head. Four thousand five hundred died that day.

On Christmas Day, Elisa rode out with the Mariscal. They passed one of the corrals on the hillside where prisoners lay in irons, exposed to Brazilian shell. Alonzo Taylor was among them.

I think she drew his attention to us, [he wrote.] López ordered us to line up before him; we approached and he asked us: 'Are you prisoners?' 'Yes,' we replied. Then Señor Von Treuenfeldt appealed to His Excellency, and he asked why he was there. Mr Treuenfeldt replied that he did not know and the President told him he was at liberty and might go. Then I stepped forward and told him I would be most grateful if he would concede the same mercy to me. López asked who I was; he seemed very surprised when he heard my name and exclaimed, 'What are you doing here? You are free.' Then the rest of the ten prisoners stepped forward and received the same reply.[32]

During the fighting of the next three days 34,000 died. On the afternoon of 28 December, one of the few surviving officers came to the Mariscal with the news that there was a gap in the Brazilians' defence through which the *état-major* could get away, and they went.

When Elisa Lynch came out of a hospital tent, she was given a message left by López for whenever, if ever, she should reappear: to gather together the women and make her way towards Cerro León. She did not know where Panchito was. The few Paraguayans left alive were leaving the battlefield. Doctors Skinner and Stewart were leaving with them.

'The words, as near as I can remember, were these,' Stewart recalled. 'Mrs Lynch said, "Do you know where the President is?" [I] replied, "I think, Madam, he has gone that road and if you want to escape you had better follow him as quick as you can." '[33]

The Allies raided the tents of dead and fleeing Paraguayans. Among the documents they found was the diary kept by General Resquin in which he listed the executions of conspirators.

Foreigners executed	107
Foreigners died in prison	113
	220
Paraguayans executed	176
Paraguayans died in prison	85
	264
Executed 22 August 1865, nationality not being expressed	85
Died (bayoneted) between San Fernando and Pikysyry	27
	112
Total death up to December 1868	**596**[34]

There were more terrible things.

> On the day following the fight of the 27th December, it was not the mounds of corpses of the combatants in decomposition that disturbed the sleep of the conquerors, but the cry of children from ten to twelve years, whose shrill voice, peculiar to their tender age, came from the military hospitals . . . whence came this astounding prodigy of the self-denying obedience of an entire people, unanimous in the one feeling of fighting until all were swept away? . . . what elsewhere would have been simply a rhetorical figure has been in this instance a terrible reality.[35]

Dr Stewart 'took to the woods for the purpose of making his escape, [but] Dr Skinner said if he took that route he would be shot, . . . he and Dr Skinner separated and . . . Dr Stewart was confronted with a number of Brazilian soldiers, who called upon him to surrender, which he did.'[36] He was taken out on a Brazilian gunboat. His part in the war was over, although his wife and infant children were in Piribebuy, still in the

Mariscal's power. At Angostura, Thompson and his officers voted to accept the Brazilians' offer of surrender in return for honourable treatment.

Madame Lynch travelled for two weeks across rough ground towards Cerro León, seventy miles away. No detail is recorded of her journey except that when she arrived in mid-January, she was disguised as a *campesina* – a peasant – with a scarf hiding her instantly recognisable hair. It was the first time she had moved without the carriage, the escort and the carts of private stores which went everywhere with the López family.

Her group was one of hundreds crawling across a countryside blasted by war to join the Mariscal; or crawling in the opposite direction to get away from him. As the Allies approached Luque, the garrison, the women, children and the wounded joined those making their way on foot and by cart eastwards into the hills. Waves of refugees, stoic fighters, deserters, prisoners of war and bandits swept back and forth across the hinterland of the looted capital through January and February. The ninety miles between Cerro León and Angostura was taken over by overlapping waves of desperate people, the roads 'covered with human corpses and the putrefaction of animals'.[37]

During the first, hot months of 1869, the Allies established themselves in Asunción. They entered to the sound of trumpets. The Argentine command moved into Venancio's house. General Osorio took the Mariscal's house on Mercado Guazú. What remained of the arsenal was packed for transport to the Matto Grosso, once more in Brazilian hands. The door to the French consulate was forced, the boxes inside were opened and the money they contained, left by the French community when they were evacuated to Luque, was 'shared out on a billiard table'.[38] Brazilian horses were stabled in the new palace on the riverbank. The Parisian furniture in Calle

Fábrica de Balas was boxed for removal to Buenos Aires, where it was put on display in the public rooms of the Palacio de Gobierno. The library was taken by booklovers or souvenir-hunters, or the illiterate who needed the pages for their campfires and latrines. Pictures by Ingres, David, Gainsborough and Goya were lifted from the walls. China and porcelain were smashed, or packed in straw and loaded with a nod and a wink on some boat heading *abajo*. Patios all over the city were disfigured by piles of recent earth. Already the hunt for buried treasure had begun but more bodies than gold came out of the ground. The river was clogged with shipping. Each day, boats of a dozen nationalities left piled high: Argentine, Brazilian, Uruguayan, British, North American, French, Italian. It was as it had been in the great days, when Asunción blossomed. Those who had thought they must die in the mud or the cordillera were working as stevedores, shopmen, shoeshiners and messenger boys. They worked for their conquerors, but they ate and drank and were not woken every night by gunfire, or the crying of child-soldiers, or the tramp of the execution squads.

But the Brazilians still did not understand the intransigent patriotism of the Paraguayans. Field Marshal Caxias had announced his triumphant retirement from the command of the Allied army. He said the Mariscal and his tattered army could not survive, out in the hills cut off from supplies. His people were begging food from the Brazilians. His city arsenal was in Brazilian hands. His army was dead in the Quadrilateral and Lomas Valentinas. The Paraguayans they spoke to in Asunción spat on his name. The Brazilians saw themselves as saviours of this country and presumed the Paraguayan nation saw the same. But as they partied through the hot season in Asunción, told each other the war was over and waited for a leader to replace Caxias, an extraordinary army was being formed at Cerro León. From all over Paraguay came cripples, children, amputees and a swarm of camp followers, across broken bridges and through deserted villages, dodging the enemy and the bandits to join the Mariscal and fight *los negros* until the end. Soldiers evacuating the Asunción garrison in December had brought the last of the arsenal machinery on their backs. A new arsenal was built in the pilgrimage town of Caacupé, fed by the foundry in Ybicui. By March, the foreign technicians who had followed orders and evacuated Asunción, then Luque, were running a replica in the hills of the costly works imported into Asunción over years. They had begun to turn out ammunition and cannon to replace those left in the southern mud. The army trained and camped at Cerro León. The village of Piribebuy had become the third capital of the republic. Between the two, Caacupé was occupied by hospitals, industrial works and depots. Families were distributed among hamlets and farms across the gentle hills around to be fed by the local population.

By April, 13,000 soldiers were being drilled at Cerro León, some taken from the hospitals or captured on the roads, others arriving to offer themselves willingly to the national effort. Each day they trained. They had no uniforms. Some had no weapons. Some were lacking a limb; others were wound about with bandages. There was a difference of over a foot in height between the veterans and the children brought by their mothers to join the army. The medical corps was reformed, for Dr Skinner had come out of the trees to join them, preferring to stay with the Paraguayans than take a British gunboat home with Dr Stewart.

Caxias had declared that the war was over, but it was not, for, by April, the Mariscal presided over a miniature state in the cordillera and Elisa Lynch was by his side.

Spies came to the Mariscal's camp from Concepción with reports of treachery. They claimed the city's notables had

sought to surrender. The commander of Concepción garrison
was brought to the cordillera, interrogated and tortured until
he confessed in his pain to something he had not done. When
news of this came to Concepción, families which had been
loyal became disloyal. Men deserted, some becoming *pasados*,
others simply non-combatants living rough on the wasteland
between Asunción and the cordillera. The Mariscal called for
Toro Pichai and told him to take five men of the Cabeza
Florida, round up the traitors and lance them. Toro Pichai
took private orders from Elisa. He was to determine the extent
and location of the wealth of certain families – she named two
in particular – and send back what gold he could to the
Mariscal, that it might be melted and rewrought as decorations
'for those who deserved them'[39].

Toro Pichai, five lancers and two priests left with a list of
the families to be killed. They crossed the cordillera and came
to Tacuatí, where many had taken refuge with friends and
relations since the Brazilians took control of the river. Toro
Pichai gave his orders: all families from Concepción were to
be produced and held in the plaza before the church. The
Cabeza Florida entered houses to search. Bewildered women
and a few elderly men were herded into the plaza and the
village was brought fearfully to watch. When all were there,
Toro Pichai read out the names of eight women and his men
crossed the plaza to bring them out. At the far end of the
cemetery, the women were stripped and lanced.

A party was held in the plaza that night. There was music
and *caña* and dancing and the lancers' caps were held out to
be filled with flowers. One Lieutenant Nuñez arrived, sent by
Elisa Lynch to gather the treasure seized and bring it back to
the camp in Cerro León. Darkness crept in and obscured the
torn flesh and the rustle of rats in the graveyard. Then the
Cabeza Florida entered houses and took the gold Elisa had
ordered.

When they were sober, they rode to the next village on the road to Concepción, entering with women seated before them on the saddle, glittering where the sun caught the gold around their necks and across their chests. They were already drunk when Toro Pichai called for the chief of police to bring thirty-three women on his list to the church plaza. As the hours passed and the women were found and brought, the men of the Cabeza Florida and their companions entered where they pleased and took what they wished. In the plaza, two scaffolds were built. Any who protested were strapped by the neck to a wooden rail. Villagers came to watch.

Some fought the Cabeza Florida with what they could. They offered the Mariscal's men a ball, as much *caña* as they could drink, entertainments and flatteries in the hope that the women in the darkening square would be spared. Music began and the square filled with couples, wordlessly dancing in the dusk around protesters in stocks and the rigid figures of those who knew they were going to die. Two priests went among them. Among the women who knelt and begged for mercy was one who had borne three children to Benigno. The priests offered their scapulars, on which the faces of Christ and Our Lady had been replaced with those of the Mariscal and Elisa Lynch. They told the women to kiss first one and then the other: '*Creed en nuestros salvadores*,' they told the women – 'believe in our saviours' – for they were the representatives of God's mercy. The macabre fiesta continued through the night and the women on the list said Hail Marys for the health of the Mariscal and Madame. The wife of the comandante of Concepción garrison went into labour. Dawn came and Toro Pichai ordered silence.

The comandante's wife was killed first. The men took her to a cattle corral 130 feet from the party, stripped her, took away her necklace and bracelets, dragged rings from her fingers, threw her face up on the ground and lanced her, twice, for there were two traitors there. Twenty-three other women were killed, one by one, naked and facing their executioners on the dank ground; then the party started again, with flowers in the lancers' hats, more women hanging from their arms and begging a share of the spoil, more children gaping. Those who remained sober and sick wished to bury the bodies but were ordered to leave them be. The fiesta continued all that day and night. When the second dawn broke, seven elderly men in irons were brought from the police station. The priests moved among them murmuring, the scapulars were brought and kissed and the seven were lanced where the women's bodies still lay.

The executions continued for days. One little girl present at the killings talked of them when she was an old lady, and recalled the chilling indifference of the spectators. 'We always went,' she said, 'as they were publicised, they were a punishment for consorting with the enemy.'[40]

Then someone came with news that the Brazilians were close. One of the priests was among the first to go, for everyone knew that the Brazilians paid deserters' wages and no pay had come from the Mariscal in a long time.

Chapter Fifteen

I n May, Madame moved from headquarters at Cerro León and took up residence in the third capital of the Republic of Paraguay.

La simpática señora Elisa Lynch has arrived in Piribebuy, [wrote the latest army newspaper, printed on the crude paper of Caacupé.] Needless to say, she was greeted with joy in this temporary capital. The benefactress of the Paraguayan country and army is received wherever she goes as an affectionate mother. The soldiers commonly speak of her as 'Our Mother'. *La Estrella* greets her with enthusiasm and wishes her stay will be a long one.[1]

The third capital was a large, undistinguished village which sat in a dip in the hills. To the north, the land sloped down to a brook, its banks now filled with hungry people and makeshift lines. In a house outside the village, the Mariscal's mother and sisters lived under house arrest. Already General MacMahon was here with Enrique, Carlos, Federico and Leopoldito Lynch. Vice-President Sanchez was in residence. So was Luis Caminos, Minister of War now Venancio was a traitor and

Fernandez dead. Consuls Chapperon and Cuverville had moved in and the wives and children of foreign families evacuated from Asunción and Luque were sleeping rough in the plaza around the church onto which the houses of Elisa, the Vice-President and the consuls looked. Elisa took a house opposite Sanchez' and moved in with the children, Mrs Venancia Stewart, and other of the wives brought by MacMahon to Piribebuy in December. There was room for a thousand people in Piribebuy; 25,000 people were there.

William Eden, head of Asunción sawmill since 1861, had left the US legation with his wife and children when Washburn fled. They were living on a verandah in Piribebuy, cold and hungry, when Elisa arrived. 'My wife went to ask her for some assistance,' Eden testified later. 'She received my wife with great tenderness, giving her some tea and sugar (the first we had had in three years) and regretting that she had not known before of our sufferings.'[2] Others recalled acts of kindness during that winter; other British women who called at the back door of Elisa's house went away with small parcels.

She had acquired a carriage and drove often to Cerro León, escorted by General MacMahon with a white flag. The three friends sat and drank wine and talked of the decadence of Europe and the rise of America; of the geological surveys the Mariscal would order when peace came and the riches which would accrue to Paraguay from the exploitation of coal fields. They discussed episodes of the war and compared them with MacMahon's experiences in the Civil War and the books the Mariscal had lately taken to reading, of theology and political science: Thomas Jefferson, George Washington, Adam Smith, Pierre Joseph Proudhon and the *Genius of Christianity*. They heard of Mitre's defeat in the Argentine elections and agreed the new president must be brought to sign a unilateral armistice. Elisa spoke to the Mariscal of the suffering British community in Caacupé and returned to Piribebuy with a job for Mr Eden in the new Caacupé arsenal. Mrs Eden remained in Piribebuy, where 'Mrs Lynch sent her many gifts'. 'I will be eternally grateful to her,' Mrs Eden declared after the war, 'I think she saved our lives.'[3]

Still the Emperor of Brazil had appointed no leader to replace Caxias. In Asunción the Allies partied, and their army relapsed into inaction. In Piribebuy and Cerro León, the anniversaries of the battles of May passed with speeches and receptions. The Mariscal's speech was rambling and his temper uncertain, for he still drowned his pain in cognac. 'I could have been the most popular man,' he told the commission which called upon him with felicitations, 'not only in Paraguay but in South America. To achieve this, nothing would have been easier than to declare a constitution. When I read those of our neighbours, their beautiful words entrance me – but when I raise my eyes from the paper to the reality, I am horrified.'[4] His listeners looked furtively at each other and retired.

When the army and its unhappy horde of followers first arrived, there was food in the cordillera, for the *traidoras* had been sent the previous year to this prison-village in the hills. They had cleared the ground, sown crops and built shelter. Officers charged with billeting families recently arrived from Luque on families in the cordillera reported to the Mariscal that the *traidoras* were living in comfort and plenty, while the loyal newcomers slept rough and ate little. He ordered the women evicted. Their huts and gardens must be given to patriots. Their destinations were the villages of Yhú and San Joaquin, eighty-seven miles to the east, already the home of *traidoras* from the early years of the war. They had become *las destinadas* – those destined for the east.

Carmen Gil de Cordal was in Piribebuy gaol with her three small daughters. The eldest, Silvia, was about six. Born into the family which told Hector Varela many years ago that Elisa

Lynch was a *malvada*, a daughter of Old Asunción, a friend of Charles Washburn, a woman whose husband had died as a prisoner of war and whose brother had been one of the garrison which surrendered with Martínez, Carmen needed commit no crime. When the *destinadas* were ordered east, she went with them, on foot, in the custody of one old sergeant and five twelve-year-old soldiers armed with lances. It took two months. The rivers were high and there were no bridges. At one flooded ford, they waited eight days. She could not take her children. They stayed in Piribebuy, sleeping rough in the care of the family slave Lolo. It was during those months that they trained their bodies to keep down bitter oranges.

The first cold weather came in June and the bodies of those who died in the night were taken away each morning.

A semblance of official ceremony was given to the occasion of la Presidenta's birthday on 24 June at the house outside Piribebuy where she and her daughters lived in semi-detention. The Mariscal did not attend but sent Elisa and the children to his mother's house, with gifts. Conversation is unimaginable. Benigno had been killed at San Fernando. Inocencia and Rafaela, recent widows, were recovering from several months' imprisonment in a closed cart. If Venancio was there – and imprisonment or syphilis probably prevented this – he was a sorry presence. And then there was Madame, well-fed, well-dressed, cold-eyed, and the four little boys, the elder ones now reaching an age of understanding, looking from their mother to their grandmother to their aunts.

The day General MacMahon was recalled was one of sadness. MacMahon truly believed in the rightness of the Paraguayan cause; he believed the Mariscal was a gentleman and a patriot who had been let down by the United States. His feelings for Elisa Lynch were stronger. Many times, he had brought with him to Cerro León some poem inspired by the orange groves or the colours of the Paraguayan sky. The last he wrote was a poem of love, dedicated to Elisa. When he left, he took a gold-embroidered poncho, Elisa's gift; a box of Paraguayan cigars from the Mariscal for President Grant; and a letter to be forwarded to the American college where Emiliano Pesoa López was studying. It was both stern and tender and mentioned almost casually the possibility that Emiliano might soon be called upon to take over the care of the younger boys from his father. He also took money: five hundred ounces of gold for Emiliano, $4,000 to be held in a US bank account for Elisa and a large number of trunks which he said contained yerba maté but were so heavy that no one believed him.

On the Mariscal's forty-second birthday, Mass was celebrated in the pilgrimage church of Caacupé, before the black virgin of Paraguay. There was a luncheon for a few and a dance for many. It was held in the afternoon that year, because there was not enough fuel to warm the plaza by night.

The man sent by Rio to finish the war was Gaston d'Orléans, son-in-law of the Emperor, grandson of the deposed king of France. He was known most often by his title the Conde d'Eu and under his leadership, the Allied army in Asunción was kicked into action. In July, they began the eastward march to take on the picaresque army in the hills and the men and women of Piribebuy dug 8,000 feet of trench around the village and in lines across the plaza. At dawn on 12 August, a vast allied force came over the crest of the hills which encircled the village.

The *casa de gobierno* and Elisa's house next door had been quietly vacated the night before. From six in the morning until half past eight at night, Brazilian artillery bombarded Piribebuy and 2,000 villagers lay waiting in the trenches. When the bombardment stopped, the Brazilian infantry marched, bayonets fixed, on to the church plaza and into the village streets, where women and children ambushed them with boiling water, heavy pans and broken bottles. By the end of the day, there was hardly a Paraguayan alive. Among the spoil taken by the Brazilians that day was the Paraguayan state archive since 1542, the treasures of Asunción cathedral and the national Treasury.

That night, Brazilian soldiers squatted among the corpses of Piribebuy, lit fires and opened the chests of clothes which Elisa had not had time to pack before she fled. They were cold and hungry and for fuel they used irreplaceable manuscripts which charted the making of the nation.

Ten miles away, hundreds of carts moved east. They collected the last *traidoras* and the families distributed throughout the hamlets of the cordillera as they went. Tatty horsemen forced their skeletal horses up and down the line, keeping order. Thousands struggled on foot. Gun carriages overturned in the ditches. Two thousand five hundred sick and wounded infantry walked in the rear with guns and regimental flags. Elisa went by carriage, the little boys in the back seat with Rosita Carreras and Isidora Díaz, Panchito riding by her side, her grand piano lashed to a cart pulled by soldiers. Her other possessions were now few, for her wardrobe was in Brazilian hands in Piribebuy. Hats were doffed and faces froze as she passed. Elsewhere in the vast convoy were the closed and stinking carts which carried the Mariscal's sisters. They were making for the camps of the *destinadas* in the east.

That day, the commanders of the Allied forces in Asunción presided over the election of a provisional government. One of the triumvirate was Cirilo Rivarola, a Paraguayan soldier who had deserted, sickened by the Mariscal's brutality. He had received his sergeant's stripes from Madame Lynch. 'May I be the one,' she had said, 'to present you with the *galones* of colonel and the *bordados* of general . . .' The new government's first decree was to banish 'Francisco Solano López from Paraguayan soil for ever as assassin of his country and enemy of the human race'.

They were *bandidos*.

So began the last retreat, north-east from camp to temporary camp.

On 10 October, 4,500 fresh Brazilian troops disembarked from a fleet of steamers at Concepción. They were commanded by the tenacious General Câmara, one of the new breed of officers brought in to end this atrociously costly war. Between him and the Mariscal was a trail of women, orphans, cripples, prisoners of war released or escaped, *indigenos* who made no distinction between *españoles* and *portugueses*, and would sell information for gold; an infinity of spies; informers, desperate mothers for whom the fate of the Mariscal was less important than bread, veterans whose minds were so shattered they no longer knew which army was theirs.

At the head of the Mariscal's army went the carts which carried his private supplies. There were wines and liqueurs, champagne, brandy and port. There was a great mound of salt. The wretched caravan behind ate bitter oranges from the endless groves, shoots and roots, coconut flesh and palm hearts dried, toasted or boiled. They ate the skin of oxen and boiled their hooves. Some covered soil in ash and ate it warm.

Somewhere among the hordes of scavenging women were the three Cordal girls whose mother, Carmen, had been sent ahead from Piribebuy. One day, two ladies in a cart came abreast of them at an arroyo. One looked at the filthy, skeletal children and asked who they were. She had not recognised them as her nieces. The slave was told she might 'go if she wished'[5]. Crying, she left the children, who continued with their aunt all that day and into the night, gnawing at bread made from palm tree flour. They were woken next morning by a messenger from the Mariscal. Who had given the ladies permission to take up these children? They must be abandoned and the ladies continue after the army as ordered.

All day the three girls sat under a tree. Another lady passed and gave them a bitter orange. Dusk had come when Lolo reappeared. That night was the first of many when Lolo went begging in the dark and brought home oranges. They fell behind the army, sickening and tiring. Silvia Cordal got earthworms. 'We made a broth from them, and when they were well cooked, the slave's mother took them out and crushed them and ate them.'[6] The youngest child died.

They continued from village to village, entering each place at the tail end of the army and begging news of their mother. Each time the Mariscal was about to march on and Carmen de Cordal was marching with him. The younger girl had forgotten why she was marching.

In early September, a patrol captured a spy and brought her to headquarters. Interrogated and beaten, she confessed she was in contact with Lieutenant Aquino of López' personal escort, who planned to assassinate him. Aquino did not deny it.

'Yes, sir,' he said. 'I wished to kill you. We have already lost our country; if we are still here, understand, it is only through loyalty to your person. Yet you are more of a tyrant every day.'

They took him away to shoot him.

'I was unlucky,' he shouted at the Mariscal, 'but sooner or later, another man will be luckier . . .'

His regiment was marched into a field and shot in the back. The Mariscal commanded the firing squad and when they were done, he went to the church, knelt outside the main door and prayed for a long time.

The army broke camp and moved on, heading north. Two women escaped and told the Brazilians that the Mariscal had with him 'twelve carts with money'[7]. Two men escaped and told them they had been tailors for Elisa Lynch; they had 'made her muslin petticoats'[8] because her wardrobe had been seized at Piribebuy. She travelled by cart or horse, they said, and when the oxen who pulled her cart were tired, soldiers took their place in the yoke. Parties sent out to rustle cattle did not return. Pickets were marched away from the camp with spades and treasury carts. They, too, did not return and the state gold of Paraguay was buried in places known only to the Mariscal and Elisa Lynch. The French shopkeeper Dorotea Duprat and her mother climbed again into the ox-cart of her friend Eugenia Gutierrez and had taken to the road one day when a messenger came with a parcel and a letter for Eugenia from Elisa Lynch:

> Señora Gutierrez, [she wrote] you should not be carrying the Duprat and Lasserre ladies in your cart. It is not my intention to interfere in your friendship; however, I cannot but tell you the harm you are doing in uttering their names.
>
> I would like to believe that these ladies do not know of the part their husbands played in the conspiracy but I must tell you what came from the revelations of these criminals. Señor Duprat, father, was one of the most active conspirators – a Brazilian spy in contact with the Baron of Santa Maria; very compromising letters written by him have been found, however His Excellency wanted to shut his eyes to this fact and leave him in liberty. Señor Lasserre is a dangerous agent of the conspiracy and received a large sum of money. Señor Aristide Duprat was one of the conspirators who wished to plunge a knife into His Excellency's heart.
>
> If you were not accompanying these ladies, you would be now at the side of your husband.[9]

Elisa Lynch knew, but Eugenia did not, that the body of Señor Gutierrez had been left at San Fernando with those of Cipriano and Aristide Duprat, Dorotea's father and brother; and Narcise Lasserre, her husband.

In early September, they reached Caraguatay, made it the fourth capital of the republic and rested.

The anniversary of the Mariscal's election to the presidency was honoured there by celebration and festivity. The mayor came to offer his best wishes. A little later, some of the young ladies of the locality did the same and revealed they had had the pleasure of conversing with Venancio, who should have been in Hilario Marcó's custody and unable to converse with anyone.

The Brazilians were dangerously close. A picket was sent to fetch Venancio. In terror, or apathy, or because the poison from his loins had corrupted his mind, Venancio sat and told his tale. He, his sisters, his mother, Pancha Garmendia, Marcó and his wife had planned to poison the Mariscal. There was no time for formal hearings. Seven members of Venancio's guard were executed and left unburied. Colonel Marcó was tied in the leather cords now used as irons, because they had no more irons.

Beneath orange trees on the bank of the Itanaramí river, the Mariscal convoked the inner circle to decide whether his mother and sisters should be tried for treason. It was agreed they should appear before a military court.

Later that afternoon, a message came to the slave Lolo to bring the three Cordal girls to the Mariscal's house. Numb and dumb, they stood before their leader, who regarded them and sent for Madame.

'I saw a beautiful woman,' Silvia recalled, 'I could not stop looking at her, she was so pretty, her clothes so lovely, everything about her was pretty and she kissed us and asked us who we were. He spoke to her and he told her to give us something for the journey because he was going to give us to our mother and she gave us a bottle of rum . . .'[10]

They took it to Lolo to barter.

During the evening, Pancha Garmendia, the Mariscal's old sweetheart, passed in front of the verandah of the house which the Mariscal, Madame and the children had taken. The Mariscal and a group of officers saw her pass and she was called.

'I take the liberty of interrupting your walk,' said the Mariscal, 'to talk to you of a matter which concerns you deeply.'[11] He told her she was to be tried and begged her to tell the truth to her judges. She replied that she was incapable of lying. Then the Mariscal dismissed her guard and invited her to join his family for dinner.

It was the first time Pancha and Elisa had been introduced. Elisa had heard much speculation about this pretty woman's entanglement with *el generalito* many years ago and Pancha had been at the heart of that group most unpleasant to her in the early days. Elisa greeted her guest graciously and then the door shut until the hour of dinner. There were no witnesses to their conversation. They ate *en famille*, with a few officers, and all the children present and on best behaviour. At about midnight, Colonel Centurión rose and offered Pancha his arm to take her into detention. She was interrogated for four days.

The Brazilians were reported to be near. The Mariscal addressed the vast crowd of people he had accumulated in his march across the country, and begged them to stay in Caraguatay, or return to their homes, for he could not feed them all. Few did so.

They continued their march through the heat and the red hills, leaving their old and sick each morning. They marched for eight days. Each morning fewer rose than had lain down to sleep. The Cordal girls struggled in the rear, both ill. They came to the hill which overlooked the army camp around the hamlet of Espadín and the younger daughter lay down. 'I am not going to see Mama,' she said. 'She always has bread and biscuits and sweet things in her cupboard. When you get there and you eat them, think of me, I am so hungry.'[12] When she died, Lolo and Silvia were too weak to dig the grave and had to pay for her burial with Elisa's bottle of *caña*. By the afternoon, Silvia, too, was fading, and Lolo, crying and weak with hunger, picked the child up and carried her down the slope. Early that evening, they found the *traidoras*, and Carmen de Cordal among them.

Later they camped on another river, in another field, this one called Guazú, of astonishing beauty: orange groves in virgin forest; silent but for birdsong. Elisa Lynch ordered the restoration of a deserted house for her family. Rudimentary chairs, tables and beds were knocked together; curtains were hung in the deep, glassless windows and locks secured to the doors. The patio was swept and snakes killed in the dark corners. The boys swam in the river with Loto. Women went for oranges, roots and berries, the men lay on the grass and boiled water for maté. Each morning, new corpses were thrown outside the camp. Soon they would be moving on, moving north and leaving the dead for the Brazilians to bury, for General Câmara's outlying Riograndense horsemen were close, sniffing at the army's spoor. And behind General Câmara was Marshal Monteiro, with thousands of fresh men at his disposal, slave and free, enlisted and mercenary; and behind Monteiro was the vast mass of the Allied army; and, on the distant Atlantic coastline, the court of Dom Pedro, emperor of eight million souls and inexhaustible credit.

This massive machine of war narrowed through the funnel of the River Paraguay, narrowed further along the eight-gauge railtracks, further still along the red dust tracks of the *serranías*★ and terminated in the skirmishing of the Brazilian riders who pounded into Paraguayan camps where fires still smoked and the dying were not yet dead.

On one of these silent, atrociously beautiful days in Guazú, Madame approached Vice-President Sanchez and asked who owned the land hereabout. Sanchez told her they were *tierras fiscales*, state lands. She asked how such lands could pass into the hands of a private proprietor. With the Legislative in recession, he said, the Executive could authorise their sale. They were transferred to Elisa Lynch for 50,000 patacones. It was an area the size of Belgium and Holland combined.

Once, she went too far in her desperate greed. Silvestre Aveiro was working in a room close to the Mariscal's one night and heard the Mariscal's furious call:

'Adjutant! Throw her out!'

She had come to him with a document for signature. There were 'shouts', Aveiro recalled, and an *escena inmortal* – a dreadful scene. The following day, the aides-de-camp saw scratches on her neck. She climbed into her coach dressed in a black veil that day, to disguise the bruises on her face.[13]

The Brazilians were close again. It was 11 December. The Mariscal was on the patio of the house he shared with Elisa and the children when Colonel Centurión approached and asked for orders concerning the female conspirators. Three were taken into the trees that night by children, tied to trees and lanced, one by one. Early the next morning, Hilario Marcó, his wife, Pancha Garmendia and the two sisters of General Barrios were killed in the same way. In their covered and stinking bullock-carts, Venancio and the López ladies waited for children's feet to approach. Instead, the cart jerked

---

★ Hilly countryside.

into movement and the Paraguayan army, now 5,000 in number, was in movement again, going north.

On New Year's Eve, they were camped on the bank of a river at Zanjha Jhu and the *destinadas* gathered together to make a plan for freedom. It rested on the children, and the fondness for them that Madame and the Mariscal had often displayed. Silvia Cordal was chosen.

Elisa received her with caresses and heard the plea her mother had taught her. Tomorrow, she told Silvia, was the best day on which to ask the Mariscal's forgiveness. She sat with the child through the afternoon to rehearse the speech she must make. She must ask pardon in the name of Panchito.

New Year's Day 1870 was celebrated by a Te Deum, spoken by priests in rags. When the Mariscal and Elisa left church, Silvia Cordal was pushed forward. She was overcome; she stood and gaped and a fearful silence fell as the Mariscal regarded her and waited, then she mumbled some childish remark, or struck some endearing attitude which made him laugh. She and her mother were pardoned that day. They attended the evening banquet, presided over by the woman Carmen had spoken of viciously fifteen years ago; the one who had brokered her freedom.

When the dying army dragged itself northwards that night, Carmen and Silvia Cordal hid in the hills. Then they walked for twenty days to reach the Brazilians in Villa de San Pedro, and their war was over.

In February, the army arrived at Chiriguelo and camped by the side of a lake. The Lynch boys swam; other boys lay down to die. Scavenging parties scoured the countryside for food. The Mariscal knew they would bring little back, if they came back at all. There was Brazilian bread a few miles south.

They remained at Chiriguelo some days. No one had plans – not even, it seemed, the Mariscal, who splashed in the lake with his sons, chatted to his troops and waited with the rest. He was calm and benevolent, treating his soldiers as sons and brothers, as he had in the earliest days of the war, before it had all gone wrong. His anger seemed to have spent itself with the latest executions.

On 7 February, Indians entered the camp and they knew its location would be known to the enemy in hours. They broke camp next morning while it was still cool and spread out in a silent, watchful line along the path to Cerro Corá, a clearing three miles away in the hills. A handful remained at Chiriguelo to guard the Mariscal's back. In Cerro Corá, camp was erected, defended and reconnoitred as it had been in too many places to recall since Piribebuy. A last hospital hut was built; a last headquarters for the Mariscal erected to one side; branches were laid over the last crude shelters under which the troops and the women would lie at midday, or all day when they could no longer rise. Skeletal soldiers dragged themselves from shade to retreating shade. Fishing parties sat by the Aquidibán brook, to catch a few fish to feed 2,000 people. Women brought in roots, baked bread from bark and made paste from wood fruits. A monkey was spotted and shot. Maté was brewed to dull hunger and bring on dreams.

Silent days went past, broken by minor incidents and the sound of the Aquidibán brook. On 14 February, an officer came from Chiriguelo with news of Venancio's death. His mind wandering and his body destroyed, he had lain down in the road and refused to walk further. An officer struck him with the flat of his sword and Venancio died in the dirt. The men played guitars at night. Elisa swam with her sons in the brook. Their grandmother's cart stood locked and stinking to one side of the clearing.

The Mariscal called a meeting. Officers sat on the grass in a circle round their leader. He had decided to strike a medal.

The medal of Amambay will be oval, 28 by 27 mm in diameter, with the national emblem depicted in the centre and an olive leaf beneath, the inscription *Disaster could not defeat us* in a circle on the upper part of the obverse; on the reverse, the inscription *El Mariscal López* on the upper part and, in the centre, *Amambay Campaign – 1870* on the lower part . . .[14]

Temporary medals had been made from scraps of red and yellow ribbon. They would be replaced by gold when Paraguay had won the war. Elisa pinned the ribbons wherever shredded uniforms could hold them on the chests of dull-eyed men. *Viva*, they said, as she passed from one to another. *Viva Paraguay. Muera el emperador.*

Late February, days of golden heat and a trickle of water beneath trees. Carlos, Enrique, Federico and Leopoldo ran between the carts, free from the eternal up-sticks and move-on. The couple had their daughter Rosita, their dear friend Isidora Díaz and their oldest companions, all together in this clearing dotted with huts and woodfires. The Allies were out there, waiting and planning and soon enough they would come.

Dr Skinner came to the Mariscal and said he could do no more. All sufferings in the camp were now caused by hunger, and medicine had no weapon against this. The Mariscal roused himself to send out a last scavenging party. Later, he called Resquin, Colonel Panchito, Elisa Lynch and Dr Skinner into his tent to hear the monthly resumé of resources.

'The ten remaining battalions total 268 comprising men and officers,' read Resquin from his papers. 'The six remaining regiments total 145 comprising men and officers. Total: 413 combatants plus 40 artillery soldiers and the officers of the *état-major*.'

The meeting broke up. Later that day, the Cai-guá Indians entered camp, drank maté with López and offered to take the army by secret paths into Bolivia. The Mariscal refused. He said he preferred to await the enemy here.

Later still, López signed a death sentence for the execution tomorrow of his mother. Darkness came.

On 1 March, the heat was stifling at dawn. Skinny creatures crept from huts on the far side of the camp and lit tiny fires for the morning's maté. Elisa was in her carriage when the first screams were heard from the southern end of the camp and a group of women burst in to tell the Mariscal that his outlying trenches were in the hands of the Brazilians. A party went immediately to investigate. Shots were heard and the men did not return. The Brazilians must be near, just beyond the trees.

'*A las armas todos!*' said López.

Immediately the camp was in commotion. Skeletons were transfigured by adrenalin and fear. The women and children were ordered into the woods and hurried words were exchanged between Elisa and the Mariscal, he ordering Panchito to get his mother's carriage away, she resisting. Panchito mounted and whipped the carriage north as López galloped towards the river, passing la Presidenta's prison-cart. He heard her voice, begging his help, and wheeled:

'Mother,' he said, 'trust in your sex,' wheeled back, and galloped on.

In a fury of hoof beats and Portuguese war-cries, the Brazilians fell upon the men at the bottom of the camp, throwing up turf, red earth and pebbles. The sounds of killing reached the carriage where Elisa, Rosita, Isidora and the boys waited, shouts of 'There goes López! Shoot him! Kill him!' from Brazilians who had been promised £100 for the dictator's head. The skirmishing was concentrated around the river, out of sight of their carriage. Bodies had piled up and begun to smell. There was no further sight of the Mariscal, last seen galloping towards the Aquidibán. Hysteria crept about the camp. Delirious soldiers and starving women came in from the woods. 'The tyrant had not yet died before his carriages were the scene of genuine frenzy,'[15] recalled a Brazilian officer. 'Women, Paraguayan officers mixed up with our own soldiers were frantically sacking the stores of food and clothing; they were leaping like wild things, distributing gold coins, burning documents, fighting over jewels. Finally, they set fire to whatever remained until it was reduced to ash.'[16]

At one end of camp, a few Paraguayan officers still fought round Elisa's carriage. A handful of Brazilians had realised it was occupied and galloped to investigate. One saw a blonde head and blue eyes and yelled:

'It's López' lover, with the bastards and the maidservants!'

There were obscene gestures and grins, men dismounted and approached the women with clear intention and Panchito drew his sword and attacked.

'Lieutenant-Colonel Martins was defending himself as Colonel Panchito López struck out blindly. "*Entrégate niño*," he said – "Give yourself up, lad". "*Ríndete Panchito, ríndete*" ' – "Surrender, surrender" cried *la Lynch*.

'A Paraguayan colonel does not surrender,'[17] Panchito screamed, and the Brazilian killed him as he spoke.

Elisa's view was blocked as the first Brazilians attempted to enter the carriage. She seized her Union Jack and kicked them back over the doorway, crying: 'I am English! Get out! Respect me!' As they fell back she saw Panchito's body, shrouded by the dust of wheeling hooves, already forgotten by Brazilians intent on spoil. She lifted and dragged him towards the carriage and laid him on cushions. 'The noise of her crying was loud. She opened his eyes, calling "Panchito! Panchito!" There were blood stains on her gown.'

Abandoning the carriage where her next eldest son was crying, 'Do not kill me! I am a foreigner, son of an English-woman!' Elisa kicked her way through the crowd to find Dr Skinner but he could only tell her what the others knew: Panchito was dead.

'Señora,' said a Brazilian officer behind her, and pointed down the field to where a group of men bore a corpse on a stretcher, 'that is the body of the Mariscal López.'[18]

He had been killed on the bank of the Aquidibán, shouting '*Muero con mi patria!*' – I die with my country.

The Paraguayan war was over.

Elisa Lynch buried her lover in the same grave as her eldest son, spurning an offer of help from Allied officers.

Four Brazilian stretcher-bearers brought the body of the Mariscal up the field; a cavalry officer supported his lolling head. 'Our soldiers,' wrote a Brazilian officer, 'looked curiously at the cadaver; the Paraguayan females danced around it until Colonel Paranhos ordered these wild women be forcibly removed.'[19] A part of López' ear had been cut off on the riverbank where he died, before the Brazilian officers put a stop to the mutilation. One of his patent leather boots was missing. 'All noted,' the officer recalled, 'the whiteness of his [naked] foot, and the delicacy of its form.'[20]

The Brazilians gave her a spade and Elisa, a Paraguayan officer, Isidora and Enrique took turns to dig the grave. Her black silk dress was red where dust clung to her sweat. When the grave was dug, she knelt beside it and reached in to smooth its walls with her hands.

La Presidenta and Inocencia came. The mother cried bitterly, knelt and kissed the forehead of both son and grandson, ignoring Elisa as she always had.

'Do not cry, Mother,' said Inocencia, who did not kneel or weep, 'for this monster who was neither son nor brother.'

Dusk fell and Elisa was still digging and smoothing. A ragged circle of prisoners of war stood around her. Some sobbed; some prayed; some simply stood and watched, then wandered away to find food and a place to sleep. She sent a last request to the officer in charge that she be allowed to cut a lock of hair and a soldier was sent to perform this service for her. He 'made sure to cut a good few handfuls for himself and distributed them among the camp to commemorate the occasion'[21]. Then the bodies were placed in the grave and red earth fell on their faces.

General Câmara sent a message to his superior at Amambay: 'Madame Lynch and her four sons are among the prisoners and are precious trophies of this victory' and went to share his bed with Inocencia López de Barrios, who bore his daughter nine months later.

Among the victims of the victory were 179 of the combatants Solano López had counted the previous evening. José Maria Aguiar, who had brought flowers across the plaza for Elisa, lay with his throat slit on the banks of the Aquidibán. The elderly Vice-President had been lanced when he refused to surrender. José Felix Pesoa López, child-captain in the Paraguayan infantry, died yards from his half-brother Panchito.

At daybreak on 2 March, Elisa, Rosita, Isidora and the little boys found their carriage ringed by curious Brazilians waiting for a glimpse of the dead dictator's mistress. Leaving camp at first light for Concepción, they passed a scene of desecration. The Mariscal's 'remains were surrounded by a crowd of women and men. A Brazilian soldier was performing pirouettes on the belly of the dead man, who lay naked above ground.'[22] Elisa threw herself among the crowd and dislodged the dancing soldier. Brazilian officers followed her and broke up the party with blows and shoves.

'Is this the civilisation you say you bring us with your cannon?' she asked them.

'Señora,' one of the Brazilian officers reminded her, 'Brazil was invaded.'[23]

She would not rebury the Mariscal naked. A white sheet was found, somewhere in the sacked and desolate camp. Its price was three ounces of gold. She wrapped the body in the sheet and officers reburied López and closed over the grave. Then the dancing soldier and the crowd of crowing men and women were shoved with fists and rifle butts into the shuffling caravan which left for Concepción and the capital. Elisa and the children rode in an ox-cart until the oxen died, and then they, too, stumbled across the red earth on foot.

One soldier watched, hidden among the trees. He waited until all sound of the Brazilians had died among the trees and came down to begin his journey across a destroyed country to see if his family still lived. Silence returned to Cerro Corá and bodies began to rot.

Chapter Sixteen

*L*a *Tribuna*, 8 March 1870:
'*Grandes noticias del Paraguay!*
MUERTE DE LÓPEZ
Su familia todo prisionera
La Guerra ha concluida.'
López is dead and this is no dream! Now the war is truly
over and the Treaty of the Triple Alliance is completely
satisfied. This man who wished to kill an entire nation has
surrendered, like all tyrants, to the imperious laws of death
. . . from a dead tyrant is born the greatest hope of a nation
which nearly died for him.

Elisa and her children arrived in Asunción in the second week
of March and found a city given to death, commerce and
fiesta. In the newspaper of the new Asunción, *La Regeneración*,
advertisements appeared from schoolmasters, architects and
engineers. An Italian shipping agent had opened offices at the
dock and Edward Hopkins was back in Paraguay, with his
saw-mill and his steamers. There were two new pharmacies in
Calle Palma, a bookseller's and shops selling clothes, fuel,
drink and guns. A hairdresser 'advises the public that, returned
from the cordilleras, his establishment is re-opened for

business'[1]. There were restaurants and a theatre and dances every night. *A la mariposa* offered ladies' fashion in Calle del Sol. Shops sold 'cheese, wine, tomato sauce in bottles, mustard, Gorgonzola, mortadella, bacalao, tongue, apricots, parmesan, gruyère'[2]. The railways ran again, under the management of the *Empresa Brasileña de Ferrocarril*.

Behind the vibrant commerce of carpetbaggers, there was misery and exploitation. The balls were 'organised debauchery'[3]. Carts were 'sent round every morning to pick up the corpses of those who have died of hunger during the night'. Four hundred women were living in the unfinished Teatro Nacional. The smell became more and more offensive until it went beyond their unwashed bodies and investigation found 'the corpse of one man that had been strangled . . . in one corner in a decomposing state'[4]. Everyone went armed, even the children, for many had been kidnapped and sent downriver as trophy slaves.

Outside the grand palace in which the Mariscal had never lived, Paraguayan veterans washed the feet of Brazilian officers. Photographs of a large-breasted bitch with Elisa's head superimposed were on sale for fifty cents. Among the women who went each night to the costume balls for the Allied officers, some wore gold wigs and the parody of a crinoline, speaking comedy French. Allied soldiers and rescued *destinadas* had already brought news of executions and the rape and starvation of women. One after another had told her story of abuse and depravity.

Within days, a letter appeared in *La Regeneración*:

when the tyrant López ordered the evacuation of Asunción . . . we were dispossessed of all our property, including jewellery, as before, under various pretexts . . . Today, the woman most responsible for this robbery, she who profited most from it, she who still holds the evidence of this crime in her hands, those valuables taken from us to satisfy her limitless greed – that woman is here. We speak of Madame Lynch.[5]

The letter continued with hatred in every word and a demand to the provisional government that Madame Lynch be prevented from leaving the country taking with her the valuables she had stolen from them. The letter was signed by ninety of the ladies who had lost their jewels to the Libro del Registro and their men to the Quadrilateral.

Hostile crowds gathered around Madame's house. Stones were thrown. Governor Paranhos could not ignore the unrest or the troublesome woman to whose existence and fortune he had somehow to find a solution. On 19 March, a decree was published by which all property belonging to the López family 'and the woman Elisa Lynch, concubine of the traitor and criminal Francisco Solano López' was confiscated. Elisa, Isidora and the children were taken to the port and went aboard a troopship. Paranhos promised to carry out an inventory of their property and men came and picked her belongings over.

40 gold and silver rings; a golden diadem; 23 gold and coral buttons; 11 watches and 20 golden chains; 19 pairs of earrings of gold, silver, sapphires, emeralds and other precious stones; a dozen maté *bombillas**; a sword with a hilt and scabbard of gold, ornamented with precious stones; 6 gold bars . . .[6]

But when the soldiers took their list back to Paranhos, he gave it as his published opinion that it consisted of 'far less than might have been expected to be acquired by Madame Lynch

---

* Ornamental gourds.

in Paraguay'. He gave no opinion on the chests taken off from Paso de Patria and Angostura, or those buried in the eastern hills beside dead soldiers. He had more important things to do than sort out who owned which gold chain and where it was. He would take no action against her.

News came from Buenos Aires. Consul Chapperon had left Paraguay aboard an Italian gunboat when the Paraguayan army took to the hills. Twice the *Arditta* had been prevented from leaving Angostura. Twice Chapperon's trunks and chests were loaded, seized and taken off again. 'The chests taken from the Italian Minister,' wrote *El Nacional*, 'are so heavy, some of them, that several men together can only move them with difficulty. *El Señor Consul* says they are "items for personal use".[7] It was not until the Italian crew kidnapped a Paraguayan sailing ship and threatened the families on board that they were allowed to leave for Buenos Aires, with Chaperron and his trunks of stolen treasure aboard. The month López died at Cerro Corá, Chapperon was murdered in Buenos Aires. A note of warning was attached to the knife which had run through his heart: '*Cosí si punisce chi dishonra l'Italia*' – 'Those who dishonour Italy are punished thus.'

More news came from Entre Rios. On 11 April, at seven in the evening, General Urquiza had been sitting on a patio with a book when he realised that he was surrounded. He called for his guard but they did not come. He retreated into his house and locked the door but the men outside came after him, knocked it down and shot him in the mouth. His daughter embraced him as he lay dying and they shot him again in her arms. The assassination had been ordered by one of the caudillos who had pressed for the relief of Montevideo and been sickened by the betrayal of the Paraguayans. The province was again in arms, troops were on their way from Buenos Aires and the assassins had fled to their comrades across the Uruguayan border.

Then, in Asunción, someone published the list of Paraguayan properties acquired by Madame Lynch in the last fifteen years. Among them were *tierras fiscales* of over thirty-two million hectares, acquired at scandalously low prices. She might have got away with the wilfully blinkered list of jewellery in her suitcase but the property acquired under conditions of war could not be ignored. On 4 May, the provisional government froze all Madame's assets and ordered 'a trial be prepared against this famous woman' for '[taking advantage] of the abnormal and painful situation in which the country found itself'. *La Tribuna* in Buenos Aires summarised the case against her, prefaced by the inevitable reminder of her immorality: 'Elisa Lynch is famous as an adventuress who had many lovers in the Old World,' Varela told his readers. 'Those indifferent to her will say: why go to such lengths to attack this woman? Because this woman,' he answered them, 'is a great criminal; because if this woman succeeds in her aims she will strip an unhappy country twice over and raise her throne on the ruins of a nation.' [8]

She immediately engaged a French lawyer resident in Asunción, Berchon des Essarts, and had all certificates relating to her property empire, including the sealed will which General MacMahon had witnessed at Lomas Valentinas, taken to his office. Essarts made it known on her behalf that property acquired from individuals during the war had been bought in order to display Madame's faith in Paraguayan victory when others began to doubt. As to the state lands, she had bought these only in order to advance the government money desperately needed during the war, using the 500 ounces of gold she had brought into the country in 1855 and put to legitimate use thereafter. Elisa knew she could not hope to keep the city properties. These, Essarts announced, she was prepared to sell back to those from whom she had bought them, at the original purchase price, without interest. His announcement provoked only fury and her Brazilian protectors advised her strongly to leave the country while she could. She had become a severe embarrassment. Protection had been offered by the military commander at Cerro Corá, as was honourable, and that protection must be continued by the civilian government in whose name he had offered it. But it was becoming clear that Elisa could not stay in Paraguay and if the Brazilians could hand her back to some European power to look after, peace would come more quickly to Asunción.

If Elisa left Asunción, however, the cases pending to determine future ownership of her vast estates would slide to the bottom of the ministry files, the property would remain frozen and its income with it. This was income Elisa needed: the time had come to return Paris and London with her New World fortune. She had children to educate and her own dignity as widow of the Paraguayan Mariscal to sustain. She agreed to leave Asunción only to go to Montevideo. She wrote a last letter to the *La Regeneración*:

> [I am] atrociously slandered by several Paraguayan ladies, whose names appear on the request submitted to the Provisional Government, most of whom I never met and do not know me. However, I also find names of some ladies who were my intimate friends, who ate at my table and owe to my actions if not their own lives, then those of their sons and relatives.[9]

She revealed, perhaps, more than she intended in this sentence.

She left aboard a Brazilian ship with her sons, Rosita Carreras and Isidora Díaz, bound for Montevideo. The banks of the River Paraguay were desolate. Villetta was still a hospital town; the white wall of its cemetery gleamed through gaps in the earthwork George Thompson had erected against the

Brazilians. At Angostura and Fortín, the defences were ruins. In the estuaries, they passed the paddle wheels of sunken steamers protruding from the mud. On the right bank, there were remnants of the great flotilla of canoes which had carried the garrison from Humaitá to Timbó beneath lilies torn from the banks. Not a living Paraguayan was seen. The place stank of death. Humaitá was a ruin. Only the hardwood telegraph posts still stood, useless, against the sky. There were yellow mounds where the batteries had been, a few cattle fed among the earthworks and waterlilies grew in the trenches.

It would take three generations to repopulate the lands destroyed by the Mariscal's war.

Abajo, the British consuls were trying to decide what to do with Elisa Lynch. Major Munro in Montevideo, to whom she had appealed for protection, was unsure of her right to this. On 23 April, with Elisa 'daily expected', he sent a confidential letter to the legation in Buenos Aires, requesting urgent instructions. Advice arrived by telegraph: Munro could not extend British protection to Mrs Lynch but was advised to talk unofficially to the Uruguayan authorities 'that she may be protected against any insult or outrage to which her participation in the late Paraguayan events may expose her'[10]. A letter was then written to Elisa herself.

> Under the present circumstances, [wrote the envoy in Buenos Aires] your position with regard to these Republics is such as to preclude me from officially claiming of their governments that security which you might perhaps otherwise be entitled to and I could not therefore . . . take the responsibility of the risk you would incur by landing at Montevideo.[11]

He gallantly suggested she alight at Buenos Aires instead, where the new president had privately told him he had 'no objection' to her presence.

Then he wrote up the whole difficult affair in a dispatch to London.

> In the event of Mrs Lynch pressing her claim upon me . . . this lady was born in Ireland, she is married to a French officer, from whom she is legally separated. She now bases her claim to British protection on the supposition that no circumstance can deprive a British-born subject of their right to British Nationality. According to the laws of this country, the claim to protection of an Englishwoman married to a foreigner and separated from her husband is fully recognised but as I do not know what course Your Lordship would wish me to adopt in this present case, I shall take no further steps pending Your Lordship's instructions . . .[12]

These soon came.

> I have to direct you should Mrs Lynch be in any personal danger, to endeavour to obtain for her all the Protection that her Position may require but as she has been married to a French Subject she has not the claim of Nationality to entitle her to be officially protected by Her Majesty's Government.[13]

Elisa Lynch was stateless: expelled from Paraguay, the protection of the British government withheld; that of the French government ceded years since when Xavier de Quatrefages signed a power of attorney on the Champs-Elysées. Perhaps only now she realised her great vulnerability; or perhaps only now did she succumb to the exhaustion of years of campaign. She reached Montevideo and did not fight, spending only one day in harbour before transshipping to the *City of Limerick*, bound for Rio. Crowds gathered in the bay to see her ship sail in. Ex-officers and notables came aboard and she received them graciously, but if they had looked for remorse, they did not find it. She defended the Mariscal against all attacks. She sent to ask the emperor for an audience, promising secrets of the war, but he refused, saying 'it was completely indifferent to him, because he neither could nor wanted to give credit to anything such a woman could tell him'.

She sailed for England.

If her spirit had not already been broken by the unremitting succession of blows dealt her over the past years, surely it admitted defeat during her first days in Europe, as an unsuccessful American returning not with a fortune, as all good Americans should, but an insistent lack of money. On 18 July 1870, Elisa Lynch, her four surviving sons, Rosita Carreras, Isidora Díaz and Leopoldito's seasick monkey came off the steamer at Southampton and took the coach to London. Emiliano Pesoa López was waiting for them there, for a strange rapprochement had grown up between Elisa Lynch and Juana Pesoa at Cerro Corá, where both saw their lover and the father of their children die. The next day, Elisa was gone again, to Paris.

It was an insane moment to visit Paris, for war fever had taken that city again as surely as it had in the months she spent there sixteen years earlier. Paris was full of troops, marching 'to Berlin' amid flowers tossed by crowds. For years, reports had come from the east that the dormant hostility of 1812 would awake and the Prussians threaten. 'We are at the mercy of an accident,' wrote a French general in 1868. In 1870, the Prussians found one, a silly affair, a manipulation of dynasties which set a candidate guaranteed to offend the French upon the vacated throne of Spain. The day Elisa arrived in Paris was the day Napoleon III declared war.

'Frenchmen!' he said. 'There are solemn moments in the life of a people when the national honour, violently excited, imposes itself as an irresistible force, when it dominates every interest, and takes in hand the destinies of the country. One of those decisive hours has just struck France.'[14]

By the time Napoleon left Paris for the front, taking the twelve-year-old Prince Imperial with him and leaving Eugenie as regent, Elisa had returned to London, for Leopoldo was dead. The convulsions had started the afternoon his mother left for Paris and he died that evening. Elisa returned to the dreariness of another coffin and another funeral in the strange grounds of Kensal Green cemetery, many thousands of miles from her other dead children in Asunción and Cerro Corá.

As she endured her first grief for Leopoldito, dreadful news came from the French–Prussian front. The French army had not been ready for war. The reserve had never been trained in the use of the newest weapons and campaign gear had never been distributed to the garrisons. Bewildered French officers who had thought their army the best in the world now struggled to find and distribute gear which had lain for years in depots. They trained recruits to use breech-loaders and sent urgent telegraphs for ammunition and food while the Prussians marched across the frontier. The Prince Imperial was sent across the channel to Hastings but Eugenie wrote to Napoleon from Paris 'come victorious, or do not come at all'.

On 4 September, he surrendered. In the Tuileries, ministers of government stared silently at Eugenie, who left in a plain carriage, to join her son and wait for news of her husband. Those who saw her leave said they heard her mutter, 'a hollow dream, a hollow dream'.

On 28 January, an armistice was signed which ceded to Prussia great chunks of land to the east, stipulated a French war indemnity of 500 million francs, the presence of an army of occupation until this was paid and a victor's entrance into

Paris. Asunción was Brazilian, Paris was Prussian and Elisa Lynch was homeless twice over. Then the violence of the Commune of Paris consumed the resentful city for eight months. On 24 May 1871 the parish priest of La Madeleine was executed by its representatives. His was one of the last deaths for at the end of the month, the Commune collapsed and Elisa returned, with Isidora. Her three surviving sons were in a boarding school in Croydon.

In January 1868, a revival had been staged of *La Dame aux Camélias*, sixteen years after it had so perfectly captured the Parisian zeitgeist. 'It was an evening of great sadness,' wrote the Baron d'Aurevilly. 'Where are the days, dear God, when those camelias were in flower? If you remember, all Paris, even the Paris of honest women, went to set their imagination on fire with this drama in which a rare *fille de joie* dies of love and grief. Oh, what a long time it is since our curiosity was so ardently, so shockingly excited!'[15] Those days had gone and with them the *lorettes* of Rue Tronchet and Caussée-d'Antin. It was twenty years since Elisa's moment of glory on Rue Tronchet. Any men and women who might have vaguely remembered her as a lovely *lorette* were gone and with them, Second Republic Paris. The froth had turned to scum. In Prussian Paris, Elisa Lynch and Isidora Díaz were not glamorous Americans of fabulous wealth but two middle-aged relics of an obscure war. Isidora Díaz was no longer the sister of a national hero but a prematurely aged spinster with dowdy clothes and an accent. Elisa Lynch was a faded second-ranker. 'Old age,' Dumas wrote, 'is the first death of courtesans,'[16] and Elisa's day was done. Few turned to stare in 1870 as they had in 1853. Isidora soon returned to Paraguay but Elisa could not.

Emiliano Pesoa López lived with or near her, maintaining a curious relationship with his father's principal mistress. His position was not easy. He had been absent during the war years, which meant that he, unlike Panchito, was still alive; but, unlike Panchito, he would never achieve the status of warrior, hero and martyr. When Elisa decided she would take the name of López, the name she had never used during the Mariscal's lifetime, Emiliano was cold. 'She now wants to give herself the name of López,' he wrote to his mother, 'I cannot stand it.'[17]

In 1872, she was living between homes in the Rue St-Lazare, Paris and Kensington, London. In 1872 or 1873, the Anglo-Argentine Robert Cunninghame-Grahame visited Paraguay and wrote of its devastation. He returned to London full of loathing for the couple he thought responsible for this degradation and spied out Elisa Lynch, although he never approached her. Contempt pours from his *Portrait of a Dictator* but the paragraph-long portrait of the woman he watched go in and out of her London house is curiously bland.

> I saw her several times in London in 1873 or 1874, getting into her carriage at a house she had, I think, in Thurloe Square or Hyde Park Gate. She was then apparently about 40 years of age. Of middle height, well made, beginning to put on a little flesh with her abundant fair hair just flecked with grey. In her well-made Parisian clothes, she looked more French than English . . . she was still handsome and distinguished looking. Her face was oval and her lips a little full, her eyes were large and grey, if I remember rightly, and her appearance certainly did not seem that of one who had looked death so often in the face; lived for so long in circumstances so strange and terrifying, buried her lover and her son with her own hands and lived to tell the tale.[18]

She may have lived in bourgeois comfort when Cunninghame-Grahame saw her but Elisa's money was dwindling. The property which would have kept her in splendour was still frozen in Paraguay and there was little prospect of its imminent release. No one knows how many of the chests of portable valuables shipped out aboard the neutral warships made their way down the area steps of her house in Kensington, thence to the discreet vaults of a London bank. Dr Stewart had defaulted on his bill for £4,000. Although a court in Edinburgh found for Elisa, and against the doctor's claims that the bill had been granted under duress, the doctor declared himself bankrupt and she got nothing. Her Washington money spent, her warship money disappeared and her Scottish money denied her, her only remaining source of income was Paraguay. However, the court case she had hoped would be soon prosecuted and won by her clever French lawyer had never been brought, for M Berchon des Essarts had been murdered by hired Italian assassins.

It was widely suspected that Essarts had been eliminated on the orders of the Minister of the Interior, in order to get hold of the papers relating to the Lynch case and destroy them. However, those documents had been immediately taken to the French consul, who was responsible for settling the estate of any French citizen, and the Paraguayan authorities could not get at them. Consul Alzac had demanded the assassins be tried. 'This will be the first time,' he wrote from the violent city of Asunción, 'since the death of López that the murder of a foreigner will have been punished.'[19] It proved impossible: the case was passed from one official to another; there were unexplained delays; papers were lost and the position of the consul, bravely continuing to press for prosecution, became dangerous. 'The expenses I have had and will continue to have to obtain the conviction of the murderers of M Berchon . . . give the measure,' wrote the consul, 'of the politicians in this country.'[20] By the end of the year, he was afraid for his life. He packed the papers relating to Elisa Lynch's case, along with the rest of Essarts' portable estate to be returned to his heirs, and made for the docks. His departure was forcibly prevented. There were two vitally important documents in his luggage which the government was determined to obtain: the Mariscal's will and another paper, which his sisters believed to have been put in the same, sealed envelope, which listed all those places where money sent out of Paraguay during the war had been deposited.

Today, [Consul Alzac wrote to his superior in Buenos Aires on 8 December 1872] I consider myself captive in Paraguay as Messieurs Cocholet and Cuverville were in the time of López ... M d'Asambuja [Minister of the Interior] will not let me leave the country before he has taken possession of the papers of Mme Lynch ... He has said I cannot leave the country without concluding Berchon's case, but by this he does not mean pass to the representative of the widow, he means pass to him, M d'Azambuja, the envelope said to contain López' will, or open it and give him a copy – this must be governed by your instructions, which I hereby request, to say nothing of those of the owner, Mme Lynch ... when I sent her official confirmation of the death of her lawyer, she appointed me proxy, but you will understand how little desire I have to become involved in these matters.[21]

He was still there two days later, frightened and desperate:

As regards the papers of Mme Lynch, I beg you will ask the Department [of Foreign Affairs] for instructions ... The document said to contain López' will is contained, as you know, in an envelope covered with the handwriting and seal of Mme Lynch. The Department must judge whether that paper must be considered to have a political value. Does this document contain the political will of the ex-dictator or only, as López' sisters believe, an indication of the places in Europe where he deposited money?[22]

When Consul Alzac finally left Paraguay, he brought only some of the papers Elisa had left with Berchon des Essarts with him and now she had no representative in Asunción to push for what she considered her rights. She would have to return, and do so herself. Isidora Díaz warned her not to come. Eliza did not heed her. In 1875, she boarded a steamer with Enrique, now seventeen, bound for Rio, Montevideo and Buenos Aires, where she would take passage to Asunción.

They disembarked at noon on 23 October 1875 and crossed the city towards Isidora Díaz's house. No one had been warned of her arrival. Heads turned along Calle Palma and incredulous word that *Madama* was back raced along the streets, but no one approached until they reached the market women squatting among their baskets and pestles in Mercado Guazú. Some rose to their feet. One spat and hostility crackled through the market. Elisa leaned from her seat, spoke urgently to some by name and handed coins through the window of her coach before moving quickly on. Messages went from house to house in the city and within hours, women from fifty families had gathered to draft a letter to the President demanding her arrest.

Sir:
we tried to close our eyes on the horror of the memory of the dreadful end suffered by our fathers, husbands, brothers and sons. In Christian resignation, we sought to soothe the wounds in our souls which will never heal, when the presence of a hateful, criminal woman . . . instigator of and accomplice in unbelievable cruelties, has appeared

insolently among us, clawing open our wounds, which bleed once more as if the blood she already has on her hands were not enough . . .

She must either be immediately, ignominiously expelled, they said, or tried as a criminal, for such she had been declared by the decree of 4 May 1870.[23]

By nightfall, Isidora's house was surrounded by a large and angry crowd. Obscene names were called and the first, small projectiles thrown. There were shouts of '*Muera!*' and news came that the market women had gathered with banners and shouts and were approaching from the port. A brave messenger emerged from Isidora's house and pushed his way down the street to the Club del Progreso, where the captain of a British ship in the bay was dining. Elisa asked his protection. He replied with dutiful gallantry that ashore, the only protection he could offer was his own. If she would go ashore the ship in the bay, he could offer her that of Her Majesty.

The market women arrived just before the police, intending to seize her, force her to carry a banner scrawled with insults and make her stand before a crowd on each street corner and shout '*Muera* Madame Lynch, López' lover!' The government had issued an order of expulsion from Paraguay, the police said. She must leave that night.

At eleven o'clock, a tram stopped outside the house. It was driven by the head of the tram service, an Englishman, perhaps because no one else could be trusted. Surrounded by the crowds, protected by police and soldiers whose affections did not lie with these foreigners, Enrique boarded, followed by his mother, pistol in hand.

'Madam,' said the driver in dismay, 'I am unarmed, I did not think arms necessary. I see you have a gun, please be good enough to give it to me as it is better, in the event of danger, that I use it.'

'It is true,' said Madame, 'that it is unusual for a lady to handle these instruments but, if the event arises, you will see that a lady can put them to good use.'[24]

When Madame left Buenos Aires for Europe, she transferred to Enrique her interest in the land bequeathed her by his father. Enrique, shrewdly, sold his interest on to an Argentine speculator and left it to him to fight the Paraguayan government for ownership. They laughed his claim out of court.

As little is known of the last years of Elisa's life as is known of the first. She left no record of it, no one from her previous life accompanied her on it, no newspaper correspondents or diarists mention it. We know only that she spent three years in Jerusalem then returned to Paris and took up the life of a respectable widow of moderate income.

The only allusion to her comes in a letter tucked into a copy of a picaresque novel in the Canning House Library, London. It was a story of nineteenth-century pluck and the hunt for the lost gold of Paraguay from secret maps and the words of a dying man who spoke of horrors during the last retreat of the Paraguayan army:

> With three troopers I had been out scouting . . . I noticed the marks of cart-wheels diverging from the road. We followed them, for my instructions were to see that nothing remained behind the column, and at the distance of about half a mile we came upon two carts, one of which bore . . . the inscription *Tesorería General de la Nación* [State Treasury]. A slight inspection showed them to be empty. We hastened forward . . . and before long reached a spot where the ground had recently been disturbed. My conclusion naturally was that the contents of the carts had been buried there . . . suddenly the narrow lane that we

were following opened out on to an open space of considerable area, in the middle of which our gaze fell upon a number of human bodies lying on the ground . . .

They were lying, with two or three exceptions, on their faces, in an irregular line, and in front of several of them, as though suddenly jerked from their hands, were their rifles and working tools.

Among them was an Italian engineer. Across his throat was a frightful gash and there were three bullet holes in his back. There were similar wounds in the backs of all the others in the line of dead, a few who must have turned upwards in their thrashing also had their throats cut . . .[25]

The novel is detailed and rumbustious; the author had talked to many veterans of the Mariscal's war. The letter inside the back cover was from the author to a Lady Jackson, dated 1887.

A Paraguayan Treasure [he wrote] is founded on fact. There is, I believe, no doubt that a considerable treasure was buried, and it is perfectly true that a number of people were shot, in order that the secret of the spot where it was hidden might not be divulged. Many attempts have been made to discover it and Mrs Lynch saw me herself on the subject and wanted me to buy the secret . . .

On 25 July 1886 she died of cancer in the stomach. Her son Federico was contacted and came to collect his mother's body. He arranged for the funeral Mass at the church of St Francisco de Sales and bought a permanent concession for her body in a grave in Père Lachaise cemetery with six other corpses. Invitations to the funeral were sent to the few who knew her:

Se ruega a Ud a asistir al cortejo, servicio funestre y entierro de la Sra Viuda Lynch de López, nacida Elisa Alicia Lynch en 1831.

Your presence is requested at the procession, funeral service and burial of the widow Señora Lynch López, born Elisa Alicia Lynch in 1831.[26]

Afterword

For fifty years after the war, opinion on the era of the Mariscal was dominated by one writer, Hector Decoud, whose mother had been held captive on the Chaco bank, whose sister had been raped by the Mariscal's soldiers, whose elder brother had been conscripted and died fighting at Cerro Corá, and whose father had been accused of treason. In 1892, he married the illegitimate daughter of Inocencia López and General Câmara, conceived the night the Mariscal died. For Decoud and the many who shared his views, Elisa Lynch and the Mariscal were murderers. Elisa's few acts of kindness during the last years of the war could not offset the far greater crimes she committed.

George Masterman, writing his hasty memoir *Seven Eventful Years in Paraguay* in 1869, was among the first to damn Elisa Lynch. He gave it as fact that her ambition was to make López 'the Napoleon of the New World' and 'as a clever, selfish and most unscrupulous woman, it will be readily understood that the influence she exercised over a man so imperious, yet so weak, so vain and sensual as López, was immense'[1]. It was she, he said, who pushed him into war to further her schemes; the blame was on her shoulders. South American writers went further.

La Dictadura del Mariscal López was written in Buenos Aires in 1874, intended for the use of primary schools in Paraguay. It contained the conquerors' views of both López and Elisa Lynch and a generation grew up believing this collection of lies and scurrilous gossip to be the truth: 'Elisa Lynch,' the book stated, 'was born in Scotland in the year 1822. She is the daughter of decent, humble people. Her father was an ironworker and her mother a dressmaker for a French *modiste* who worked in London, to which capital the Lynch family had moved.' At the age of twelve, already beautiful, literate and bilingual in French and English, Elisa Lynch became a shopgirl 'where she was soon surrounded by worshippers'. Without heeding 'the tears of her mother or the caresses of her father' she ran away with young Lord L— and soon became 'general in chief of the immense army of 70 lorettes who constitute the court of Venus in England'[2]. She became famous; she forced Lord L— to take her all over Europe and, when she had spent all his money, she left him in Madrid for a tenor of the Teatro Lírico, whom she left for an English banker and so on, until she married poor Xavier to get into good society. He married her secretly, was disinherited by his family and forced to go to Algeria. Here she started seducing his senior officers. The stories went on and on, perverted versions of the already perverted gossip of Doña Pura.

Even wilder stories than this were circulating about Elisa. It was said Lord Palmerston had been her lover; that she had plotted to exterminate all Paraguayan women and replace them with a mass immigration of Scotswomen; that she was bald and had her hairdresser arrested because he told his cronies so one night when in his cups; that she had allowed her children, during the last months of the war, to pay the starving 'an ear of corn or a handful of flour'[3] for the pleasure of whipping them; that she was responsible, through sheer malice, for inventing the conspiracy against López; that she had had many lovers in Paraguay, among them General José Díaz, whose bandages she had ripped off so he would bleed to death and keep the secret . . .

In 1921, a book was published by Paraguayan historian Dr Juan Emiliano O'Leary. This was a startling new version of the war, the Mariscal and, by association, Madame Lynch. In O'Leary's version, the Mariscal was not the destroyer of Paraguay but its saviour: a statesman of vision who fought bravely and brilliantly against the aggression of his neighbours. His death, and that of the Paraguayans who had followed him into battle, had been the sublime act of patriotism. O'Leary's vision, too, was given force by his background for he could match Decoud in pedigree: he was the son of a *destinada*. O'Leary's *Historia de la Guerra del Paraguay* was the start of a revisionist movement which blossomed under the military juntas of twentieth-century Paraguay. A floundering nation required a focus around which to build an identity and what more appropriate to a military dictatorship than the cult of the Mariscal who had died, sword in hand, crying '*Muero con mi patria!*' – 'I die with my country!' in a hail of Brazilian bullets?

It was O'Leary who began tracking down survivors of the war and persuading them to write their memoirs. Silvestre Aveiro was found and persuaded to dictate his *memorias militares* just before he died in 1919. Padre Maíz, still administering the sacraments, wrote *Etapas de mi vida* at the age of ninety-one, a book of absolute denial to face the truth or accept responsibility for his actions.

In 1929, the *Comisón Pro-Reivindicación del Mariscal* was created. The soldier who had crouched in a tree and watched Elisa Lynch dig a grave for the Mariscal and Panchito was traced and led the commission to the spot he remembered. Bones were found and the first monuments went up to mark

the battle-site. In February 1936, General Morinigo surrounded the Chamber of Deputies in Asunción with troops
and half a century of military rule began. 'A revolution was
necessary,' wrote Asunción newspaper *ABC Color* in its
centenary edition (3 March 1970) 'for the Mariscal finally to
be glorified by an act of government.' General Morinigo
provided that revolution – and another bloody and 'patriotic'
war, this time with Bolivia.

The revisionism continued: 'the Marshal *was* the nation'
and his army was 'the nation in arms'[4]. No possibility of
dissent was allowed. These views were both interpretation of
the past and support for the strong-man governments under
whom the revisionists wrote. None of the small club of
dictators which ruled Latin America would disapprove of an
ideology by which the commander in chief of the armed forces
is the incarnation of the nation and all those who defy him are
traitors. Nor would the General Presidents ignore the memory
of Elisa Lynch when they saw the effect of Evita Perón on the
Buenos Aires masses. Street names were changed and
municipal statuary erected; text books were altered and the
works of Decoud were banned.

When the revisionists turned to Elisa Lynch, they attributed
to her the feminine virtues which complemented the mascu-
line in the world of Stroessner, Perón and Franco: motherhood, self-sacrifice, unquestioning loyalty to her man. But the
raw material remained unobliging and 'fictionalised bio-
graphies' appeared to supply womanly interludes. The most
hagiographic was by an Argentine woman, Maria L
Concepción de Chaves, after whom an Asunción street has
been named. Her *Madame Lynch: Evocación*, written in 1957,
transposed their meeting to Algeria. Xavier de Quatrefages
became an unfeeling brute who denied her children and the
love affair with General López thus became the rescue of a
maiden by a gallant knight, with no possibility of unfortunate

behaviour in Paris. Once in Paraguay, this Elisa laid her little blonde head on Francisco's shoulder while he lectured her on the balance of powers in the Plate; and galloped at the head of his troops in a fetching pair of breeches.

As the centenary of the Mariscal's death approached and the Panteón de los Héroes filled with the bones of warriors, the Paraguayan embassy in France contacted the Municipality of Paris and asked permission to exhume the remains of Elisa Lynch. The file containing their correspondence, kept in the Centre des Archives Diplomatiques de Nantes, will not be opened until 2013 so we cannot know what official reasons they gave. The grave in Père Lachaise was opened, dust and bones exhumed from its seven bodies and the urn which contained them sent across the Atlantic. After her ceremonial reception from President Stroessner in 1961, she sat for several years on the plinth of the Museo Militar until a monument was erected for her in La Recoleta cemetery. She was transferred on a gun-carriage to the largest plot on Avenida C of La Recoleta, to which is attached a plaque: 'Homage of the people, government and armed forces to Elisa Alicia Lynch'. It is little visited now. President Stroessner scuttled across the border to a millionaire's exile in Brazil after a coup in 1989 and since then, military heroes and heroines have gone out of fashion. Paraguay, however, is a strange and restless country. Elisa Lynch may yet be elevated again, by some other soldier determined to be a great man of history.

Endnotes

Foreword
[1] *La Tribuna*, Asunción, 25 July 1961.

Chapter One
[1] Elisa Alicia Lynch, *Exposición y Protesta*.
[2] Theophile Gautier, *Voyage pittoresque en Algerie*.
[3] Elisa Alicia Lynch, op cit.
[4] Hector Varela, *Elisa Lynch de Quatrefages por Orion*.
[5] ibid.

Chapter Two
[1] *The Times*, 10 December 1853.
[2] *Historia Argentina – Curso Elemental*.
[3] J C Chavez, quoted in Jorge Rubiani, *La Guerra de la Triple Alianza*.
[4] Charles Quentin, *Le Paraguay*.
[5] Quoted in Pelham Horton Box, *The Origins of the Paraguayan War*.
[6] *The Times*, 24 May 1853.
[7] ibid.
[8] ibid.
[9] Quoted in Joanna Richardson, *The Courtesans, the demi-monde in nineteenth-century France*.
[10] Juan Crisóstomo Centurión, *Memorias o Reminiscencias Historicas sobre la guerra del Paraguay*.
[11] Declarations of Brizuela reproduced in, among others, Fernando Baptista, *Madame Lynch: mujer de guerra y de mundo*.
[12] ibid.

319

[13] Public Records Office (PRO) FO 59/10.
[14] ibid.
[15] George Frederick Masterman, *Seven Eventful Years in Paraguay*.
[16] Public Records Office (PRO) FO 59/10.
[17] Quoted in B Jerrold, *The Life of Napoleon III*.
[18] National Archive of Asunción (NAA) historia I 30, 28, 19
[19] Quoted in Jorge Rubiani, op cit.

Chapter Three
[1] Quoted in Pelham Horton Box, op cit.
[2] George Frederick Masterman, op cit.
[3] Ildefonso Bermejo, *Repúblicas Americanas: Episodios de la vida privada, política y social en la República del Paraguay.*
[4] Lieutenant Page, quoted in Charles Ames Washburn, *The History of Paraguay, with notes of personal observations, and reminiscences of diplomacy under difficulties.*
[5] Ildefonso Bermejo, op cit.
[6] George Frederick Masterman, op cit.
[7] Ildefonso Bermejo, op cit.
[8] *Le Monde Autour de 1871*, quoted in Fernando Baptista, op cit.
[9] Hector Varela, op cit.
[10] Declaration of Encarnación Bedoya quoted in Guido Alcalá, *Destinadas, Residentas y Traidoras.*

Chapter Four
[1] Hector Varela, op cit.
[2] ibid.
[3] ibid.
[4] ibid.
[5] ibid.
[6] ibid.
[7] Reproduced in *La Tribuna*, Buenos Aires, 25 February 1856.
[8] PRO FO 59/12.
[9] Centre des Archives Diplomatiques de Nantes (CAD), Buenos Aires, Legation 21.
[10] PRO FO 59/12.
[11] ibid.
[12] Hector Varela, op cit.
[13] ibid.
[14] ibid.

[15] *La Tribuna*, Buenos Aires, 26 February 1856.
[16] Hector Varela, op cit.
[17] ibid.
[18] NAA historia 320/7.
[19] Hector Varela, op cit.
[20] ibid.
[21] ibid.

Chapter Five

[1] CAD assomption-a-12.
[2] Charles Quentin, op cit.
[3] PRO FO 59.
[4] ibid.
[5] PRO FO 59/12.
[6] CAD, Buenos Aires, Legation 21.
[7] ibid.
[8] Jorge Rubiani, op cit.
[9] CAD, Buenos Aires, Legation 21.
[10] George Frederick Masterman, op cit.
[11] ibid.
[12] Marion Mulhall, *From Europe to Paraguay and Matto-Grosso*.
[13] George Frederick Masterman, op cit.
[14] Commission of Enquiry questioning General MacMahon, reproduced in Osvaldo Bergonzi, *El Circulo de San Fernando*.
[15] Bartolomé Bossi, *Viaje pintoreco por los ríos Paraná, Parguay, San Lorenzo, Cuyubá y el Arino tributario del grande Amazonas*.
[16] ibid.
[17] ibid.
[18] George Frederick Masterman, op cit.
[19] ibid.
[20] Fidel Maíz, *Etapas de mi vida*.
[21] PRO FO 527/9.
[22] ibid.
[23] Charles Ames Washburn, op cit.
[24] ibid.
[25] PRO FO 59/20.

Chapter Six

[1] Jorge Rubiani, op cit.
[2] *La Tribuna*, Buenos Aires, 9 November 1859.

[3] *La Tribuna*, Buenos Aires, 27 November 1859.
[4] Osvaldo Bergonzi, op cit.
[5] Quoted in Josefina Plá, *The British in Paraguay*.
[6] George Frederick Masterman, op cit.
[7] ibid.
[8] ibid.
[9] ibid.
[10] ibid.
[11] NAA historia.
[12] NAA historia 331/29.
[13] Charles Ames Washburn, op cit.
[14] ibid.
[15] ibid.

Chapter Seven
[1] Fidel Maíz, op cit.
[2] ibid.
[3] ibid.
[4] Charles Ames Washburn, op cit.
[5] NAA historia 444/12.
[6] Charles Ames Washburn, op cit.
[7] Juan Crisótomo Centurión, op cit.
[8] George Thompson, *The War in Paraguay*.
[9] NAA historia 130, 27, 84.
[10] NAA historia 332/7.
[11] Charles Ames Washburn, op cit.
[12] ibid.
[13] Fidel Maíz, op cit.
[14] CAD Assomption-a-12 'lettres des particuliers'.
[15] *La Tribuna*, Buenos Aires, 13 June 1863.
[16] Charles Ames Washburn, op cit.
[17] ibid.
[18] George Frederick Masterman, op cit.
[19] Fidel Maíz, op cit.
[20] ibid.
[21] Charles Ames Washburn, op cit.
[22] ibid.
[23] ibid.
[24] ibid.
[25] ibid.

[26] ibid.
[27] ibid.
[28] ibid.
[29] ibid.
[30] Juan Crisótomo Centurión, op cit.
[31] Charles Ames Washburn, op cit.
[32] George Frederick Masterman, op cit.
[33] ibid.
[34] ibid.
[35] ibid.

Chapter Eight
[1] Charles Ames Washburn, op cit.
[2] ibid.
[3] ibid.
[4] Quoted in Jorge Rubiani, op cit.
[5] Pelham Horton Box, op cit.
[6] Quoted in Jorge Rubiani, op cit.
[7] Quoted in Fernando Baptista, op cit.
[8] Quoted in Pelham Horton Box, op cit.
[9] Charles Ames Washburn, op cit.
[10] NAA historia 340/7.
[11] *La Tribuna*, Buenos Aires, 14 September 1864.
[12] ibid.
[13] *La Tribuna*, Buenos Aires, 13 October 1864.
[14] Charles Ames Washburn, op cit.
[15] ibid.
[16] George Thompson, op cit.
[17] Charles Ames Washburn, op cit.
[18] ibid.
[19] ibid.
[20] *The Times*, 21 January 1865.
[21] Ivan Boris and Manlio Cancogni, *El Napoleón del Plata*.
[22] George Thompson, op cit.
[23] ibid.
[24] Quoted in Fernando Baptista, op cit.
[25] Hector Decoud, *La Masacre de Concepción ordenada por el Mariscal López*.
[26] Juan Crisóstomo Centurión, op cit.
[27] George Thompson, op cit.

Chapter Nine

1 Charles Ames Washburn, op cit.
2 Jorge Rubiani, op cit.
3 ibid.
4 *The Times*, 1 June 1865.
5 George Thompson, op cit.
6 The Treaty of the Triple Alliance is reproduced in, among others, Jorge Rubiani, op cit.
7 ibid.
8 Quoted in Fernando Baptista, op cit.
9 Charles Ames Washburn, op cit.
10 ibid.
11 Silvestre Aveiro, *Memorias Militares*.
12 *La Tribuna*, Buenos Aires, 21 October 1864.
13 Quoted in Jorge Rubiani, op cit.
14 Quoted in Josefina Plá, op cit.
15 *La Tribuna*, Buenos Aires, 3 September 1864.
16 ibid.
17 George Thompson, op cit.
18 George Frederick Masterman, op cit.
19 *La Tribuna*, Buenos Aires, 22 September 1864.

Chapter Ten

1 Quoted in Milda Rivarola, *La polemica francesa sobre la guerra grande*.
2 ibid.
3 George Thompson, op cit.
4 Juan Crisótomo Centurión, op cit.
5 Juan Bautista Rivarola, *Diagonal de Sangre*.
6 George Thompson, op cit.
7 Hector Decoud, op cit.
8 Declaration of Rafaela López reproduced in Hector Decoud, op cit.
9 George Thompson, op cit.
10 Justiniano Rodas Benítez, *Testimonios de un Capitán de la Guerra del '70*.
11 Silvestre Aveiro, op cit.
12 Leon de Palleja, *Diario de las Fuerzas Aliadas contra el Paraguay*.
13 George Thompson, op cit.

[14] *Buenos Aires Standard, Official papers seized by the Allies on December 28 1868.*

[15] Mr Taylor's narrative reproduced in George Frederick Masterman, op cit.

[16] Quoted in Fernando Baptista, op cit.

[17] PRO FO 59/25.

[18] George Thompson, op cit.

[19] Leon de Palleja, op cit.

[20] ibid.

[21] Fernando Baptista, op cit.

[22] Alfredo de Taunay, *Diario do Ejercito*, quoted in Fernando Baptista, op cit.

Chapter Eleven

[1] George Frederick Masterman, op cit.

[2] Milda Rivarola, op cit.

[3] Elisa Alicia Lynch, op cit.

[4] Richard Burton, *Letters from the Battlefields of Paraguay.*

[5] George Thompson, op cit.

[6] NAA historia I 30, 27, 84.

[7] ibid.

[8] ibid.

[9] ibid.

[10] ibid.

[11] Quoted in Fernando Baptista, op cit.

[12] George Thompson, op cit.

[13] *Buenos Aires Standard*, op cit.

[14] Jorge Rubiani, op cit.

Chapter Twelve

[1] Fidel Maíz, op cit.

[2] Charles Ames Washburn, op cit.

[3] ibid.

[4] *The Times*, 24 December 1869.

[5] NAA historia 347/17.

[6] Charles Ames Washburn, op cit.

[7] ibid.

[8] ibid.

[9] ibid.

[10] *Buenos Aires Standard*, 2 March 1870, clipping in PRO FO 59/30.
[11] ibid.
[12] PRO FO 6/268.
[13] ibid.
[14] PRO FO 59/27.
[15] PRO FO 6/268.
[16] ibid.
[17] ibid.
[18] Juan Crisóstomo Centurión's unpublished declaration reproduced in Osvaldo Bergonzi, op cit.
[19] George Thompson, op cit.
[20] *Buenos Aires Standard*, 26 June 1867.
[21] PRO FO 6/268.
[22] ibid.
[23] George Thompson, op cit.
[24] Quoted in Osvaldo Bergonzi, op cit.
[25] Charles Ames Washburn, op cit.
[26] Quoted in Osvaldo Bergonzi, op cit.
[27] George Thompson, op cit.
[28] PRO FO 59/27–67.
[29] PRO FO 59/28.
[30] George Frederick Masterman, op cit.
[31] Dorotea Duprat de Lasserre, *Sufferings of a French Lady in Paraguay*.
[32] CAD, Buenos Aires, Legation 16.
[33] ibid.
[34] ibid.
[35] *El Semanario*, 25 February 1867.
[36] NAA Libro del Registro.
[37] ibid.
[38] Declaration of Mercedes Roca in Guido Alcalá, op cit.
[39] George Thompson, op cit.
[40] NAA Libro del Registro.
[41] ibid.
[42] George Thompson, op cit.
[43] ibid.
[44] NAA historia 347/17.
[45] PRO FO 6/268.
[46] NAA historia 253/26.

Chapter Thirteen

[1] George Thompson, op cit.
[2] Juan Crisóstomo Centurión, op cit.
[3] ibid.
[4] Dorotea Duprat de Lasserre, op cit.
[5] Declaration of Padre Acosta reproduced in Osvaldo Bergonzi, op cit.
[6] Osvaldo Bergonzi, op cit.
[7] Charles Ames Washburn, op cit.
[8] ibid.
[9] ibid.
[10] George Thompson, op cit.
[11] ibid.
[12] ibid.
[13] ibid.
[14] ibid.
[15] ibid.
[16] ibid.
[17] ibid.
[18] ibid.
[19] Gordon Meyer, *The River and the People.*
[20] Juan Crisóstomo Centurión, op cit.
[21] Osvaldo Bergonzi, op cit.
[22] Silvestre Aveiro, op cit.
[23] ibid.
[24] ibid.
[25] ibid.
[26] ibid.
[27] George Thompson, op cit.
[28] CAD, Buenos Aires, Legation 16.
[29] Juan Crisótomo Centurión, op cit.
[30] Silvestre Aveiro, op cit.
[31] ibid.

Chapter Fourteen

[1] Mr Taylor's narrative in George Frederick Masterman, op cit.
[2] ibid.
[3] Charles Ames Washburn, op cit.
[4] Mr Taylor's narrative in George Frederick Masterman, op cit.
[5] Juan Crisóstomo Centurión, op cit.

[6] Silvestre Aveiro, op cit.
[7] ibid.
[8] George Thompson, op cit.
[9] Mr Taylor's narrative in George Frederick Masterman, op cit.
[10] ibid.
[11] ibid.
[12] Hector Decoud, op cit.
[13] Arturo Rebaudi, *Un Tirano de Sud América: Francisco Solano López*.
[14] ibid.
[15] Silvestre Aveiro, op cit.
[16] Mr Taylor's narrative in George Frederick Masterman, op cit.
[17] Richard Burton, op cit.
[18] George Frederick Masterman, op cit.
[19] PRO FO 59/28.
[20] George Frederick Masterman, op cit.
[21] PRO FO 59/28.
[22] George Frederick Masterman, op cit.
[23] ibid.
[24] ibid.
[25] Reproduced in H. Koebbel, *The Romance of the River Plate*.
[26] George Frederick Masterman, op cit.
[27] *La Regeneración*, 19 November 1869.
[28] ibid.
[29] George Thompson, op cit.
[30] ibid.
[31] Reproduced in many books, Fernando Baptista (op cit) among them.
[32] Mr Taylor's narrative in George Frederick Masterman, op cit.
[33] *Times*, 24 December 1869.
[34] *Buenos Aires Standard* (official papers), op cit.
[35] Ibid.
[36] *Times*, 24 December 1869.
[37] Dorotea Duprat de Lasserre, op cit.
[38] CAD, Buenos Aires, Legation 16.
[39] Hector Decoud, op cit.
[40] Interview in *La Tribuna*, Asunción, 1 March 1970.

Chapter Fifteen

[1] Quoted in Fernando Baptista, op cit.
[2] Declaration reproduced in George Frederick Masterman, op cit.

[3] ibid.
[4] Juan Crisóstomo Centurión, op cit.
[5] Declaration of Silvia Cordal reproduced in Guido Alcalá, op cit.
[6] ibid.
[7] *La Regeneración*, 27 October 1869.
[8] ibid.
[9] Dorotea Duprat de Lasserre, op cit.
[10] Declaration of Silvia Cordal, op cit.
[11] Silvestre Aveiro, op cit.
[12] Declaration of Silvia Cordal, op cit.
[13] Silvestre Aveiro, op cit.
[14] Juan Crisóstomo Centurión, op cit.
[15] Alfredo de Taunay, *Diario do Ejercito*, quoted in *La Tribuna*, Asunción, 1 March 1970.
[16] ibid.
[17] ibid.
[18] ibid.
[19] ibid.
[20] ibid.
[21] ibid.
[22] ibid.
[23] ibid.

Chapter Sixteen
[1] *La Regeneración*, 1 October 1869.
[2] *La Regeneración*, 28 December 1869.
[3] Clipping of *Buenos Aires Standard* in PRO FO 6/290.
[4] ibid.
[5] *La Regeneración*, 19 March 1870.
[6] Elisa Alicia Lynch, op cit.
[7] *El Nacional*, Buenos Aires, 6 December 1870.
[8] *La Tribuna*, Buenos Aires, 29 October 1870.
[9] Elisa Alicia Lynch, op cit.
[10] PRO FO 6/290.
[11] ibid.
[12] ibid.
[13] ibid.
[14] Quoted in B. Jerrold, op cit.
[15] Quoted in Joanna Richardson, op cit.
[16] Alexandre Dumas, *La Dame aux Camélias*.

[17] Letters of Emiliano Pesoa López reproduced in Elisa Alicia Lynch, op cit.
[18] Robert Cunninghame-Grahame, *Portrait of a Dictator.*
[19] CAD, Buenos Aires, Legation 16.
[21] ibid.
[22] ibid.
[23] *La Regeneración,* 24 October 1875.
[24] *La Tribuna,* Buenos Aires, 1 November 1870.
[25] Alexander Baillie, *A Paraguayan Treasure.*
[26] Quoted in article in *La Tribuna,* Asunción, 5 October 1975 by Victor I Franco

Afterword

[1] George Frederick Masterman, op cit.
[2] Jacinto Vicencio, *La Dictadura del Mariscal López.*
[3] ibid.
[4] Arturo Bray, *Solano López, solado de la gloria y del infortunio.*

Bibliography

Alberdi, Juan Bautista, *Historia Argentina – Curso Elemental Historia de la guerra del Paraguay*, Buenos Aires, 1962.

Alcalá, Guido, *Destinadas, Residentas y Traidoras*, Asunción, 1991.

Aveiro, Silvestre, *Memorias Militares*, Asunción, 1970.

Baillie, Alexander, *A Paraguayan Treasure: The Search and the Discovery*, London, 1887.

Baptista, Fernando, *Madame Lynch: mujer de guerra y de mundo*, Buenos Aires, 1987.

Barrett, William Edmund, *Woman on Horseback: The Biography of Francisco López and Eliza Lynch*, New York, 1938.

Baylé, Jacqueline, *Quand l'Agerie devenait francaise*, Paris, 1981.

Benítez, Justiniano Rodas, *Testimonios de un Capitán de la Guerra del '70*.

Bergonzi, Osvaldo, *El Circulo de San Fernando*, Asunción, 1998.

Bermejo, Ildefonso Antonio, *Repúblicas Americanas: Episodios de la vida privada, política y social en la República del Paraguay*, Madrid 1873.

Francia: Luis Napoleon III, Madrid, 1854.

Boettner, Juan Max, *Música y músicos del Paraguay*, Asunción, 1946.

Boris, Ivan and Cancogni, Manlio, *El Napoleón del Plata: Historia de una heroica guerra sudamericana*, Barcelona, 1972.

Bossi, Bartolomé, *Viaje pintoresco por los ríos Paraná, Paraguay, San Lorenzo, Cuyubá y el Arino tributario del grande Amazonas*, Paris, 1863.

Box, Pelham Horton, *The Origins of the Paraguayan War*, New York, 1967.

331

Bozzo, Emanuele, *Notizie storiche sulla repubblica del Paraguay e la guerra attuale*, Genoa, 1869.

Bray, Arturo, *Hombres y epocas del Paraguay*, Buenos Aires, 1943. *Solano López, soldado de la gloria y del infortunio*, Buenos Aires, 1945.

Brodsky, Alyn, *Madame Lynch and Friend, the true account of an Irish adventuress and the dictator of Paraguay who destroyed that American nation*, London, 1976.

Buenos Aires Standard, Official papers seized by the Allies on 28 December 1868, Buenos Aires, 1869.

Burton, Richard, *Letters from the Battlefields of Paraguay*, London, 1870.

Canard, Benjamin, Cascalar, Joaquín and Gallegos, Miguel, *Cartas sobre la guerra del Paraguay*, Buenos Aires, 1999.

Cardozo, Efraím, *Breve historia del Paraguay*, Buenos Aires, 1965.

Centurión, Juan Crisóstomo, *Memorias, o Reminiscencias Historicas sobre la guerra del Paraguay*, Asunción, 1987.

Chaves, Maris Concepción, L. de, *Madame Lynch, Evocación*, Buenos Aires, 1957.

Cooney, Jerry W. and Whigham, Thomas L., *El Paraguay bajo los López*, Asunción, 1994.

Cunninghame-Grahame, Robert, *Portrait of a Dictator*, London, 1933.

Decoud, Hector, *La Masacre de Concepción ordenada por el Mariscal López*, Buenos Aires, 1926.

Dumas, Alexandre, *La Dame aux Camélias*, Paris, 1856.

Duprat de Lasserre, Dorotea, *Sufferings of a French Lady in Paraguay*, Buenos Aires, 1871.

Gautier Theophile, *Voyage pittoresque en Algerie*, ed. Madeleine Cotton, London, 1973.

Goldfranck, David M., *The Origins of the Crimean War*, London, 1994.

Hillairet, Jacques, *Dictionnaire historique des rues de Paris*, Paris, 1963.

Jerrold, B., *The Life of Napoleon III*, London, 1874.

Koebbel, William H., *The Romance of the River Plate*, London, 1914.

Lano, Pierre de, *The Secret of an Empire: The Empress Eugenie*, London, 1895.

Lynch, Elisa Alicia, *Exposición y Protesta*, Asunción, 1987.

Maíz, Fidel, *Etapas de mi vida*, Asunción, 1996.

Masterman, George Frederick, *Seven Eventful Years in Paraguay: A narrative of personal experiences amongst the Paraguayans*, London, 1869.

Meyer, Gordon, *The River and the People*, London, 1965.
Micó, Tomás, L., *Tesoros enterrados en el Paraguay*, Asunción, 2000.
Mulhall, Marion McMurrough, *From Europe to Paraguay and Matto-Grosso*, London, 1872.
Nicola Siri, Eros, *Por quién llora el urutáu, Francisco Solano López, Elisa Lynch y la Guerra de la Triple Alianza*, Buenos Aires, 1978.
O'Leary, Juan E., *Historia de la guerra de la triple alianza*, Asunción, 1992.
El Mariscal Solano López, Madrid, 1925.
Nuestra Epopeya: La Guerra del Paraguay, Asunción, 1919.
Page, Lieutenant Thomas J., *La Plata, the Argentine Confederation and Paraguay*, New York, 1859.
Palleja, Leon de, *Diario de las fuerzas aliadas contra el Paraguay*, Montevideo, 1865.
Pardella, Agustín Perez, *Cerro Corá*, Buenos Aires, 1977.
Pinkney, David Henry, *Napoleon III and the Rebuilding of Paris*, Princeton, 1958.
Plá Josefina, *Los Británicos en el Paraguay*, Asunción, 1984.
El Teatro en el Paraguay, Asunción, 1967.
Quentin, Charles, *Le Paraguay*, Paris, 1865.
Rebaudi, Arturo, *Un Tirano de Sud América: Francisco Solano López*, Buenos Aires, 1925.
Richardson, Joanna, *The Courtesans, the demi-monde in nineteenth-century France*, London, 1967.
La Vie Parisienne 1852–1870, London, 1971.
Rivarola, Juan Bautista, *Diagonal de Sangre*, Asunción, 1986.
Rivarola, Milda, *La polemica francesa sobre la guerra grande*, Asunción, 1988.
Rubiani, Jorge, *La Guerra de la Triple Alianza (ABC Color)*, Asunción, 2001.
Thompson, George, *The War in Paraguay*, London, 1869.
Varela, Hector, *Elisa Lynch de Quatrefages por Orion*, Buenos Aires, 1870.
Vicencio, Jacinto, *La Dictadura del Mariscal López*, Buenos Aires, 1874.
Washburn, Charles Ames, *The History of Paraguay, with notes of personal observations, and reminiscences of diplomacy under difficulties*, Boston, 1871.
Young, Henry Lyon, *Eliza Lynch, Regent of Paraguay*, London, 1966.
Zinny, Antonio, *Chronología de los obispos del Paraguay*, Buenos Aires, 1887.

Zubizaretta, Ramón, *Dictamen sobre el valor legal de los titulos de Madama Linch en la reclamación de las 3,000 y pico de leguas,* Asunción, 1888.

Newspapers and periodicals

London
The Times

Buenos Aires
Buenos Aires Standard
La Tribuna
El Nacional

Asunción
La Tribuna
El Eco
La Regeneración
ABC Color

Unpublished sources

Public Records Office (PRO)
PRO FO 527 – Correspondence from Asunción.
PRO FO 59 – Political and Other Departments: General Correspondence before 1906, Paraguay.
FO 527 – Consulate and Legation, Asunción, Paraguay: general correspondence.

Centre des Archives Diplomatiques de Nantes (CAD)
Buenos Aires, Legation 16.
Buenos Aires, Legation 21.
Assomption-a-12.

National Archive of Asunción (NAA)
Libro del Registro
'Historia' series 315–33.
Loose documents I 30, 27 and I 30, 28.

Index

335